THE
BIG DARK

Pamela Elaine Telford

Library of Congress Control Number: 2025912496
ISBN: 979-8-89228-586-5   (Paperback)
ISBN: 979-8-89228-587-2   (Hardcover)
ISBN: 979-8-89228-588-9   (eBook)

Book Ordering Information:
Atticus Publishing
548 Market St PMB 70756
San Francisco, CA 94104
(888) 208-9296
info@atticuspublishing.com
www.atticuspublishing.com

ATTICUS
PUBLISHING

Printed in the United States of America

TABLE OF CONTENTS

DEDICATION

To Jack—

Who gave me two beautiful years of love and deep emotional connection that helped me survive the three decades of abuse and who visited me several times in my dreams to remind me that I am worthy of all the love that the Universe has to give and that I deserve to give myself the same love and compassion that I give every one else.

And to Barbara—

Who graciously and lovingly helped me to navigate and process the pain with hard questions and loving support. Thank you for seeing me, hearing me, and holding space for my healing.

PREFACE

There is a silence so heavy, so suffocating, that it doesn't echo—it absorbs. For over thirty years, I lived inside that silence. On the outside, I was capable, put-together, functional. Inside, I was unraveling. And no one knew.

I never imagined I'd be the woman writing these words. Not because I lack the voice—but because for decades, I believed I didn't deserve to be heard.

This is not a story about a bad relationship. This is a story about the unseen wounds, the quiet gasps in the dark, the thousand subtle manipulations that add up to a life stolen in plain sight. It's about how trauma doesn't always come crashing through the door. Sometimes, it seeps in through the cracks—smiling, patient, wearing the mask of love.

I write this not to accuse, but to illuminate. Not to shame, but to awaken. I write this for the woman sitting in her car in silence, afraid to go home. For the friend who suspects something is wrong but doesn't want to intrude. For the mother who gave everything and forgot herself in the process. For the daughter who learned too early how to fly under the radar to avoid disappointment.

I write this for the person who still doesn't have the words—but knows the feeling all too well.

This book is not neat. It is not tidy. It is not polished or softened for your comfort. It is jagged, raw, and unapologetically honest—because abuse is none of those things. The truth doesn't need to be pretty. It just needs to be told.

Through these pages, you will walk with me through the darkness—through control, betrayal, manipulation, and isolation. You will witness the slow erosion of self, and the long, arduous climb back toward light. But you will also find, in these same pages, fragments of fierce love. For my children. For my younger self. For every woman who has ever whispered "enough" into the night.

This isn't just a story of what happened. It's a reclaiming. A resurrection.

I am no longer hiding. I am no longer apologizing. And I am no longer afraid to take up space with my truth.

If my story mirrors even a sliver of yours—know this: you are not alone. You are not crazy. And you are not weak. You are surviving something many wouldn't believe unless they lived it.

Now, I invite you to walk with me. Not because the path is easy. But because, at last, it is mine.

Pam

Part One: Foundations

1. ME

I forgive myself and I am worthy of love, happiness, and respect.

I was a victim of domestic abuse for over thirty years. It seems absolutely incredible to think that I endured three decades of a toxic, abusive marriage and didn't become dark or turn to self-harm. Never, ever in a million years would I have thought this would happen to me. I'm a smart, strong, independent person, and I'm very capable of taking care of myself. Whenever I heard about someone being abused, I couldn't understand why they would stay. I would confidently tell myself *that would never happen to me—and if it did, I would just walk away.*

How ignorant and naïve I was. Only people who have never experienced domestic violence can say that with any kind of smug confidence. Unless it is physical, most victims don't even recognize other forms of abuse being directed at them. We just know that the abuser makes us feel "less than." We walk around with sadness always behind our smile.

It did happen to me. And it happened so insidiously. It was slow and methodical. It was calculated. There were red flags, but I was too young, with too little life experience, to recognize them. By the time I put all the nuanced events together and realized the abuse and the damage that had been done, I was trapped. I had no job, no money of my own, and three little kids who depended on me.

The crazy part is, I still didn't fully realize the scope of the abuse until nine years after I had left him. I was still giving him the benefit of the doubt—nine years later—that he didn't realize how much he had hurt and traumatized me.

I thought just leaving him was all I needed to do to heal and move on. I was starting a new life with a new love. I had a great job and had regained my independence. I didn't count on the past trauma to ooze its way back into my consciousness nine years later and cause me to have anxiety attacks.

It was March 2023. I woke up in the middle of the night after reliving one of those traumatic events in my dream. I was sobbing, and my throat tightened to the point where I couldn't breathe. My Dearest woke up, scared for me. I could hear the concern in his voice as he tried to find out what was wrong. I couldn't speak. I could barely breathe.

He sat up in bed and wrapped his arms around me, trying to help me calm down.

I had no idea where that reaction had come from. There was nothing recent I could point to and say, *That's the reason why I had that dream and that reaction.* I had trouble falling back to sleep—and then had to get up and go to work a couple of hours later.

I found myself getting triggered by scenes in movies, or by conversations with patients, family, and friends. I had trouble falling asleep and staying asleep. My Dearest recommended that I see a therapist, but I didn't want to. It hurt too much to remember the abuse. I couldn't imagine having to recount thirty-plus years out loud to someone. I didn't know how deep my scars were, and I was afraid to find out.

So I endured the rise and fall of the suppressed emotions as best as I could, alone.

I bought a spiral notebook and allowed myself to feel the anger. I let my stream of consciousness flow, writing feverishly every emotion I was feeling. I started recounting specific traumatic events in more detail as I searched for answers to the question, *Why* me?

Was I being punished for something I did in a prior life? Is this what they mean when they say, "Karma is a bitch"?

I'm a good person. I've always tried to stay connected to my fellow man with compassion and empathy. So why did I go through so much abuse at the hands of someone who was supposed to love and protect me?

I just kept writing and searching, trying to find the answers. I went way back into my childhood, looking for a connection—some thread that explained how I got caught in that web of torture.

What I discovered was that my personality was a perfect match for Mike's abusive personality. It was the perfect storm. Once I was in it, I had very little chance of getting out. I quickly became ensnared in the cycle of abuse and didn't even realize it until it was too late.

So, what made me the perfect partner for his abuse? It was all the good qualities you want in a person. I am kind, empathetic, compassionate, and understanding. I give people the benefit of the doubt, and I always look for the good in others. I'm forgiving and easygoing.

My problem was that I didn't have strong personal boundaries.

I was raised to put my own needs second to those of others. I was taught that I was only worthy if I pleased the people around me. I grew up in a family of six kids, all close in age. This was long before microwaves and disposable diapers. I can only imagine the workload my mother had every day, and the stress and worry my dad must have carried trying to provide for all of us.

We all had to help around the house from an early age. My parents were obsessed with perfection. If something wasn't done the way they wanted, you got scolded and had to redo it. I believed I was a bad person, unworthy of love, simply because I didn't know how to wash the dishes correctly when I was five years old.

I learned early that the best way to get praise and loving attention in a busy household was to please my parents. If I ever tried to prioritize my own needs, I was told I was selfish or self-centered. If I voiced something I was proud of, I was told I was conceited.

I became uncomfortable with compliments. Accepting them felt like vanity—something I was taught was unacceptable. I learned to fly low under the radar, hoping not to disappoint anyone. And I tried hard to please others so I could earn some positive attention and feel worthy.

I was always concerned with doing the right thing, and I took injustices very personally, even when they weren't directed at me. I would plant myself firmly in the middle of a fight to try to break it up. I never worried about getting hurt.

If I saw someone who seemed vulnerable, who couldn't stand up for themselves, I jumped in to fight their fight.

My problem was that I didn't feel like I had the right to fight for myself.

My personal boundaries were weak. They prevented me from standing up for my value and self-worth. In the past, when I told someone they had hurt me, they got upset, defensive, and pushed back. Instead of acknowledging the hurt, as I would have done for them, I was made to feel bad for even bringing it up.

There was a big part of me that lacked self-love and self-compassion, even though I seemed to have an endless supply of it for everyone else.

Until... eventually, the real Mike began to emerge—bit by bit, as he tested my boundaries.

I would be caught off guard by his shifting personalities. It caused confusion and mental distress. *Was there something I did to provoke this response? Why is he upset over something so small?*

I was raised to be mindful of others' feelings, and here it seemed I was making someone upset. I felt like I had to fix it—do whatever I could—so he wouldn't be mad at me.

I didn't realize it at the time, but I was trauma-bonded to Mike very early.

It was rooted in my deep-seated need not to disappoint anyone—to make them happy, even at my own expense. To put it plainly, I was a giver with weak boundaries, and Mike was a taker pretending to be a giver—until he couldn't keep up the charade any longer.

One by one, he plundered my weak boundaries until I had almost none left, and he had nearly total emotional control over me.

It was the perfect mix of personalities for a toxic, abusive marriage. Lucky me.

And the irony of it all? We weren't even supposed to be together. It was supposed to be temporary. I was just looking for someone to explore my sexuality with.

Connecting with Mike was the single most destructive decision I ever made in my life. It sent me down a path of darkness that took me thirty-three years to escape.

I decided to write this book after many months of journaling and seeking internal peace. I became driven to recall every slight by him and to find meaning in the pain I endured. I needed to answer the questions that dogged me: *How did I let this happen? Why me? Why didn't I leave sooner? How did I miss the signs? Why did I even seek out Mike in the first place when I already had a kind, loving, and emotionally safe relationship with an amazing man who would never, ever purposefully be cruel to me?*

The more I scoured my past, the more I realized how intentionally cruel Mike had been. No one saw it. He was very careful to make sure no one was around when he said or did those things.

For a long time, I chalked it up to his depression and made allowances. That's me—always giving the benefit of the doubt. But then it hit me: if it were really about his depression, wouldn't he behave the same way in front of others?

But no. He didn't.

He knew how he treated me was not acceptable. He knew that if anyone saw or heard his abusive ways, he would be condemned. That's why he carefully selected his moments—when we were alone—to unleash his ire.

That's when I realized the depths of his abuse. It was calculated. It was intentional.

When he said he loved me, it caused me so much confusion. I thought, *If he is okay with hurting me, and he is calculated in his abusive treatment toward me, then how can he ever say he loves me?* That is a sick, twisted form of emotional and mental abuse.

Two completely contradicting behaviors can't possibly both be true. Which is it? Is he a nice guy who is also abusive to his wife? No. He is an abuser who pretends to be a nice guy.

That was a watershed moment for me.

I realized, ten years after I had left him, that he never loved me. He used me to make himself look good. I gave him social credibility. Others would think, *What a wonderful guy he must be to have such a great wife as Pam.* No. He never loved me. He lied to me and betrayed our vows. He humiliated me and threatened me.

He made me afraid to sleep with my back to him at night.

I wasted over thirty years of my life with a man who ultimately detested me—because I was everything he wasn't.

Through my personal journey of healing, I have determined that my ex is 99.99 percent a covert narcissist. Apparently, only a licensed psychologist can diagnose someone officially as a narcissist; otherwise, I would give it 100 percent certainty.

The covert narcissist is the worst of all the narcissistic types because they are wolves in sheep's clothing. They pretend to be this amazing, loving person, but they are actually cruel and selfish, with no empathy or compassion. They have no ability to self-reflect or see their hurtful role in a relationship.

They don't care.

All they want is attention and adulation. They will play the victim in every scenario so you will feel sorry for them. This makes them the center of attention—even if it is only to receive sympathy. They are experts at pretending to be humble while emotionally manipulating the person closest to them to give more and more of themselves, allowing them greater and greater control.

Since I was an empathetic people-pleaser, I was the perfect person for him to sow the seeds of his perceived victimhood.

I was also dealing with my own shame—shame over falling into this relationship and a sense of obligation to help him work through his demons as my penance. I thought if I could "fix" him, I would somehow be relieved of some of the shame I had cloaked myself in.

But he kept moving the goalposts, keeping me forever chasing the need to help him through his struggles.

What an evil bastard.

I was just his accessory for the world to see. I was nothing more than what I could do for him.

The taker, taking from the giver.

I have read that narcissists prey on empathetic people. They look for those who are the most empathetic and who have the weakest boundaries. That would be me.

The biggest difference here, though, was that Mike didn't go looking for me. I went looking for *him*.

It just so happened that my personality was the perfect match for his personality to create a toxic and abusive relationship.

Mike loved to tell people, "She came after me. I didn't go after her."

It would send shivers down my back every time he bragged about it. It would remind me how I hurt the beautiful soul of Jack. I was so innocent about who Mike really was.

It was like I was this silly little bug, curious about a shiny web flickering in the wind. I had no idea that my curiosity would get me caught in something so dark, so fast, that I wouldn't be able to get out.

This empath–narcissist relationship didn't happen because he stalked me and then made a move. No. I was just a silly little bug that walked right into the trap he didn't even know he was setting for me.

Here's something very tragic to keep in mind about victims of domestic violence: almost 75 percent of them (mostly women) are killed by their abusive partner *after* they leave the relationship.

If you ever wonder why victims don't "just leave," this is one reason. The intimidation, the threats to the victim and the kids—they are very real.

The abuser's mindset is, *How dare you leave me? I'll show you who gets the last word.*

This isn't the only reason a victim stays, but it is one that I felt all too well.

I knew I had to have a foolproof plan in place before I could leave. He made that very clear when he demonstrated how fast he could grab his gun, load it, and be ready to use it.

He made it very clear when he was holding that loaded gun, making threats about shooting himself—and the dog.

I hate him for that.

The trauma that remains embedded in my brain will be with me forever.

You will read and see how insidious the abuse can be. You will see how emotional manipulation takes on many different forms.

You may be incredulous at how long I lasted in that toxic, poisonous marriage.

But let me remind you: when you are emotionally, mentally, and psychologically spun in so many different directions, and all you can do is survive moment to moment, you don't see the big picture.

You certainly don't see the total cost to your mental well-being.

And suddenly—it's thirty years later.

The realization that you spent over half your life in trauma with someone who never loved you and was purposefully cruel is devastating.

Thirty-three years with him. And no one knew about the abuse.

I held it all in and hid it from the world. I had no one I felt I could trust. I had no one I felt would even believe me.

You can't imagine how incredibly alone you feel when half of you is hidden.

I felt invisible. I felt abandoned.

I endured thousands of deep psychological cuts, and no one saw my pain. No one heard my voice.

Now, I have a chance to be heard after thirty-plus years of silence.

I get one chance to write my story. That's it. I get only one chance to honor myself and all that I went through.

Half of my existence has been lived in silent torment, and I won't be silent anymore.

I have put my whole energy into writing my story. With this one chance to get it right, I fretted over sentence structure and paragraph flow. These may seem like little things, but I needed to make sure I honored my experience by making it as perfect as I possibly could.

Long after I'm gone, my voice will still be heard. And I will feel like my life was validated.

I knew the book would never be perfect. I just wanted it to be "good enough"—good enough for my standards, no one else's.

I wanted a record of my life that was real and brutally honest.

I wanted at least one book printed and bound so I could have it as a tribute to my suffering—and my survival.

So, I dug deep. I relived, moment by moment, the abuse, so I could accurately convey the emotions and context to the reader.

After all, every cut I endured was an emotional wrecking ball.

I tried to paint that emotional picture the best I could, so the reader could feel some of my pain.

I struggled to find the right words, because some emotions ran so deep that I didn't know how to describe them.

In the end, I'm very proud of what I accomplished.

All this so my story can finally be told. So my voice can finally be heard. So my life—and my pain—can finally be witnessed by others.

I recognize that there will be those who feel uncomfortable reading about my abuse for their own reasons. I anticipate that some people I know may turn their backs on me because they can't reconcile that this "great guy" was actually a monster.

In other words, I am anticipating that some people will exit my life.

Their choice.

I will tell my story loud and clear to anyone, and I will swear that it all happened just as I have written.

I realize now that those who leave weren't meant to be with me on this part of my journey anyway. I wish them well.

I didn't realize how emotional I would get writing some of the more intense passages.

There were times I had to get up and walk away— sometimes for a couple of days.

But even with the pain of opening old wounds, I was so proud of myself for facing each traumatic event in depth and head-on.

I had to go through the pain to get to the healing.

I had to go through it all so I could sleep again.

And, with as much as I have revealed in the book, there were still many anecdotes I left out—purely for the ease of the reader.

In other words, my experience was actually worse than what is written, simply because of the scope and length of the abuse.

I didn't have the emotional bandwidth to pull everything back from the depths of my memory and put it into words.

This is an example of reaching the point of "good enough."

I will end this with a plea:

If you suspect someone is being abused, please keep communications open with them.

Don't let them feel isolated and alone.

Believe them when they tell you that this "wonderful guy" is really a monster.

Look for signs like hyper-independence, where the victim is forced to take on more and more responsibility in the marriage.

Look for visual cues:

- Do you see a mom pushing a stroller and carrying the bags while the dad walks alongside, doing nothing?

- Do you see the mom tending to the kids' needs at dinner while the dad sits nearby, unaffected, eating his meal without interruption?

These are outward signs that the power dynamic in their marriage is skewed—and that a form of domestic abuse may be flying unnoticed.

Question the imbalance in parental responsibilities.

Contact the National Domestic Violence Hotline at 1-800-799-7233 or visit www.thehotline.org for more information and support.

You are strong. You are powerful. You are worthy. You are loved.

You deserve a happy and emotionally supportive relationship.

You have already survived the worst—and you are still standing.

You are *not* at fault for getting into this abusive relationship.

You were tricked into believing he was a wonderful person who was also a victim in life. You were made to believe that you were the only one who could help him overcome his perceived emotional injuries.

The only thing you did was try to love someone who was not capable of loving you back. You will eventually learn that the whole point of you suffering through this abuse is to realize that you deserve the same compassion and empathy you give everyone else. You will learn that personal boundaries are not selfish but your right. And you will learn that you won't let yourself get into an abusive relationship ever again.

I send my deepest love to you all.

*   *   *   *   *   *   *   *   *   *   *

It's not just the narcissist who hurts you. It's the people who take their side. It's the people who look the other way. It's the people who tell you to move on or get over it. It's the therapists untrained in personality disorders. It's the lack of healing help. It's the victim blaming. It's everyone who doesn't understand narcissistic abuse.

@ SuzzannaQ

2. How We Met

Behind every woman stuck in an abusive relationship is a little girl who never felt good enough and the narcissists' love bombing temporarily eases her pain. ~frankiestherapy

We met in college, where we had a similar group of friends, but we didn't hang out. I was in a serious two-year relationship with a great guy. It was the end of my sophomore year, and I was preparing to transfer to the dental hygiene school in Yakima to finish my last two years.

Somehow, I got it into my young, twenty-year-old head that I wanted to experience being with another guy before I fully committed to my then-boyfriend. I just wanted it to be a short fling. But with whom? I thought about the few guys I knew, and Mike was the only one on campus I was aware of who didn't have a girlfriend.

The school year was ending in three weeks, and with summer break approaching, I felt like I had to act quickly.

Jack, my boyfriend, had once told me about his good friend Rob and Rob's wife, Lori. They had temporarily broken up so she could experience other relationships, and then they got back together and got married. That story was dancing around in my thoughts. *If it worked for Rob and Lori, maybe it will work for Jack and me,* I told myself.

Yes, this was a stupid idea. It was also totally out of character for me.

I would never purposely hurt someone. I would never play with someone's emotions. But I was caught up in the time crunch and the idea that this had worked out for someone else.

I could never cheat on Jack, but this silly urge to expand my sexual experience took hold quickly. Unfortunately, I was moving so fast that I didn't see how the whole thing would backfire. I just thought: *If I'm going to do it, do it now with someone I sort of know—before school ends—or I'll forever wonder what it would've been like to be with someone else.*

Jack and I spent that Memorial Day weekend together in Yakima. He was home for the week from school, and as usual, we spent our free time together.

I felt bad about what I was going to do. That should have been enough of a sign that it was reckless and wrong. But after living a life centered on pleasing others, I wanted to take this small opportunity to explore my curiosity—just for myself—before totally committing to Jack.

He drove me back to school—only thirty minutes away— and I don't remember either of us saying a word during the drive. I remember thinking the entire time about how much I dreaded having to tell Jack what I wanted.

We walked side by side up the three flights of stairs to my dorm room in total silence. I wonder now if he sensed something was off—if he was ruminating, too, trying to make sense of what he was feeling.

Once inside my dorm room, with the door closed behind us, I told him.

It hit Jack hard.

He asked if I had slept with someone else. I hadn't. I had barely ever spoken to Mike.

Crazy, right?

If I could have floated above the scene and heard myself, I would've thought I was out of my mind.

In that moment, I thought I was being mature—breaking up temporarily instead of cheating. Wasn't that better? I didn't even know if Mike would respond to my advances. I didn't even know how I was going to go about it.

I must have been crazy—breaking up with an amazing man without even knowing if I could pull off this so-called "fling."

I broke Jack's heart. I saw his eyes well up.

I can't imagine the thoughts that ran through his head as he tried to make sense of what had happened. I can't imagine that long, lonely drive back, filled with confusion and emotional pain. I don't know what he must have told his mom and his family when they asked what happened.

And he would've been right: nothing *had* happened. Jack never did anything wrong. There were no fights. No arguments. We always had a beautiful connection whenever we were together. He made me feel safe, loved, seen, and important. He supported all my goals and was my biggest cheerleader.

I can only imagine how hurt and confused he must have been, searching for answers. And all I wanted was to see what it was like to have sex with someone else.

How ridiculous of me to believe that Jack and I could find our way back from that.

Just because Rob and Lori made it work didn't mean we could.

I only saw how foolish I had been after the damage was done.

Life isn't like the movies. The guy and the girl don't always get back together and live happily ever after. Some things, once broken, can't be repaired.

So just like that, my life veered in the wrong direction—and it would take me over thirty-three years to regain control.

But at the time, I was oblivious.

I set out to find Mike. And then...?

I didn't have any idea what I was doing. I just went looking. I found him studying for finals in the library with our mutual friends. I pulled up a chair and started studying too, not knowing how I was going to "make a move."

Somehow, he ended up in my dorm room, where I mustered the courage to ask him for sex.

Who *was* this girl? Who *was I*?

What was I thinking and doing? I had never done anything like this. I didn't recognize myself.

This wasn't me—but in that moment, it was me.

How did I do something so out of character? I don't hustle guys. So what was I thinking?

This is the moment in my life that I still don't fully understand.

What was going through my mind that caused me to be so reckless with my relationship with Jack?

I may never know.

This is the moment that—if I could go back in time—I would stop myself. I would listen to my higher self and never leave Jack. But it's too late.

There's no going back. There's only going forward.

I immediately knew I had made a mistake.

The sex was unfulfilling.

This isn't a criticism of Mike's sexual abilities, but rather a realization: if you don't love someone, if you don't share an emotional connection, sex is like eating air.

There's nothing there.

Nothing that fills your soul.

My curiosity led me down this path, and when I got there, I realized it was a dead end.

Panic set in the moment I realized what I had done. Panic—and shame.

Now what?

Do I call Jack and tell him I'm sorry? Do I beg for his forgiveness? That's what I should have done. I *should* have risked his rejection. But instead, a sudden wave of shame flooded my body.

Here I was—someone who had always been attuned to others' emotional needs—now realizing the magnitude of my mistake and how deeply I had hurt Jack.

What did I just do?

How could I have been so naïve to think that doing this would be okay?

I was so ashamed of what I'd done that I believed Jack wouldn't want me back. How could he, after what I'd done to him—without cause?

To make it worse, Mike began professing his love for me almost immediately. He told me how he knew I wouldn't leave him the way his last girlfriend had.

Holy smokes.

What had I just gotten myself into?

I started spending my days in confusion, caught between two impossible paths.

How do I let Mike down without hurting him?

How do I ever get back to Jack?

I tortured myself internally. I felt obligated to spend time with Mike and find a way to break things off without hurting him. I buried myself in final exam prep, trying to distract myself and find a way out of the emotional trap I had created.

Mike was skilled at playing with my emotions. He told me how excited his mom was to meet me—how she was thrilled to see him finally with a girlfriend.

A girlfriend?

It had only been a couple of days.

But already, I was in too deep. Mike sensed I was pulling away, so he played the victim to my sympathies.

"My last girlfriend was just using me. She had another boyfriend I didn't even know about. It hurt a lot when we broke up. I'm so glad you're not like her."

Oh boy. Now what?

I hadn't thought about the fact that I was using Mike. And now, here he was, confiding in me about someone who had done the very thing I was doing.

How could I back out without hurting him—and without destroying the image I held of myself?

I didn't have the self-love to say no. I ended up going home with him for the weekend to meet his mom.

I would rather hurt myself than someone else.

His mom was eager to connect. She pulled out family photo albums and showed me pictures of Mike as a little boy. His two sisters were excited to meet their baby brother's new girlfriend.

Everyone bombarded me with attention and warmth, welcoming me into their family.

Not even a week—and this is where I was.

I was caught between the heavy weight of what I'd done and the desperate desire to escape the mess without creating more casualties.

I had no one to talk to.

The shame and guilt were overwhelming.

I was going home for summer break the next week, and I hoped that the physical distance from Mike would give me the space I needed to untangle myself.

When I got home, my mom asked about Jack. "He hasn't called in a while. Is everything okay?"

When I told her I'd broken up with Jack, she was furious.

She didn't call me a whore or a tramp—but that's how I interpreted it.

I remember her words vividly:

"Jack is such a nice guy. How could you do that to him? Nice guys don't like girls who do that. He probably won't take you back now, after what you've done. You'd better not do to Mike what you did to Jack—and you better hope this is the one!"

Holy smokes.

What had I done?

Am I a whore? A tramp? Am I really that bad of a person?

Am I now stuck with Mike? Do I have to make this relationship work? What about Jack?

How do I get back to him?

I let my mom's words sink in—and they stayed with me for many years.

Now I fully saw what I had done, and I was so, so ashamed.

I had broken up with Jack thinking I was doing the right thing—being honest as I explored my sexuality.

I believed I was being mature and respectful by breaking up rather than cheating.

Even though my intentions seemed "honorable," I hadn't considered the reality: I was being dishonorable by using Mike for my own needs.

How disgusting.

I felt sick—literally sick. I wanted to vomit.

I was ashamed of myself.

I understood, finally, how I had hurt the beautiful soul of Jack—and how I was about to hurt an innocent soul in Mike once I was "done" exploring.

How could I go back to Jack now? I felt so unworthy of him.

I punished myself in my thoughts. I told myself how horrible I was.

How did I get into this position?

I knew, deep down, that I was a loving, empathetic person.

But how could I reconcile that with what I had just done?

How could I claim to be a decent human being after orchestrating something so hurtful and selfish?

After what my mom said, I truly believed there was no going back to Jack.

So, I carried my shame quietly.

I felt I had to prove to myself that I was a decent human being.

And to do that, I needed to make this relationship with Mike work.

I moved forward in a state of mourning—but kept it hidden from everyone.

In the beginning, Mike showered me with attention and gifts.

He opened every door for me. No one had ever opened doors for me before, and that made me feel special.

He made me feel like I was the most important person in the world to him.

His parents and family also lavished me with kindness—shopping trips, concerts, dinners.

I had lived such a frugal life that I wasn't used to these kinds of extravagances.

It had my head spinning.

I now know that I was being *love*-bombed—not just by Mike, but by his entire family.

I didn't realize then how quickly that kind of emotional bond could form.

I wanted so badly to stay in their favor, to not disappoint anyone. Their attention and approval became an external validation that I was still worthy—even though inside I was punishing myself every day for what I had done to Jack.

Looking back, I believe my determination to prove my goodness clouded my judgment.

I threw myself into a relationship with Mike, even though the red flags were everywhere.

The old me would have seen those signs and run. But this new, shame-filled version of me felt I was being too judgmental, too unforgiving.

So I gave him the benefit of the doubt—again and again.

Now I can see the warning signs clearly.

They were obvious to anyone with the life experience to interpret them.

But I was too busy drowning in shame.

I wanted so desperately to be washed clean that I ignored what was right in front of me.

The red flags that crept up early were small, subtle slights. Most of the time, I couldn't quite put my finger on why I felt bad in the moment.

Like the time we were driving somewhere in his Bronco, and I slid over to sit next to him while he was driving. He spoke to me harshly—like my dad would have.

"Get back over to your seat and put your seat belt on," he snapped. "You will have your seat belt on in the car whenever I'm driving. The last thing I want is for you to go through the windshield."

Okay, fair enough. He snapped at me "for my own good." He wanted to make sure I was safe. How could I feel bad about that?

But I did.

It was the way he said it. He made me feel like a stupid child the way he barked at me. I immediately felt like a silly little girl being chastised by her father. He could have lovingly told me he preferred I wear a seat belt—for the same reason—and I would have responded without feeling ashamed.

But instead, he made a habit of retelling this story to anyone who would listen, and I found myself humiliated over and over again. I felt like I had displeased him. I told myself, *I'll show him I'm not silly. I'm an adult. I'll just work harder to be better in his presence.*

Another time, we went out to dinner with his family, and I took a while to read the menu. I wasn't used to going out to dinner, and menus overwhelmed me. Too many choices—and I was worried about how much money I would cost them. Everyone else was ready to order, except me. I felt the weight of their eyes on me.

Mike made a small comment that I needed glasses to read the menu.

When he saw that I was bothered by the comment, he said, "I was just kidding. It's just a joke."

Then the table started laughing—and once again, I felt stupid.

Mike helped me move into an apartment in Yakima to start my first year in dental hygiene school. It was early September 1981. He had borrowed a truck from a friend, and we had to make the long trip from Camano Island to Yakima and back. Plus, Mike still had to return the truck to his friend. It would be a long day.

He confessed to me during that drive that he had taken speed.

What did he just say?

I was shocked that he had done it—and even more shocked that he told me about it. He said he needed it to stay awake.

I told him I didn't want him to do that again.

He brushed me off. Said it was no big deal. That I was being too sensitive.

The rest of the trip, I was on edge, trying to anticipate what might happen next.

On our way back from Yakima, Mike started telling me he believed my mom didn't like him.

"Your mom doesn't like me. She probably wishes you were still with Jack."

How do you even respond to that?

He was painting himself as the poor boyfriend—the one the parents didn't like—comparing himself to Jack so I would rush to his defense.

He was baiting me to inflate his ego. To prove my love by denouncing both my mom and Jack.

At the time, I couldn't understand why he needed to coerce and manufacture affection like that. It made me feel like maybe I wasn't doing enough to make him feel special.

I asked him why he said that.

"Because I think she likes Jack better than me," he answered.

He had no real reason to say it.

He was grasping for drama. I knew it then. I felt uncomfortable with his emotional manipulation, but I didn't want to make him mad—especially when I was stuck in the truck with him and would have to endure the long ride home with a sullen attitude.

I said something like, "She doesn't hate you," and left it at that.

Then there was the time I wanted to make out in his car somewhere.

He stopped my advances, grabbed my arms as I was about to wrap them around him, and pushed me gently but firmly back to my side of the car. Then, in a very serious, concerned tone, he said,

"Our relationship is too special for us to make out in the car. I don't want anyone to catch you in a compromising situation. You deserve better than that—and I'll make sure I protect you."

Wow. That was a powerful statement.

I didn't quite know how to feel about it.

On one hand, I felt rebuked—like I'd done something wrong. On the other hand, he sounded like a high-principled man who didn't want me to be caught in an embarrassing situation.

I sat back on my side of the car, trying to process the confusing emotions going through my head.

Once again, I felt like a silly girl he had to correct.

But then I told myself: *I've never had anyone declare that kind of virtuous protection for me.* Not even Jack.

I began to believe that Mike's stern ways were his way of showing he would stand up for me. That he would protect me.

Who wouldn't want to believe that in their partner?

So my emotional attachment to him grew stronger.

In the meantime, there were many other little nuanced attempts by Mike to feel out my boundaries—a little here, and a little there. If he ever felt like he was going too far, he would back off and shower me with gifts again. At Christmas, he gave me a beautiful jade necklace. No one had ever given me such a beautiful and expensive gift like that before. He paraded me around to his family to show them the gift, and everyone gathered around me with their own words of approval.

I was living in Yakima, and Mike was going to school in Ellensburg. The winter slowed down our visits, so I would call him on the weekends when the rates were cheaper. I didn't have a lot of money, so calling him was an expense, and I thought he would appreciate the financial sacrifice I was making for our relationship. After talking to him for a bit, I discovered he wasn't even listening to me. He was watching TV and pretending to listen. I was so furious. I thought about hanging up on him and seriously contemplated breaking up with him.

The next thing I knew, he surprised me with a kitten. I was eager to avoid any confrontation with him, so I accepted the kitten with joy and let go of his slight to me. I had a hard time believing that someone who was thoughtful enough to get me a kitten could possibly ever mean to be dismissive to me on the phone. I gave him the benefit of the doubt and let it go.

The reality of the kitten was that I now had to financially care for it. I had vet bills, cat food, and cat litter to buy. It was an easy gift on his part. The cat was probably free or cost him very little. The weight of the caretaking and the bills were all on me. His gift was cloaked as a sweet expression of love for me, but it really was a financial burden.

This wasn't the only time that Mike didn't take into consideration my measly bank account. When he would come to visit, he didn't like the fact that "there's nothing to eat in the house." What he meant was that I didn't have any treats or snack foods other than popcorn. Of course, I didn't have any of that stuff. I didn't have the money for anything that wasn't necessary. So off we went to the grocery store looking for ice cream, cookies, and chips. I was shocked that he expected me to pay for it.

My grocery budget for an entire month was under fifty dollars. Here I was, paying close to twenty dollars for garbage food. His mom always gave him whatever money he needed without accountability, and I was the opposite. I had to make what little bit of money I made during the summer last all school year. And the frustrating part was, Mike knew that. He knew that my money was limited. We talked about it often because it was always at the forefront of any of my decisions.

I didn't say anything about the purchases because of my own weak boundaries. It made me feel disrespected, but I still didn't say anything. I was so trauma bonded with him already. I was afraid of him being upset with me because I would point out how he didn't respect my finances.

The truth is, it was a combination of my weak boundaries and my own poor self-worth that stopped me from standing up for myself. Part of my personality is believing the best in everyone. I believed that Mike would have been so in tune with me that he would have known not to drag me to the store to buy unnecessary groceries. I was counting on him being just like me. After all, early in our relationship, that is how he portrayed himself to be: just like me.

On the other hand, Jack and I were so in tune with each other that he was very sensitive to the fact that I had little money. He would have either paid for the groceries himself or he would have just settled for the popcorn I already had. I was giving Mike the benefit of the doubt that he would be sensitive to my situation just like I would be to someone else, but he wasn't.

That hurt. I felt very unseen by Mike. I should have read the tea leaves then and let him go. I still believed that I didn't deserve any better, so I put up with the little breadcrumbs of consideration I got from Mike and allowed myself to believe that it was enough. Looking back, I can easily recognize the red flags now. Even in the many moments I knew it didn't feel right, I knew something was wrong, but I had a hard time putting my finger on it. At the time, I just shrugged it off and looked for the good intentions.

All the while, Mike was testing me and my boundaries. "If she is willing to let me get away with this, then let's see if she will put up with even more." With every little ceding of my boundaries and not voicing how what he was doing made me feel less than, Mike just took more and more. I was getting trapped deeper and deeper into an emotionally abusive relationship, and I didn't realize it.

We really didn't have anything in common. Mike was an extravagant spender and thought money came in an endless supply, while I worked so hard for the small wages I made to pay myself through college. Where Jack was always so accepting of who I was, Mike would point out flaws and then make suggestions on how I should behave in front of others. He would privately chastise me about silly things that made me feel like I was a stupid little girl, and then it would make me want to work harder to prove to him that I wasn't.

I was swimming in so much shame over what I did to Jack that I accepted all of this behavior, and I would simply try harder to be what Mike wanted. Looking back now, I can see that I was in a trauma bond with him early on. The back-and-forth of his love and attention mixed with his criticism and shaming made my head so confused. I accepted that I was not good enough and that I needed to try harder in our relationship. I hung in there longer than I should have because I was so mentally messed up and determined to prove that I was a good person.

I had a tough dental hygiene program ahead of me, and I was in my last two years of college, so I just put my head down and moved forward. This should have been a beautiful time for me and Jack. He was now back in Yakima after finishing school in Seattle, and he was going to be taking a few courses at the same college where I was attending dental hygiene school. We were finally going to be able to spend more time together as we moved closer to our forever commitment to each other.

But now, there was a constant dark cloud walking with me. I was very aware of the possibility of running into Jack, and I was terrified of it. I was so ashamed of myself and so sure he was disgusted with me that I didn't know what he would do if we came face-to-face. I was so afraid of him rebuking me. I didn't think I could take his rejection, even though I felt like I deserved it. So, I purposely didn't wander too often from the dental hygiene building on campus.

There were two times in those next two years that I ran into Jack. Both times I was walking home, and he was in his car as he slowed down to say hi. Both times I froze. How could he be so nice to me, especially after what I did to him? I don't believe I ever said a word. My shame kept me silent. He might have taken my silence for indifference when, in fact, it was just the opposite. I was screaming inside, but no one would know. My eyes just welled up with tears as he drove off.

The second time he stopped, it was late February 1983, almost two years since I broke up with him. This time he offered me a ride home, and I took it. I still didn't say anything to him; I was too frozen in my shame and confused about his kindness toward me. I was surprised when we got to my place and he jumped out of the car and came into the house with me. He stood in the living room, looking around, and said, "Good memories."

I had already discovered in January that Jack was engaged. I had run into his fiancée, someone I had gone to high school with, and she told me. Here we were, Jack and I both engaged to someone else, and I was still anguishing over what I did to him. Since I had no words for him that could make a difference at this point, I just ended up giving him a big hug, and he gave me a big smile and left.

Going back to that moment thirty years before, when I saw Jack drive away for the last time, I remember feeling such deep sadness knowing that we should have been together. Crazy, but on my wedding day, getting dressed at the church, this voice in my head said very loudly and clearly, "Don't do this." I took a moment to wonder where it came from. I was definitely taken aback by how clear and strong the voice and the message were. I just pushed it aside and continued to get dressed, wondering if I was doing the right thing marrying Mike. Too late, I told myself. Too many things in motion to go back now.

The same message came back to me as I was walking down the aisle with my dad. I remember thinking that if I said anything to anyone, they would just say I had "cold feet." So, I said nothing and just continued to walk down the aisle.

I have since discovered through my healing journey that you must listen to your intuition. It is your higher self telling you what is best for you. When that voice comes loud and clear, it is imperative that you listen. You don't have to understand why. The answer will come later. All you have to do is trust yourself. My higher self knew that Mike and I should not be married. It was an exit ramp being offered to me, and I was too afraid to take it. I didn't trust myself.

I now know that above all else, I need to trust and love myself. After all the hell that I have been through, I realized that I am the only one who will truly have my own best interests in mind. I needed to shake off the old belief systems that I inherited as a kid that told me that it was wrong to put myself first. Unfortunately, it would take me over three decades to finally do it. What an absolute shame that it took me that long to realize that I am just as worthy as all the people that I extended grace to in the past.

So now I'm married and moving away to Virginia. With Mike being in the Marine Corps, there were going to be quite a few moves in the first couple of years and Virginia was just the first stop. This was the first time that I was going to be away from my family and the only life that I knew. I had convinced myself that I was excited but deep down I was nervous and scared. All I could do was to put on my big girl pants and leave my beloved Yakima for what would be a long thirty-one years.

*   *   *   *   *   *   *   *   *   *   *

Trauma bond is a psychological addiction in the same way a drug addict becomes addicted to a drug, your brain becomes addicted to another human being. The way it usually develops is through narcissistic relationships where there is push and pull, hot and cold with affection. There is someone who has been manipulated dreaming of the relationship returning to the love bombing stage. It creates a paranoia mentally that if they aren't happy, you take it personally that you are responsible. You will do anything in your power to make them feel great again. It is created through the hot and cold dynamic of the abuser.

Jlcowdrey and coachcowdrey

3. Early Years

Peace comes when you realize everything that is out of your control should be out of your mind too. ~IMAGINARYPLANETTT

In the early years, we moved five times in three years. It seemed like every six months we were moving, and I could feel my body shifting and getting ready each time. There is an inherent amount of stress that comes from moving and relocating. I would feel it in the preparations that had to be made before each move. I knew that Mike was feeling it as well.

But Mike's controlling and abusive ways were starting to manifest differently and with more intensity. He was getting easily ticked off by simple daily challenges. I started anticipating his mood swings whenever a perceived challenge came his way. I would tell myself that he was under a lot of stress from his flight training, and instead of holding him accountable for his moody, abusive ways, I would let it go. I believed that it was just temporary and that he would return to the great guy I knew before we married once he got out of the training command.

Our first duty station was in Quantico, Va., "The Crossroads of the Marine Corps." This is where all Marine officers come, regardless of their specialty, to train to become officers in the Marine Corps. Mike was going to school at TBS, The Basic School. This school teaches all Marine second lieutenants the basics of ground tactics—basically training them in the tactics of an infantryman.

Their schedule started early before daylight and finished many times well into the evening after dark. I was home alone quite a bit, but the wives in our group would get together for fun activities to help us through that period. We organized softball teams and played against other wives' groups. I have always loved sports and have been fairly athletic, so I dove right into these functions and had a blast.

Mike came home one day from work and told me that TBS was sponsoring a "Jane Wayne Day" for the spouses. The wives would be able to run the obstacle course, ride in the back of military vehicles with gear on, and do some light infantry activities. I love competition, and I was looking forward to doing whatever the Marine Corps had lined up for me to try.

A couple of days before the event, Mike took me out to get some boots. He said that I needed boots that would protect my ankles from any rollover from the uneven terrain that we would be facing. He then took me out to the obstacle course and had me put the boots on and make a run through the course.

I had an absolute blast doing it. I was a strong and fast runner, and I was agile, so it was easy for me to vault over the many wooden hurdles that were in place and make my way to the rope ladder that went way up and over to the other side. It was fun, fun, fun. I was ready to smoke all the other wives on Jane Wayne Day and claim my own personal victory at the end.

Unfortunately, I woke up on the morning of the event with the flu. I hadn't had any symptoms the night before when I went to bed, so I woke up in total surprise and full-on misery. Mike was so mad. The husbands were going to be allowed out of classes for the day to be with their wives; now Mike had to be in class all day, and he wasn't happy.

He slammed stuff down as he was getting ready and told me it was a waste of money to buy the boots since I wasn't going to compete. My head was killing me, and I could barely move in bed. Instead of voicing his concern for my illness, he spent the morning venting about how he was going to have a miserable day because he had to go to classes. He made it seem like I had purposely gotten sick just to make his day miserable.

I remember being so sick that I barely reacted to his selfish tantrum. But I did remember how he made me feel, and I couldn't understand why he was acting so hostile toward me when it wasn't my fault that I got the flu. This was the first time—but it wouldn't be the last—that Mike would show no empathy for me and my misery. He was solely focused on how it affected him, not how it affected me.

We moved to Florida six months later, where Mike was attending Aviation Ground School and Basic Flight

School. These schools are very tough, and some pilots don't make it through this next step. They end up being removed from their flight contract and then forced to find another specialty in the Marine Corps. Mike would study hard to be prepared for the next day's task and would sometimes ask me to quiz him to get him ready.

I would spend my evenings and weekends quizzing Mike on whatever he asked me to do. We would go out to the airfield on the weekends, and he would climb into a mock cockpit so I could quiz him on the controls and procedures. When he came home after a flight check where he received a poor score, he would be emotionally frail. I recognized that flying jets was a difficult skill, and I knew it was his passion. I understood how he would feel the weight of these flight checks as he tried to progress through to the next round. It was unusual for me to see him emotionally crumble, but I understood why.

Then Mike would start to bad-mouth the flight check and talk about how it was flawed. He would cry foul when he described what he believed were other pilots getting special treatment and not having to go through what he had to endure. I was getting upset with him because I wanted him to have fair and equal treatment. I have always been about justice and standing up for others.

So when one of his fellow pilot friends—who Mike said was getting special treatment—came over to offer some condolences, I stepped in and gave him an earful of my thoughts. Mike stood by and watched me be his pit bull for him. The pilot friend was taken aback by my fiery defense of my husband and left with apologies.

This was the first time that I ever had cause to step in and stand up for my husband. His description to me of how he was being ill-treated sparked an overemotional response to defend him. What I eventually learned was that Mike was prone to exaggerate his circumstances and would often paint himself to be the victim. This time, I played perfectly into his performance and gave him the much-needed energy supply he wanted for his wounded ego.

Mike knew that my empathetic nature would swoop in to soothe and defend him when he felt like he needed it. I would end up falling for his victimizing ploy many more times in our marriage before I recognized that it was a form of emotional manipulation. But before I saw through his intentional self-victimizing ways, he got to watch me jump up and deploy my sympathies to soothe him. He got to see how he could easily manipulate my sympathetic tendencies for his benefit, and he didn't hesitate to use that tactic whenever he felt like he needed attention from me. In other words, he enjoyed watching me jump into action to placate him.

We moved to Beeville, Texas, six months later, where Mike was attending Intermediate and Advanced Flight School. This was going to be a longer tour—approximately eighteen months compared to the six months in Florida. Due to the longer tour, I was able to get a steady position substitute teaching at the high school. It would help us with extra income and keep me busy while Mike was busy with flight school.

Again, I would help him get ready for his flight checks by quizzing him. There were many late nights of me staying up to help him, then turning around and getting up to teach at the high school. I gladly did it because that is what you do for each other. If your spouse needs you, then you step in wherever you can to help. It didn't always get reciprocated by Mike. If I needed something, he would be too busy with his studies to stop and help me. Again, I would let it go, rationalizing that his studies were more important. I would have to find ways to deal with things myself.

We had moved to Texas in September 1984, and now it was February, and I learned that I was pregnant with our first child. The baby was due in early November. The first couple of months were hard on my body. I felt like I had the flu. I slept all the time; I got nauseous but, surprisingly, never threw up. My breasts swelled up and were super tender, and my whole body was getting thick. It was hard to recognize myself in the mirror.

Mike's schedule kept him busy during the day and then studying at night. I went to all the doctor appointments alone and was left to plan for the baby by myself. I had found a crib just a couple of doors down from someone who didn't need one anymore. Luckily, it was very cheap and still in good condition. Then I found a dresser for the baby at a yard sale. It was very simple, with just four drawers, and it needed to be repainted.

I was going to paint it myself, but Mike insisted on doing it. He wanted it to be done correctly, and he felt that it should be air-sprayed instead of painted with a brush. I didn't care. I just wanted it painted. If he wanted to do it, then I would let him. I had plenty of other things to do before the baby was born.

We didn't have an air sprayer, so we were going to have to rent one. Our finances were always tight, so we had to wait until payday to get it done. Mike and I planned to create a spray tent outside where he could spray the dresser and keep it protected from the wind and airborne debris. We had the day set—it would be on a Saturday in late September. We would be able to rent the sprayer in the morning and then return it by the end of the day. It was going to cost us enough to make it hurt a bit in this pay cycle, but overall, we were still saving a lot of money instead of buying a new dresser.

Saturday came, and I had the dresser washed down and the drawers removed in advance of the paint. Then a fellow pilot friend who lived down the street came to the door and asked for Mike's assistance in fixing something with his car. Mike immediately abandoned our project and left to go help Rob. I put up a small protest, and Mike said it wouldn't take long and then he would be back to paint the dresser.

In my mind I was *thinking, If it won't take that long, then paint the dresser first, then you can go help Rob.* I was

49

concerned that we wouldn't get the dresser painted in time to return the sprayer and then we would be charged for an extra day. But Mike had an opportunity to show how handy he was with auto repairs and gain valuable external credit and validation from a friend. It would become an unwelcome scenario with him over the years, where he would have all the time in the world to help others but not me. In his eyes, helping me would only benefit me; helping others would benefit him because of all the public adulation he would get for his selfless service to them.

The Saturday was rolling along, and the hours were ticking away. Mike was still busy working on Rob's car, and the wind was now picking up. I thought about doing it myself, but I knew that if I did, Mike would rail into me for not waiting. Twice, I walked down the street to see how much longer it would take, and each time he told me it wouldn't be much longer.

I was getting very perturbed when I saw the clock at almost 4 p.m., and we had to have the sprayer back by 5 p.m. closing time. Mike still had to erect the spray tent, and the wind was going to be a problem. Close to 4:20 p.m., Mike and Rob came running down the street and started feverishly trying to erect the spray tent in the wind. Mike quickly gave the dresser one blast of the paint and that was it. He didn't have time for the paint to dry and apply a second coat like we had planned. It was all he could do to take the sprayer apart, clean it, and return it to the rental place in time.

I was not a happy person. The dresser was okay. It wasn't the best paint job. I felt like I could have done better with a brush, but Mike insisted on spraying it. And I was okay with that. It's just that he made the dresser a nonpriority in place of Rob's car. I had been left to plan and organize the baby's room by myself, and I was counting on at least having Mike's contribution with the dresser. It got done, but it was done haphazardly. This was our first baby, and I wanted it to be right. I learned that day that Mike's priorities were fluid when anyone other than I asked for help.

The baby came two weeks early. My water broke when I went out for an evening walk. Luckily, I was only two blocks away, so I returned quickly to tell Mike. I'm standing in the kitchen, gushing buckets of water, when I told Mike that my water broke. He said, "Are you sure? Maybe you just peed your pants." No, I'm sure. Water was pooling all around me, and he finally got motivated to get up and go get some towels for the floor. I had called the doctor, and they told me to make my way to the hospital.

Mike was getting ready for night carrier landing qualifications and was about to leave for his flight when my water broke. I figured it might take me several hours to deliver, so I gave him permission to go on to his flight and I would get a neighbor to take me to the hospital.

As it was, the baby didn't come for another eighteen hours, and Mike was able to be there for the delivery. He loved telling people how he went on to do his carrier qualifications while I went to the hospital without him. I did feel a little annoyed at him since I always felt like I was taking a back seat to his career. But I let it slide.

The baby was a girl, and we named her Jillian. My life was immediately turned upside down. In addition to the normal house chores, I now had to add all the needs of a new baby without the help of her dad. Mike would complain about Jillian's crying and how he couldn't concentrate and study. He kept telling me how dangerous his job was, and he needed to be prepared for the flights. I knew his job was dangerous; I just didn't know what I was supposed to do to get Jillian to stop crying. He was expecting me to take the baby out of the house and go somewhere so he could keep studying. I wondered why he didn't just leave to go study somewhere else.

And so, this continued every night when Jillian's tummy would get gassy, and Mike would get angry. I felt like I was on my own, and I didn't get any consideration from Mike for all the sleepless days and nights that I had to endure.

His parents came to visit a couple of weeks after Jillian was born. They insisted that they take us all out to dinner. I said no. I knew that Jillian would turn into a pumpkin at night, and it wouldn't be fair to everyone in the restaurant to have to hear a crying baby. I kept insisting that I stay home, and his parents kept insisting that they take me out. Mike stepped into the discussion and insisted that I go with them to dinner. He said I was being ridiculous and that there would be plenty of people to help with Jillian if I needed it. I, having weak personal boundaries, gave in to their demands.

It was a disaster. As I expected, Jillian was screaming the whole time. It was ridiculous. I had her outside the restaurant, trying to soothe her while everyone was inside ordering. Eventually, I was told to come in and place my order. I get overwhelmed with menus and have a hard time choosing on a good day. Now I had a screaming newborn in my arms, so it didn't go well. People in the restaurant got mad and made ugly comments. Mike's parents acted like nothing was wrong, and no one offered to take Jillian from me. So back outside I went until the food came.

Mike was not happy that Jillian was crying and ruining his dining experience. I was not happy for obvious reasons, and neither were the other people in the restaurant. After Mike had finished his dinner, he came outside and took Jillian from me. Everyone else was done eating by the time I came back in. I looked up at the window and saw Mike pacing back and forth with Jillian. He stopped to give me the biggest daggers with his eyes and made it clear that he was not happy with me for Jillian's crying.

To top it off, Jillian had a massive blowout, and she got poop all over him. Yes, that sucks. I tried to tell all of them that it wasn't a good idea, and now I was getting blamed for Mike not having a good dining experience. What about me? Anybody? What about me?

I saw a whole new side to Mike when Jillian was born. He had no desire to help me with her or give me a break. I was even expected to take her with me grocery shopping because Mike had to "study." Mike's life never changed. It never really skipped a beat. He resented any attempt by me to have him contribute. He always cited how important it was for him to be ready for his next flight and made me feel like I could never ask him for any help.

When we eventually moved to Yuma, Arizona, in February 1986, I found myself isolated, thirty minutes outside of town on an Army base. We only had one car, and Mike used it to go to work. I was left to take care of Jillian by myself. I had to walk everywhere on the base if I needed something. Mike's schedule was brutal. He was flying six days a week. That meant we both only had one day off. I tried to use his one day off to run errands in town and to just get out. Mike would have a fit and say he deserved that one day off to run his own errands. After all, according to Mike, I was home all day with Jillian and had it easy. He was busy with his dangerous job of flying and deserved to have that one day off more than I did.

Of course I gave in. I believed that he needed rest so he would be fully ready for his training flights. There was already one pilot who had died in a crash, and Mike said it was because he didn't get his rest the night before due to their baby crying. I don't know if that really was the reason for the accident, but I was willing to bite the bullet and endure no breaks from Jillian if that meant Mike would have a safe flight.

And so, I lived for six months way out in the desert on an Army base with no car and no husband to give me a break. I was learning that I could not depend on him for anything and that it would all be up to me. I became hyper-independent and congratulated myself on making it through each day with all that I accomplished—with no help from anyone. Sadly, this would become my normal for the next thirty years.

After six months in Yuma, we were finally ready to move to North Carolina. This would be our fifth move in three years, and Mike would finally be assigned to a gun squadron. This next move would have Mike deploying on aircraft carriers and leaving me alone to run the house and the family. I was exhausted from the last three years, and I was hoping that this next move could give us some stability. I had no idea how hard it was going to be on me as I followed Mike around in his career. I know it would have made it easier for me if he had given me some indication that he appreciated the sacrifices I had made. But that was a no.

Instead, I continued to make excuses for him and his nonexistence as a dad and husband. I kept thinking that it would ease up once he got through with the training command and made it to the gun squadron. But all it did was get different. I was still counting on the loving and considerate Mike to turn up, so I kept putting one foot in front of the other, making it day by day, waiting for his transformation.

I would be waiting forever.

    *   *   *   *   *   *   *   *   *   *   *

The person who should matter most to the narcissist is the one they treat the worst, while strangers get their best performance.

@JENNALEA_COACHING

4. Finances and Folly

You didn't imagine it. The gaslighting, the manipulation, the emotional whiplash - it was real. Your intuition wasn't wrong. Trust yourself. ~evolvewithsophie

As I had mentioned earlier, we had moved five times in three years for his training—from Yakima to Virginia, then Florida, Texas, Arizona, and North Carolina. If I wanted to work as a dental hygienist, I would have to take a new state board exam in every state we moved to. Unfortunately, I was only able to get my license in Florida and North Carolina, so I didn't have the opportunity to work consistently. The pay for a new officer in the Marine Corps is not very much, and having the extra income when I could work made a difference.

My first inclination with this "bounty" of extra income I made in Florida was to save the money or, at the very least, pay cash for the things we needed. I knew my extra income wasn't guaranteed wherever we moved to, and I didn't want us to extend any financial obligations based on it. I felt saving the extra money was the wise thing to do.

Fortunately, I was able to convince Mike early on in our marriage that we needed to invest my earnings and some of his. We would live on his paycheck alone, since my income supply was not consistent. What a coup on my part, since he made it very clear many times later in our marriage that he resented having any of "his" money going into investments. Nonetheless, the monthly investments that we set up early were a godsend when it was time for me to leave him.

The first couple of years were probably the best—but far from great. We were married adults with no kids, so we were able to take off and do things couples would do like go to restaurants and movies. I was able to work for only six months in a dental office in Pensacola, and then I found work as a substitute teacher in Texas when I couldn't get my hygiene license in the state. It wasn't a lot of extra money, but it felt great to finally be a professional and to make money. I had been required to pay my own way since I was in the third grade, so money came very hard for me; consequently, I was always very appreciative for every cent I made, and I was very mindful of how money was saved and spent.

I learned early the difference between wants and needs. My parents would pay for my needs, but I would have to pay for my wants. I also learned that "needs" can be interpreted differently by each of us. When I told my parents I needed new shoes because mine had holes, I was told that they still fit me—or I could buy new ones with my own money. If I outgrew the shoes, they told me I could wear my older brother's shoes or, again, buy new ones with my own money.

I learned to sew in the fourth grade so I could afford to have the clothes that I wanted. I paid my way through a private high school and then college—and I even paid for our wedding. There were times while I was in college that I didn't have the money to eat on the weekends. I was so thin and stressed all the time, worrying about money and having to pay for everything at such an early age. Since I had always earned money and paid my own way, I expected nothing less from myself when I was married.

Now that I was finally working as a professional and making more money than I had ever made up to that point (still not very much but, by comparison, it was a lot), my stress and worry about money had gone down a bit. But I never quit being vigilant about managing the flow of our income. I knew that you couldn't spend more than you made. I knew that it was important to have a healthy savings account. I knew how to economize, since I had been doing it from such an early age. The problem was—Mike was the opposite.

His parents paid for everything. They paid for his tuition, his rent, his groceries, and gas money. He bragged about making five thousand dollars in a summer while in college and then had nothing to show for it when the next school year started. His parents never required that he be responsible with his money, so they kept footing the bill and he never learned fiscal responsibility. What he learned was that money was an endless supply and that whatever he wanted he could just go out and buy. Obviously, he and I were not in sync with our view on finances, and that became a constant source of anger and resentment between the two of us.

He resented being on a budget. He didn't consider that I was sacrificing my own needs as well. I put off getting a haircut, and I wore my shoes and clothes until they were almost threadbare. I was trying to squeeze as much money out of his paycheck as I could to keep him happy. I clipped coupons and cut corners with recipes so our groceries would last longer. I kept errands to a minimum so that our gas would last longer.

His verbal assaults on me and our finances made me feel like I was at fault for the little money that we had. He totally abdicated all financial responsibility to me, so every pay period I would have to be the one to tell him we didn't have the extra money he wanted.

One time I broke down in front of him, crying, and told him that I didn't deserve to spend any money on myself since I wasn't working. He surprised me by responding tenderly, "It's not my money, it's our money, and I don't want you to think otherwise." This was followed by a warm embrace from him. I thought, *Finally, we are on the same page. He gets it, and he understands the pressure I've been under.*

But that sentiment didn't last long. His indiscriminate spending would often lead us to an overdrawn account and back in the red. I had to constantly move money from our piddly little savings account to cover the overage. When I brought up the fact that the account was overdrawn, he chastised me for letting it happen.

I never seemed to be in a good spot with him. Just when he led me to believe that we were a team with our finances, he pulled the floor out from under me and laid me low with his verbal barrage. I started to cringe every time I had to give him our financial updates. I was prepared for a verbal flogging each time, but I wasn't prepared for his explosive episodes of pounding on the furniture, slamming cabinets and doors that left me intimidated and shaking.

I couldn't help the fact that I couldn't get work consistently due to the frequent moves. But I still carried the responsibility for paying the bills and being the bearer of bad news. Eventually, he had enough and decided he was going to get a credit card and buy a dirt bike. Did he discuss this with me? Of course not. I was blindsided when he brought the dirt bike home and declared it was only going to cost us an extra eighty dollars a month. I didn't know where I was getting the extra money from, but now I had to scramble.

The total cost of the dirt bike kept creeping up when you added in the insurance and the trailer he needed to haul it. He didn't care that we were stretched super thin. He just wanted what he wanted, when he wanted it, and that was all there was to that.

He was happy as long as you didn't require too much from him. He was a child stuck in a man's body—selfish and self-centered. It became more apparent after we were married that his wants and desires would become a priority over anyone else's needs. If you dared to bring to his attention the reality that money was not in an endless supply, he would melt down and have tantrums. He would stomp his feet, tighten every muscle in his body as he pounded his fists on the furniture or the wall. His eyes, normally blue, would turn dark from his pupils dilating as his anger grew, and his face would get puckered tight as he glared at me and shoved his chest forward in an attempt to intimidate me.

In the beginning, I pushed back against his anger toward me. I didn't think it was fair that he took it out on me. After all, I was just the messenger—I was just telling him the truth, the reality that money wasn't in an infinite supply. But I learned quickly not to challenge him. He became scary. He turned into a human being I had never seen before, and my shock turned quickly into fear when he said, as he made his way toward me in a threatening manner, "It's my goddamn money, and I can spend it as I goddamn well please." (So much for it being both our money.)

I took an instinctual step back and started to cry. He softened his body language, wrapped me in his arms, and apologized. It was the first time that he made me feel physically unsafe and afraid. His quick change in mood and his softening behavior helped me to calm down a bit, but I was still so taken aback by his visceral reaction that I became very cautious from then on not to trigger him. This became a pivotal event that would further strengthen the trauma bond I had already developed.

A whole new dynamic was shaping up between us without me realizing it. He had been pushing my boundaries little by little up to now, but this event took everything to a new level. Now I was very afraid of doing anything to trigger him. It wasn't long after this that he went off on me again about the finances, and it left me shaking and crying. This time, instead of calming down and comforting me, he doubled down and said, "No! You are not going to use crying to get me to apologize."

And so, he didn't. He just let me cry and yelled at me for crying.

There weren't too many times in our marriage that I let him see me cry after that, but every time I did, instead of trying to comfort me, he would just yell at me for crying. I got no comfort from him when I was down— only berating. How could someone who says they love you not be compassionate toward you when you need it the most?

I can tell you how... they never really loved you at all.

That was an unfortunate truth that I didn't fully internalize for many more years to come. The truth was always there, but I didn't acknowledge it. He didn't really love me. My higher consciousness knew. It sent me a message that his behavior toward me wasn't right by placing a sadness that hovered right behind my eyes. Since I was so mentally confused by his behavior, I didn't understand the message. Instead, I just became accustomed to the sad feeling without putting a definition to it, and I carried it with me until I left him thirty years later.

He was obsessed with spending money. It's not actually the acquisition of stuff that he liked—he just liked to spend money. I thought if I sent him grocery shopping, he could get the thrill of spending money and yet it would be on the food we needed.

What a mistake.

He came back with my list completed, but he also spent close to an extra fifty dollars on junk food: ice cream, chocolate sauce for the ice cream, ice cream cones, cookies, chips, cereal, soda, juices. All of those indulgences are nice to have—but not when we're on a tight budget, and an extra fifty dollars spent is a huge chunk out of our budget.

That was the one and only time he went grocery shopping for me.

Mike's parents indulged him in whatever he wanted, so I am sure he associated spending money with his definition of self-worth. He felt good about himself when he spent money. He would get really excited about the prospect of buying anything. He got a rush of endorphins when he spent money. His mood would elevate from excitement to almost euphoria. It seemed like his body would quiver when he spent money. He would come home so giddy and excited, eager to show me what he got. He would always claim that he got a "great deal" and that he saved us a lot of money!

Eventually, the realization would set in that we couldn't afford it. He would reluctantly take it back for a refund, and then he would sulk and pout like a little kid.

He would chastise himself out loud for me to hear: "I'm a fool. I know I can't afford it. I'll never be able to afford it." Or, instead of his verbal self-flogging, he would resort to slamming doors and drawers to let me know he wasn't happy. He would walk around with a scowl and barely acknowledge me, making me feel like I was the reason for his misery. Looking back now, I can see how I took on the role of a parent in the marriage and he took on the role of a child. That parent-child dynamic in a marriage is always headed for ruin.

Throughout the marriage, he would constantly buy and return—or buy and sell—after he got his euphoric fix. Then he would replace that emotion with self-loathing. His mood became predictable. It added more anxiety to my life when I had to brace myself for the inevitable blitz of mental torture he hurled toward me as if I was the reason he couldn't afford it. He was always the victim. He played it well. He would say things like, "Well, I guess you're glad I took it back. I guess you're happy to see me without any pleasure in my life." Then he would follow it up with, "I can't seem to do anything right. I'm always messing things up for us."

He was challenging me with these statements, fishing for a consolatory response. Of course he was messing things up—but do I tell him I agree with him? Of course not. Only if I was interested in intense retaliation from him. So do you lie and say, "No, sweetie. Of course you don't mess things up for us"? Or do you say nothing and let the silence be interpreted as agreement? He was going to make me wrong no matter what my reaction was. Acting as the parent in the marriage, I felt like I had to put a bandage on his wounded ego to diffuse a potential meltdown.

It took many years of this behavior—him playing the poor victim—before I understood his M.O. I eventually quit taking the bait and would not respond. I would just be silent. I discovered that narcissists hate silence. They want attention. They want a response to their pitiful self-loathing statements. Even if it's not the response they want, they will use any response to their advantage—either to assuage their self-inflicted wounds or to use it against you. Either way, they feel superior to you—and that is what they want.

This buy-sell, buy-sell addiction of his would get ridiculous. When we started making more money, he started spending bigger dollars. Shopping on Craigslist became his favorite pastime. He would bring home some big power tool and tell me what a great deal he got.

"It was only $500."
"It was only $800."
"It was only $1,200—and that was a steal!"

Next thing I knew, he was reselling it on Craigslist, but for less than he paid. Why, I asked. He had no answer. But I eventually figured it out. First, once he realized we couldn't afford it, he would verbally punish himself for the extravagance. Second, to make himself feel better, he would manufacture praise from strangers by offering them a really great deal—selling the item at a loss. It made him feel valued and important that someone, even if it was a stranger, walked away having a positive view of him. He was essentially buying adoration from strangers by sucking up the money he lost when he originally bought the item.

Obviously, this buy-then-sell-for-less strategy is not favorable to your finances. It left me constantly trying to plug the financial holes that he created.

Another favorite thing for him to do was to buy his own birthday, Christmas, or Father's Day gift. Usually, around six weeks before, he would say with great excitement, "You don't have to get me anything for my birthday—I already got it." Then, when his birthday got closer, he would go out and buy something else and declare it was also for his birthday, as if he had forgotten the earlier purchase.

When it was his actual birthday, he would be bummed if I didn't get him anything substantial. I would have to remind him that he had already bought his own birthday gift. Plus, there wasn't any money left in the checking account to get him anything anyway—after he had already spent it on himself. That wasn't a good enough answer for him. And so, I had the pleasure of enduring several days of silent treatment from him.

There was one Christmas in 2010 that I had finally had enough. Three kids in college and the budget was tight.

I had communicated to him early about the state of our finances so he would be mindful about purchases. He came home less than a week before Christmas with a new gun. He walked in the door and said, "You don't have to get me anything for Christmas—I already got what I want."

He spent over $800 on that gun when we didn't have the money to spend. Plus, who spends that kind of money on themselves? Our son, Craig, was with him when he bought it, and he told me that he asked his dad, "Are you sure Mom is going to be okay with that?" Craig knew it was an irresponsible purchase, but it obviously didn't deter Mike since he walked through the front door so elated and telling me he got "a killer deal!"

I was so disappointed. I knew it was an extravagant purchase at such a wrong time in our lives—a purchase we couldn't afford. So I found a quiet place upstairs in the office and figured out a way to tell him he had to return it. I decided that I had to treat him like a little child and talk to him gently but firmly—that he had to return it. I would not have any hint of disappointment in my voice, but I was going to be firm. I knew I was going to have to endure his punishment in whatever form he decided to give it, but I didn't care. Eight hundred dollars to spend on yourself at Christmas when we have three kids in college is ridiculous.

He surprised me in that he didn't go full ballistic, but he was very upset. He said, "I can never do anything right. You are always right, and I am always wrong."

I replied, "I'm not always right."

Then he said, "There you go. You're right again and I'm wrong again."

Geez, always the poor victim in his own story. How do you get anywhere with someone like that? I stood my ground and gently told him he needed to return it.

He came home the next day, hanging his head low, and told me the gun store had a no-return policy. So he placed the ad on Craigslist, and on Christmas Day, some stranger rang the doorbell to buy it from him. As usual, he sold it for way less than he bought it for. He gave me a deep look of disgust as he shut the door behind the stranger. He wanted me to know that I was the reason why his Christmas was ruined. It became just another holiday draped in his sulky mood, floating above our celebration.

He was selfish and didn't care if you knew it. He did not want the kids to get braces or help with their college tuition, since it would divert money away from him. He would destroy us financially over and over again, and I was left to try to figure out how to pay the bills and provide for the kids.

When I needed extra money to buy Claire a computer for college, I looked over the entire house to see if I could find anything I could sell to make money. All I had of any value was my wedding ring and my china. I looked out in the garage and saw thousands of dollars' worth of stuff that he had bought for himself. Over twenty years of marriage up to this point, and I realized I had basically nothing of mine to claim.

I sold my china, then bought Claire her computer, and just kept moving forward with my head down, trying to provide for the kids.

Our checking and savings accounts were a constant dark cloud that hung over me our entire marriage. How can I leave the marriage with three kids if I don't have the money to do so? Thirty years of financial abuse. Thirty years of me trying to plug holes and pay bills. Thirty years of watching him prioritize himself with extravagant purchases while I struggled with buying myself a twenty-dollar bra.

This constant beatdown of our finances is one of the main reasons that propelled me to leave after thirty years. Unfortunately, I still had a long way to go before I saw the way out.

* * * * * * * * * * *

Whether it's controlling your access to money, discouraging you from pursuing better opportunities, or making unwise financial decisions, the narcissist will often put you in a position of financial dependency...all while claiming they're supporting you.

@JENNALEA_COACHING

5. The Big Secret

Sometimes you have to give up on people. Not because you don't care, but because they don't. ~modernframeofmind

We had been married for almost three years when I discovered his dark secret.

We had recently moved from Yuma, Arizona—where Mike was undergoing advanced flight school for the A-4M Skyhawk—to Cherry Point, North Carolina, where he would be stationed at his first gun squadron, VMA-223. We moved into our base housing on December 23, 1986, and we were busy trying to decorate for Christmas with whatever we could find in whatever store was still open. All our decorations were still in boxes somewhere in the house, and we were half camping out while opening boxes and settling in. Crazy time—but we made it work.

Jillian had turned one in October, so she was walking around a lot by then. It was a challenge to keep an eye on her and unpack at the same time. Time passed quickly with the move and the holidays, and I was starting to feel very fatigued, and coffee was starting to make me nauseous. A pregnancy test confirmed that I was pregnant with our second child, and I was due in early September. Mike had such a hard time adjusting to our first baby—with the crying and sleepless nights—that I had planned on waiting at least five years before having another one.

But the universe had a different plan for me. Baby number two was coming in September.

I was very apprehensive about this pregnancy because Mike was not a supportive father at all. He had no patience for Jillian's crying in the evening when he was trying to study. I tried hard to comfort and quiet her so he wouldn't get angry—but what do you do? Babies are going to cry. And now there was going to be another baby to irritate him. I wanted the baby, but I was also very much on edge about how Mike was going to treat me with the extra crying in the house.

It was early January 1987, and we were still unpacking boxes. I had a list of errands to run, and it was going to take me a couple of hours. Mike was going to do more unpacking and didn't want to watch Jillian at the same time, so I took her with me. Off we went to run our errands.

After about thirty minutes, I had to go back to the house because I had forgotten something I needed. I don't remember what it was, but I know I needed it to complete my errands.

I pulled into the driveway and kept the car running with the heater on. Jillian was still in her car seat as I ran into the house to grab what I needed. I walked in quickly and expected to find Mike in the dining room unpacking boxes. He wasn't there, so I quickly looked around as I headed toward the bedroom.

I walked into the bedroom and froze just inside the doorway. There was Mike—standing in front of me wearing my lingerie.

Holy crap. What was this in front of me?

I was so shocked. I stood there with my mouth hanging open. The look on Mike's face was one of fear and anger. His face twisted up and his body got tense as he closed his fists. He started to breathe heavier, his lips slightly parted, and I could see the movement with each inhale and exhale. I didn't know what to say. I was frozen. But I recognized that body language—he was ready to explode. I instinctively knew not to say a word for fear of physical harm.

He was a master at manipulation. There was no "I'm sorry," no "Let me explain," no "I should have told you sooner." None of that. Instead of any apology or humbling response, he twisted everything around on me by saying, "I guess you must hate me now. I guess 'for better or for worse' means nothing to you."

And just like that, he turned the situation around so that it focused on me and my supposed judgment of him—instead of focusing on the fact that he was a cross-dresser and had kept it from me.

I started questioning my own judgment. Is this what "for better or for worse" means? Am I supposed to be okay with this? Am I the one who is being unreasonable? Am I wrong for judging him?

Mike was successful in getting me to start looking inward for a resolution to this soul-shattering surprise instead of holding himself accountable for his deception. I wasn't able to get into any discussion with him at that time—Jillian was still strapped in her car seat outside in the running car. I was numb from what I had just discovered, and my head was swimming with so many thoughts at the same time. There were no words that came out of my mouth. I just grabbed whatever I had come in for and turned around and left him standing in my lingerie.

What a blur going through my head. Did I just see what I thought I saw? How long has this been going on? I didn't sign up for this. This is not what I had wanted in a partner—someone who was a cross-dresser.

What do I do? Do I leave?

Wait, I'm pregnant with our second baby. How do I take care of two babies on my own with no money? I would need help from someone—family. If I got out and got help from someone, then I would have to tell them why. And I would be too ashamed to reveal why I was leaving him.

I had to be careful about what I did next. I couldn't say anything to anyone on base—not even the base chaplain. Are you kidding? A United States Marine fighter pilot is a cross-dresser? Do you realize what kind of tsunamic wave of disruption that discovery would make in the air wing?

Forget the air wing—how about the entire Marine Corps? What career implications would it have for him? He would be ostracized.

This was 1987. There was very little tolerance in society for the queer population—let alone in the ultra-masculine world of military fighter pilots. His career would be toast. He could lose face with his family. How do I get away to start over with two babies and no money? How do I do that and not set off a series of events that would be devastating to him and humiliating to me?

Even then, with this huge shift I was experiencing from the revelation, I was starting to think more about him and how the world would respond to him than I was about me. I was so shocked, and I was so confused as to what to do. Right now, I had to focus on completing my errands and then figure out how I was going to respond to him when I got back home.

Then I remembered something relevant from the past. It wasn't long after I started seeing Mike that his two older sisters shared with me how they used to dress Mike up in little girl clothes when he was little. They laughed at how they turned their brother into a girl and said, "He was so cute." What would they say now that he is a cross dresser?

In addition, Mike repeated the same story to me a couple of different times. I wondered now if he was testing my attitude towards it and grooming me to accept this obsession of his as an adult.

All these little fragments of memories came back now with more clarity as I searched for the "why's" and the "what's": why does he do it – why didn't he tell me before we were married - what do I say to him – what do I do now?

I had no idea about what makes a man want to dress up as a woman. There was no internet at the time to search for a psychological explanation and certainly no one I could trust to ask. I only knew that I felt bewildered and betrayed.

When I returned from my errands, he was in his own clothes again. He was unpacking some boxes and was deadly quiet. He looked up at me and gave me one of his signature "I dare you to say anything" looks. I walked past him and took Jillian to her room to change her diaper and put her down for a nap. I still didn't know what I was going to say, but I knew I had to say something. My heart was beating fast and out of rhythm. My breathing became quick and shallow as it took over my senses.

I shut Jillian's door behind me and walked down the short hall to where he was unpacking boxes. He stopped and looked up at me with an intimidating look on his face. I found myself apologizing for making him feel bad. He was still, and his demeanor didn't soften. I didn't have anything planned to say to him—it just came out as I continued, "I still love you. But I don't want to know about it. As long as I don't see it or know about it, then I don't care." His shoulders relaxed a bit, but he still didn't say a word. I didn't know what else to say, so I just turned around and left to busy myself with unpacking boxes.

The truth is, I didn't know if I still loved him. I said it out of habit and to diffuse any eruption that might be brewing in him. I had witnessed him exploding on me several times, and I was afraid of him and what he would do to me if he felt threatened.

This was not the man I thought I married. I didn't recognize this person called my husband, and I was intimidated by this stranger's body language. I felt like I had shifted into another dimension, and I was unfamiliar with this world I was now experiencing. I may have said I didn't care if I didn't know about it—but I did care. I just couldn't see a path out for myself, Jillian, and this baby I was now carrying. I was responding in that moment by bringing down the temperature in the room and protecting myself from any fallout. I would try to make sense of this craziness later when I had a chance to calm down and reflect.

Fast forward: many years later, Mike asked me to watch him get dressed up as a woman. He said I would better understand. I told him I would never understand—because it was not what I had agreed to before we married. It was hard enough for me to find the strength to have sex with him due to the abuse, but I could never

77

have sex with him and not get physically ill if I saw him dressed as a woman. It would feel like I was having sex with a woman, and the thought of that was repulsive to me.

I never saw him in women's clothes again after that encounter in January 1987, but I was sure he was still dressing up when I wasn't around. I started to find pieces of my lingerie missing, and some of my dress shoes were stretched out. I suspected he was still dressing up.

I searched and searched for the evidence but could never find it. It wasn't until January 2023 that my daughter, Claire, told me she had found his stash of clothes while snooping around. She was in middle school at the time, and she told me that her dad warned her to stay out of his sea bag that was tucked in the closet of the office upstairs. She said that his warning was all the encouragement she needed to snoop. She opened it up and looked inside and couldn't understand why "Mom's" dresses were in the sea bag or why Dad thought it was such a big deal to keep them hidden. She just put everything back and shrugged her shoulders.

I personally could care less if someone wants to be a cross-dresser. If that's what makes them happy, then they should do what makes them happy. But for me, it was a huge betrayal. Mike never gave me a choice. He took that away from me before we were married. If he had told me about his obsession with cross-dressing, I would have broken off the engagement and wished him luck in finding someone who could fully support him.

Mike knew that. He knew I wouldn't marry him if I knew he was a cross-dresser, so he kept it quiet. When I said "for better or for worse" in our vows, it was without the realization of the kind of person he wanted to be. I entered into a marriage that was a lie from the beginning.

I unfortunately discovered it at a time when I was the most vulnerable. I had a one-year-old baby, was pregnant with another, had no money of my own, no real opportunity to work and provide for them, and no one I could go to for help. All my family was on the West Coast, so I felt alone. I was betrayed by him. I was betrayed by the man who promised to love and protect me. I don't know why, but I felt great shame in myself for letting it happen.

So where do I go from here?

I was already dealing with his yo-yo personality and mood swings. I had been making excuses for him due to his perceived stress with work and flying. Every time I let something slide—every time I didn't hold him accountable for his actions toward me—he used that as permission to take more from me. My weak personal boundaries were no match for his take-take-take personality. He was adept at using my empathy and compassion against me, making me feel like I was the one with the problem.

I easily took on guilt—and Mike was more than happy to oblige me. I was an innocent caught up in his narcissistic web of insecurities.

This deep secret of his was now known by me. Mike didn't like that I held this dark secret in my hands, and so he dug deeper into his bullying and abuse to gain even more control over me. I was hoping for our life to gain stability—especially after all the recent moves and changes to our family. Instead, my life took an abrupt turn. There would be more tension and drama with him around.

I would learn to look forward to when Mike had to go away for training or a deployment. With Mike being gone, it would be the only time that I felt safe and relatively happy in our marriage. That is an absolute shame.

What to do now? There was only one thing I could do: get up every day and take care of Jillian and this unborn baby and make my way through to the next day. That was it.

Since I didn't feel like I was allowed to put my own needs first, I fell even further down on my own list of importance. I believe my lack of self-importance kept me from seeing a way out of this marriage. It kept me chained to my own toxic belief that this was all that I deserved—after what I did to Jack.

I would move through each day in sadness and with a mental fog, so much so that I would cease to notice it and accept it as my new normal. I had become a smaller version of myself in just three years.

But I kept the eternal hope that Mike would change. He had to.

Now I was left to try to wipe out the image of him in my lingerie and move on.

*　　*　　*　　*　　*　　*　　*　　*　　*　　*　　*

The Narcissist's Dirtiest Trick: Reframe the script to make you convinced that your feelings are invalid. It switches the attention from the narcissists' behavior and focuses on your reaction. This is Reactive Abuse.

Jill Wise, Narc Abuse Recovery Coach

6. Single Married Parent

Let it end.

Let it hurt.

Let it heal.

Let it go.

~poets.and.writers

It's June 1990—three years since Mike shocked me dressed in my lingerie. Our second baby, Claire, was born three weeks late in early October 1987, and our third baby, Craig, was born on his due date in March of 1989. Our family had grown to five, and Mike had kept a steady pace of detachments and deployments the entire time. In 1988, Mike had been home for a total of three months. In 1989, he had been home for only two months. The endless pace of training was exhausting for all of us.

It was a good thing I was a strong and capable woman used to taking care of myself, because this pace was brutal. There were many wives who couldn't handle it anymore and divorced their servicemen because of it.

I don't blame any of them for realizing it was too much to ask of the families. In fact, I'm impressed that those women had enough self-worth to realize they deserved more from a marriage—and then had the courage to start over. That was what I lacked: courage.

There was an odd dichotomy working against me. On the one hand, I was very strong, independent, and courageous. But on the other hand, I lacked the self-worth to believe that I had the right to demand more for myself. That lack of self-love kept me a prisoner in this marriage far longer than I needed to be.

In a normal, healthy marriage, there would be a shared load of responsibilities. Both husband and wife would feel heard, valued, seen, and respected. Neither would feel like they were carrying an uneven burden, and they would both know that if life got tough, the other would be there to help them get through it. A lengthy departure by one spouse would shift an unbelievable amount of responsibility onto the other. It would be stress that seemed never-ending and could make anyone crumble under the weight of it all. I understood the motivation many spouses had to call it quits and start over.

As for me, I looked forward to Mike being gone. He added more stress to my daily life because of his self-centered ways. He refused to have his life change just because we had kids. He had hardly any responsibility with the daily chores, and he didn't seek out any active engagement with the kids. What he did bring to our lives was unpredictability and tension.

He never knew what his work schedule would be for the next day until after seven o'clock in the evening when the flight schedule was posted. I never knew what the next day was going to bring, so it was hard to plan anything—even something simple. I would try to plan activities and personal errands but then have to scratch it all because of Mike's schedule. I couldn't blame him. He was at the mercy of the military's demands, and I understood that. But it didn't lessen the burden it put on me.

So whenever Mike would go away for a long weekend, or a detachment, or a deployment, I would be in heaven. I didn't have to plan meals around him. I didn't have to be home at any given time to greet him. I had less laundry, and there were fewer chores to do. And I didn't have to walk around on eggshells afraid I might do or say something that would tick him off. It was like I was on vacation. I loved having him gone.

What I didn't love was being a single, married parent.

I wanted the Hallmark version of marriage. I wanted a spouse who valued and respected me. I wanted a spouse who recognized my daily sacrifices and showed me consideration—and treated me like I was the most important person in the world to him. I had so much love to give, and I was trying my best to lather Mike with it all, but my efforts seemed to roll right off him like rain on a window.

He rarely acknowledged any of my efforts and was only concerned about what I could do for him. He was never interested in my day or what the kids were up to. He never once came home from work and asked me how my day had gone. Never. I can only imagine that he must have thought I had it easy—being with the kids all day and running the house. And he must have believed that what he was doing was more important, so I was the one who needed to cater to him. He never recognized how invaluable I was to our family's success.

I had been making plenty of excuses for him because of his military schedule. I told myself that if Mike wasn't so preoccupied with work, he would have the mental and emotional capacity to be more present in our marriage and more actively engaged with the kids. Now, Mike's schedule was getting a bit of a breather. There were no deployments or detachments scheduled through the summer. I thought it was the perfect time for us to get away from the military distractions and reconnect as a family.

We decided to take a long summer vacation home to Seattle. It had been at least five years since we'd been home, and we were due for a reset.

We flew into Seattle at the end of June 1990. The sky was blue, and Mt. Rainier was out to greet us on our return. It was immediately healing to feel the Pacific Northwest air. It always felt clean and full of energy.

My favorite time was the morning, when few people were up. Being on East Coast time allowed my body to be up early, rested, and ready to go. I would take advantage of having my in-laws to watch the kids as I took off on a morning run or a walk along Alki Drive. The morning air and relative quiet filled my body with so much-needed healing energy. My body soaked up all the peace it could before I had to go back and face the chaos of the day.

It was heaven.

The first few days of being back were filled with excited reunions. The kids were so small, and they had hardly seen any family while we lived in North Carolina, so it was a tad overwhelming for them. They eventually fell into the flow of all the extra attention they weren't used to.

Mike had several high school friends still in the area, and they all found their way over to Mike's parents' house to catch up. Everything was all smiles and handshakes and hugs. They may have been Mike's friends, but I also took advantage of the energy they were bringing and allowed it to fill me as much as it filled Mike.

The guys made plans to get together for the Fourth of July and walk down to the beach to watch the fireworks from Ivar's. Mike didn't include me in the making of the plans; he just assumed I would be okay with it. And I was. I was easygoing, and if Mike's parents were okay with watching the kids, then it didn't matter to me.

A little side note here. I was still young and eager to please Mike. I didn't think anything about the fact that he made plans without consulting me. At that time, I wasn't bothered by it. But as the years went by, I resented that I wasn't consulted and was expected to just go along with whatever he planned. That same consideration was never reciprocated by Mike. He made it clear that he didn't want me to make plans for him without asking him first. He's right. But I guess that rule was only meant for him and not for me.

I would eventually push back on anything where I was not included in the planning. It both irritated him and amused me that he couldn't see his double standards.

So, now it was the Fourth of July, and we had gotten together with a group of his high school friends near Alki Beach to watch the fireworks at Ivar's across Puget Sound. His parents were willing to watch the kids. Since it didn't get dark until 10 p.m., the kids were going to be well off to sleep by the time we left for the beach.

There were at least eight of us. We were standing around visiting and watching fireworks when a friend of his, Ken Stockton, put his right arm around my shoulder. I thought nothing of it. I turned to him and smiled. Then, without any hesitation, he slipped his right hand down my tank top and grabbed my right breast.

I reflexively elbowed him and moved closer to my husband. Mike gave me a look that said, "Chill out," then he elbowed me so that I had to back away from him.

I was shocked! Shocked that his friend did that to me—and shocked that my husband pushed me away when I moved toward him for safety and comfort. Our friends, who had seen the assault take place, started shifting their gaze between both me and Mike, waiting for Mike's reaction.

Nothing! He did nothing!

My shock and disgust from this sexual assault by a "friend" was now replaced with humiliation and betrayal. My honor had been compromised in front of everyone, and the man who swore he would never let anyone put me in a compromising situation did nothing. I was humiliated, embarrassed, and I felt devalued.

Later that night, getting dressed for bed, I brought it up again to Mike. He was perturbed that I hadn't just "let it go," and he let me know it in the tone of his voice when he said to me quite sharply, "It's not that big of a deal. You're making too much about it. He just had a couple of beers."

I was so hurt. I felt betrayed. Mike's reaction made me feel like I was nothing. How could Mike downplay this disgusting sexual abuse by one of his friends? How could he minimize this assault by saying, "It's not that big of a deal"?

Immediately, my mind went back to before we were married when he made such an emphatic and chivalrous declaration: "I will never let anyone take advantage of you. I will never let you be caught in a compromising situation."

Now he had the chance to defend my honor. Instead, he turned his back to me and said it wasn't that big of a deal. I felt totally disrespected, devalued, humiliated, betrayed, confused—so many feelings that describe how the person who is supposed to love and protect you ultimately betrayed you. I felt so small and insignificant.

More than twenty years later, during a bout of self-deprecation and multiple attempts to project himself as a victim to me—all in an effort to get me to exhibit pity for him—he brought up the 1990 assault again. He said, "I should have done something about it."

Mike said this in a pitiful tone as he was walking past me, not stopping to look at me or say it to my face, not giving me the opportunity to hold him accountable and tell him how deeply it still hurt me. No real apology. No real remorse.

Up to now, I have seen this act of his so many times over so many years that I knew exactly what he was trying to do.

He was motivated by only two things:

1. He wanted to come across as the pitiful victim in his self-flogging.

2. He wanted me to chase after him and tell him something like, "It's okay, you poor dear who has been tortured by it all these years. Come, let me remove the guilt and tell you what a great person you are."

If I had done just that, then he would have used that moment to confirm more emotional control over me. After all, if I could let him off the hook that easily for this disgusting betrayal, then there would be no limit to what he would say and do to me, knowing he was guaranteed forgiveness.

In the past, I would end up feeling sorry for him and then try to put the blame on myself for his despicable behavior. I would have felt like it was my job to "fix" him and give him grace so he could let go of the self-loathing. I would tell myself that it *couldn't be that Mike would purposely be an asshole to me. He swore to love and protect me. I must have done something to bring it on.*

It had become routine for me to blame myself somehow for his abuse toward me. I had been conditioned over the years not to do anything to provoke him. To carefully tiptoe around his feelings. I would usually swallow the pain and keep it to myself because I had witnessed his wrath of destruction over the years if you dared to hold him accountable.

Keeping the peace had become more important than holding him responsible for his actions.

Now, Mike was counting on me to once again discharge him of any responsibility for his ill treatment of me.

Not this time.

I watched Mike pass by me as he made his pitiful statement about what he should have done, and I, in response, said and did nothing. Nothing!

This is one of the things that frightened him the most—anyone showing indifference to him and acting like he wasn't even in the room. That's because Mike craves attention. He wants any attention, good or bad. If it's good attention, then he can puff up and confirm to himself that he is entitled to say and do what he did. If it's negative attention, then he can twist it to make me look like I was an ungrateful person who couldn't accept his version of apology and accountability.

By giving him no response, I was able to strip the power he had over me. I just let him slink away into the family room by himself. I let him sit and wait and wonder if, at any moment, he would see me run into the family room and get on my knees to forgive him.

Instead, I just went about my day as if he wasn't even there—and with that, I took his fuel away from him.

But now we're back to where we started: July 4, 1990, Alki Beach, Seattle, around 11:00 p.m. Watching fireworks. Disgusting guy grabbing my breast. Spineless husband shrugging it off. Just more lies and betrayal from him. Just another crack in his deceitful mask.

This is when I realized I was alone. This is when I first started to fully understand that he was not the person he portrayed himself to be before we were married. It was all lies. I started to lose faith in his commitment to me and our marriage. There was a realization that I could not trust him to stand by me and have my back.

And this was just the beginning of our summer vacation.

Jillian was four and a half, Claire was two and a half, and Craig was just fifteen months that summer of 1990.

A lot to manage on my own. I was married, but I felt like a single parent because their dad was constantly deploying. Finally, we had several weeks in the summer to be together as a family. I was looking forward to having their dad act as a partner and be engaged with the kids and me.

Unfortunately, Mike didn't feel the same.

He had a different agenda, and it didn't include us. He was looking forward to this trip to take off on his own and do whatever he wanted. The kids and I just got in his way.

After staying the first couple of weeks at his parents' house in West Seattle, it was time to go up and visit my parents on Camano Island. My mom and dad were hosting my mom's family reunion. All my aunts and uncles and cousins and their kids were going to be there. I was so looking forward to seeing everyone, and I wanted Mike to be there so my family could meet him. Other than at our wedding, my relatives hadn't met him. Now was the perfect opportunity.

Mike ended up having other plans. He didn't want to go up to Camano Island. He wanted to stay in Seattle. He conveniently forgot that we had planned this part of the trip before we left North Carolina. He couldn't see that this visit as a family was important to me—even if I compromised and cut our visit with my family to just a few days.

When I pushed back, he tried to justify his decision by saying how he hadn't been home in several years and there were things he wanted to do in Seattle. My disappointment just made him angry, and he accused me of being selfish.

This had become a common tactic of his. He would often turn the situation around on me and try to make me look like I was the unreasonable one. I may have easily taken on guilt that I shouldn't have—because of my weak boundaries—but I felt this emotional cut very deeply.

I, too, had been gone for many years. He wasn't the only one. There were things that I wanted to do too—but they were all centered around family. Mike wanted it to be centered around him.

Before we were married, Mike constantly told me how much family meant to him. He passionately expressed his love and commitment to family. He told me how honoring family was so important. So important that it motivated him to go into the military like his brother, his dad, and his uncle.

He put on a great performance back then. He convinced me that he was an honorable, committed, and caring guy who would always protect me and make me feel safe and loved. Apparently, that was a lie.

Here he had a chance to put his words into action—and all he could see was what was in it for him. He had manipulated me into believing he was this amazing person so I would become emotionally attached to him. So attached that I would ignore the red flags that would surface.

So now there were two lies exposed: the lie that he would never let anyone put me in a compromising situation, and the lie that family was so important to him.

That beautiful family we created didn't seem important enough for him to spend a few days together. He also didn't think that spending time with my family was critical. "They're your parents, not mine."

So, this guy—who passionately proclaimed the importance of family before we were married—was a liar. He only told me what he knew I wanted to hear. "I know, I'll tell her how important family is. Chicks dig that stuff!" It was all just a lie.

The mask he wore before we were married was cracking, and I was left confused and hurt as to who this man really was that I had married.

I searched for a compromise and got him to agree to at least meet the kids and me next week at the Woodland Park Zoo for a family outing. "Next week" was now tomorrow, and I called him at his parents' house to figure out a place and time to meet. *All is good*, I thought. *Maybe tomorrow will be different. Maybe family time at the zoo will be a turning point, and Mike will be more emotionally connected and involved with our family.*

I was hoping that somehow the amazing guy I knew in the beginning of our relationship would return.

But then, that's me. Always giving someone the benefit of the doubt. Always looking for the good in people. Unfortunately, someone with a narcissistic personality like Mike will take advantage of those generous qualities. They use the grace given to them not to reflect and reciprocate, but to selfishly take even more.

Mike wanted to see how far he could go before I pushed back. I had already been on the receiving end of his dark side when I dared to stand up to him in the past. He could go into a fiery rage in an instant and intimidate me by destroying objects around him—or threatening to do so. As strong as I thought I was, I was terrified of what he could do to me if I got him mad.

I learned quickly that to keep the peace and preserve my well-being, I had to avoid any subject he would interpret as a critique of him or his actions.

Instead, I kept hoping that great guy I knew before our wedding would return. I pushed out the negative thoughts and placed big expectations on tomorrow's family day at the zoo.

The next day, my mom drove the kids and me into Seattle. The kids were excited to see the animals—and excited that their daddy would be joining us. Mike and I had agreed to meet in front of the zoo, near the rose garden.

We got there close to the agreed time, and I let the kids run around the grassy areas as we waited for their dad to show up.

Fifteen minutes passed the meeting time, and I started to get worried. I found myself vigilantly watching the kids and the parking lot at the same time.

Thirty minutes passed, and he still wasn't there.

I gave him the benefit of the doubt. *Maybe* he had the time wrong. Maybe traffic was bad coming from West Seattle through the city. This was a time before cell phones. All I could do was wait.

Now nearly forty-five minutes in, the kids were starting to get tired and cranky. We had to go ahead into the zoo without him.

My soul felt very heavy. I couldn't understand why he didn't show. I was a bit embarrassed that my mom was there to witness it. I truly doubted that anything bad had happened to him. I was left trying to figure out what could have caused him to totally stand us up.

Maybe, I thought, *there was a problem with his parents' car, and he couldn't make it.*

I was still making excuses for him, still trying to give him the benefit of the doubt—that he wouldn't just blow us off.

Over the years, I found myself consistently giving him too much credit for what I thought he would do—based on his past emphatic declarations about family and honor. I wanted to believe that he wouldn't let anything get in the way of family commitments.

There was no way I could ever wrap my mind around the fact that we were just an inconvenience to him.

So I held back my full disappointment in his absence until I talked to him.

I called him later that day after we returned to my parents' house on Camano Island. I was hoping there would be some really good reason why he didn't make it. I was hoping that he would be apologetic and truly contrite—that he left us waiting and wondering where he was.

I was wrong again. He offered no apology for making us wait and worry.

Instead, he gushed over what a great day he'd had when an old family friend of his parents, Lee Brewster, popped in to say hi. Mike decided to stay and visit with Lee instead of meeting us at the zoo. I would have been less disappointed if he had at least acknowledged that he'd let his wife and children wait and worry and had apologized for it.

But there was no acknowledgment. No apology. He didn't even ask how the kids enjoyed the zoo. He just raved about what a wonderful time he had visiting with Lee.

I hung up the phone, dejected.

He made me feel like the kids and I were not a priority in his life. I was the one expected to be understanding and supportive of his choice to stay in Seattle, while he totally dismissed us and our feelings. Family and family commitments were not important to him. It didn't matter what he had said in the past—his behavior told the real story.

A huge crack appeared in his mask.

I felt the fundamental discard he had for me and the kids. Who is this guy? How can he be so self-involved that he can't even slightly consider the disappointment he had delivered to me?

It's a lonely and devaluing feeling to be on vacation with your family when your spouse prefers to have a separate vacation experience from you and the kids. I had already spent months upon months acting as a single parent due to his crazy deployment and detachment schedule over the last couple of years. I had gotten used to raising the children and running the house alone. The last thing I expected was to be alone on a family vacation.

I made the assumption in good faith that Mike was looking forward to spending time with us. That's one of my toxic qualities—always assuming that everyone is like me. I assumed that everyone would be thinking about how their actions affected others. I assumed that everyone would be in tune with others' needs and then be mindful in how they treated them.

But Mike shattered that assumption.

He made it very clear with his behavior that his family was not a priority. We just got in his way.

Eventually, Mike did come up to my parents' house to visit—but he only stayed about an hour. He and his dad were still spending time with Lee Brewster, and their activities brought them close to Camano Island. His visit was so short that it could hardly be counted as quality time.

Mike acted like an acquaintance who just stopped by to say hi. He didn't put in any emotional effort to connect with my parents, and he barely acknowledged the kids. He made a show just so he could say he was there. It was always a minimal effort with him. He was just sowing his breadcrumbs of attention.

It was now the first of August, and Mike was returning to North Carolina a week before we did. There was no hope of creating any family time with us. I was fed up. My mind was swirling with so many emotions as I tried to figure out my next step.

I knew I didn't want my marriage to continue with a husband who wasn't invested in it. I didn't want a husband who wasn't interested in creating meaningful connections with me or the kids.

The truth is, I was used to raising the kids alone. The only advantage of being married to Mike was that it gave me financial security. I didn't have to worry about working *and* being the sole financial provider for the kids. But the kids and I deserved more than just his financial contribution. We deserved a man who wanted to be around us—a man who couldn't wait to get home and hear about our day. A man who made each of us feel valued and important in his life.

There was a sense of abandonment creeping in.

I was starting to feel like the dog no one really wanted to take care of—the one you barely put food in the bowl for and give a slight pat on the head every once in a while.

I frightened myself when I started to allow thoughts of leaving him to enter my mind. I started imagining what it would take to leave the marriage and raise the children alone. I didn't get very far with those thoughts, though, because of the ever-changing needs and demands that come with three kids under the age of four. There was always something that diverted my attention away from internal thoughts and toward the kids' outward demands.

Soon, it wouldn't matter what exit plans I tried to make.

Somehow, among all the chaos in my head and all the emotions churning in my stomach, I still managed to hear the TV in the background say something about Iraq invading Kuwait. In the next week, our lives would be directly impacted by this tiny country in the Persian Gulf halfway around the globe.

My marital concerns would have to wait.

*   *   *   *   *   *   *   *   *   *   *

The saddest part about us, is that every single time I tried explaining to you how I felt, you just thought I was trying to start an argument when all I wanted was for you to understand how I was feeling.

flying_on_a_brokenwing

Part Two: Struggles and Survival

7. Iraq War

Nobody in the world, nobody in history has ever gotten their freedom by appealing to the moral sense of the people who were oppressing them. -ASSATA SHAKUR

When Mike returned to Cherry Point from the Seattle trip, Iraq had invaded Kuwait. The squadrons were soon in a whirl as they all prepared for the possibility of a high-scale ramp-up of their defense capabilities. My thoughts of planning for an exit in our marriage quickly took a backseat to the feverish news reporting and speculation about a large-scale military deployment of all branches to support Kuwait.

The kids and I returned a week later. We had been back home only one day when Mike came home from work and said, "I've been transferred to 331 (VMA-331 squadron), and I'm S-4 (logistics—responsible for packing everything), so we'll be busy every day until late, packing up supplies and loading the ships."

Just like that, a tornado of emotions and personal preparations took over. There was no breathing room for any discussions about what happened in Seattle and how it made me feel insecure about the future of our marriage. Just emergency spouse meetings and appointments with the JAG to be sure we had a personal will and power of attorney signed. It was a blur of elevated priorities designed to get the squadron deployed in one week.

Then—poof—he was gone. No end date to this deployment. No idea when they would be in port so I could anticipate a phone call. Just—poof. A total of three Harrier squadrons were deployed along with all the support personnel. The base became eerily quiet with all the service members suddenly gone.

The early weeks of what was to be called Operation Desert Shield were a blur, filled with a blistering pace of meetings and personal adjustments at home. So many phone calls from concerned friends and family had me relaying the same story of our whirlwind last week together and fending off questions about what was going to happen next.

I experienced complete physical and emotional exhaustion from repeating the same story. My body was vibrating at a higher level of anxiety, and it was difficult to focus on the immediate needs of the moment. I knew I couldn't continue another day immersed in the chaos and stress of this unprecedented deployment, so I decided to take the kids with me on a weekend getaway to Wilmington, where phones couldn't follow me.

It was a surprisingly peaceful weekend. I had three kids under five years old with me, traversing around an unfamiliar city. You'd think it would be a suicide mission—being on a mini vacation with all three little ones by myself. But I had so many months of practice being on my own that it was actually very relaxing. I didn't have any agenda other than to focus on letting the kids have fun.

We spent the days playing in the sand, getting ice cream, hanging out at Chuck E. Cheese's, and spending unlimited time in Toys "R" Us. It was just what we all needed. We returned home relaxed and ready to define what it would mean to be on our own for an indefinite period.

I suspected that the squadron would be gone for at least six months, since that is usually the minimum that an aircraft carrier would be out. So many others were speculating that they would only be gone for three months and that they'd be back by Thanksgiving. The thought was that the Iraqi army would back down in the presence of the American military. That attitude reminded me of the Battle of Bull Run at the beginning of the Civil War, when many thought the Union would easily win after that battle. Those people were wrong then, just as these people were wrong now. I just knew it would be at least six months. As it turned out, the squadron didn't even dock and get off the ship for the first time until Thanksgiving.

This was 1990—long before cell phones. The only way to communicate was to wait for them to take shore leave and call home, or they would write a letter. I got my first phone call from him around Thanksgiving, three months after the squadron had left. It was the first time I was able to talk to him. I had no idea when he would be calling again. I was just lucky to be home when he did. Because of the unpredictable nature of their deployment, I decided to get an answering machine so I wouldn't miss any future calls.

I had made a commitment to write to him every night, and I started the first day he was gone. We—the wives left behind—were told that the mail could be erratic and that we should number the letters on the outside of the envelope so, in case the service member got several letters at one mail call, they would know the sequence to read them in. I stayed up past midnight every night to write about the day's events. I was so busy with the kids and the chores that I didn't get a chance to relax and reflect until late.

I fully believed that writing every day would make a difference in his combat readiness. I believed it would directly contribute to the success of the military mission by keeping his spirits high. I only wrote about the positive events happening—since there wasn't anything he could do about my daily struggles anyway. I wanted him to have only uplifting messages from home. I very quickly erased any thoughts of leaving him and focused my energy on the kids and on my impact on the mission's success by writing those letters every night.

Fast forward: he kept them all, and now my kids have them as a diary of that year.

The holidays came and went, along with all the extra craziness that accompanies them. Now we were starting the new year of 1991. The squadron had finally made it to the Persian Gulf and was in a constant state of combat readiness. The pilots had daily flying exercises to help keep their skills sharp. It was during one of these training exercises at the end of January that we got word we had lost one of our pilots.

Captain Manny Rivera crashed his AV-8B into the beach while returning to the aircraft carrier. He didn't eject and was killed instantly. It was a complete shock throughout the squadron and the entire aviation community.

This fatal accident created a heightened sense of anxiousness among everyone: the command, the pilots, the squadron personnel, the squadron wives, and the families back home. Even the American public, who heard about the fatality via the news, started to realize how much of a personal sacrifice was going to be made by our troops once the war started. If a training exercise could prove fatal, then what number of fatalities could we expect from the war?

The entire Gulf War was televised on every network, with CNN being our primary source of news coverage. Family and friends would call and ask what I knew about their mission or operations. No one knew anything. We were getting our information from CNN just like everyone else. I quickly realized that the constant news coverage was consuming me and creating extreme exhaustion. I made the decision to break away from the coverage. I knew the military would contact me if anything happened to him. I always said, "No news is good news." If I didn't have the chaplain knocking on my door, I knew my husband was all right.

I was able to calm down and feel less stressed once I broke away from the constant news coverage. I found that I started to sleep better. I got back into a meaningful daily routine for me and the kids. I was able to fend off all the external anxieties that family members were directing toward me as they tried to cope with their own emotions about the war. My mental, emotional, and physical health improved greatly once I made the intentional effort to reduce the external noise I allowed to penetrate me.

Then we got the news that another one of our pilots had been shot down on a bombing run on the last day of the war. Captain Reg Underwood's AV-8B was hit by a surface-to-air missile, and his wingman couldn't be sure if he had ejected. For several days, we all kept watching CNN, hoping to hear that he had been captured. Unfortunately, the news was the opposite. The tragedy was amplified when you realized that Reg's wife had given birth to a baby girl while he was deployed—and now, father and daughter would never meet.

The war was over. Forty-three days. From January 17 to February 28. The other squadrons on base returned first, and you could detect the palpable difference as more and more servicemen began to reappear on base. Mike's squadron was finally on its way back home. It would be the last to return. VMA-331 would take a couple of weeks longer, since they were coming back via aircraft carrier. I took advantage of the extra time to get everything ready for his arrival.

I was super excited. The kids and I made posters, and I filled the refrigerator with his favorite groceries. Extended families of the servicemen from all over the U.S. were making their way to Cherry Point. The spouses were busy shopping for "welcome home" clothes for themselves and their children.

I didn't tell the kids that their daddy was coming home until the day of his arrival. I had learned the hard way that you can never count on a set day and time for the military to return from a detachment or deployment. The kids were too young to understand the disappointment of their dad not being there when we thought he would be. So, I waited until that morning, when I got the final word that the planes were ready to fly off the carrier.

It was exciting to watch the planes fly over us in wing formation as they made their approach to land. So much anticipation was in the air as we all readied ourselves for our pilots to land and be reunited with them. I knew the two girls were super excited, but I wasn't sure about Craig, since he was only sixteen months old when his dad left. Now, he had just turned two, and all he had were pictures of his daddy. But when Mike finally landed and greeted everyone with a hug, Craig hugged him so tight that his little fingers were red. He obviously knew who his daddy was, and he obviously missed him very much. It was such a sweet moment—and one that I'm glad I got on camera.

Eight months after their departure, VMA-331 finally returned home. They were the last squadron to return to the base, and they had a hero's welcome. The commanding general of Cherry Point showed up to welcome them home, and local media were there to interview the families. It seemed like we had been navigating emotional extremes for such a long time. Now we were all riding on this huge emotional high with the squadron's return. This high, however, was tempered by the solemness we felt for the loss of Manny and Reg.

The reunion was fabulous. Mike was so happy to be home, and he told me how the war had put his life in perspective. He told me how much family meant to him. I was so happy to hear that. I truly felt that our relationship would grow stronger because of this experience. I allowed myself to believe that I would not have a repeat of the disastrous events that had unfolded last summer in Seattle.

It didn't take long after the squadron's return for the service personnel to start receiving orders for their new assignments. Many in our squadron, including Mike, were chosen to go to the Amphibious Warfare School (AWS) in Quantico, Virginia. This was an advanced warfare school, and this particular year was especially designed for veterans of the Gulf War. It would only be a one-year tour, and then we would be back at Cherry Point.

I was looking forward to this move. There were too many tough memories here. It felt like breaking away from the familiar would be healing for all of us, even if only for one year. I was counting on this next duty station to allow us to come together as a family. Mike would be home for dinner every day, and there would be no worry about any deployments.

I had such high hopes for this change in our lives. It was so nice to have our family together again. Unfortunately, it wouldn't take long for the reunion high to fade. Mike couldn't seem to be happy for long, and I would, once again, become the recipient of his personal frustrations.

*   *   *   *   *   *   *   *   *   *   *

You keep trying to explain to them how you feel until you finally realize, that it's not a matter of them understanding, it's a matter of them caring.

Maria Consiglio

8. Quantico, VA 1991-92

Everything you've ever wanted is sitting on the other side of fear.
-George Addair, Daily State of Mind

Amphibious Warfare School (AWS) was at Quantico, Va.—"The Crossroads of the Marine Corps." We had already been stationed there before, right after we were first married in 1983. I was familiar with the base and the surrounding area, so it made the move easier. I was surprised to find out that the Marines hosted other military officers from around the world. We had a neighbor and his family from France, and there were officers from Ecuador and Spain. It was such a treat to get to know them and to be introduced to their cultures. I was really looking forward to this year.

Jillian was now starting kindergarten, and Claire and Craig were at home with me. I tried to settle into a nurturing routine of being a present mother and supportive wife. For a short while, life was running smoothly. The kids made friends on our street, I would have morning coffee with my neighbor on her front porch, the parents organized a carpool to take and pick the kids up from school, and we had a family dinner every night. It was an easy and relaxing time. *Is this what it feels like to be a normal family?* As wonderful as it was, it didn't take long for Mike to turn sour and put me through more emotional challenges.

It always starts with subtleties—little comments or attitude shifts. Those subtleties were always hard to figure out. *Did he really mean to say that? Does he realize how he hurts me with those comments?* I couldn't fathom that he would purposely be hurtful to me. My first inclination was to think of it as a "one-off." In response, I would make excuses for him due to the "stress" that he was under at AWS.

It started with little things, like his refusal to watch the kids so I could go to the store. Or maybe he would give me the silent treatment. I was always very confused about where this attitude and behavior shift had come from. Since I couldn't believe that he actually meant to be hurtful, I wouldn't call him out for the emotional mistreatment. I would be in a bit of shock, not knowing how to respond. Then I would end up giving him the benefit of the doubt and cutting him some slack.

As he constantly shifted from being cooperative to hurtful, I began to show more signs of cognitive dissonance. My brain said that he loved me and wouldn't cause me any harm, but here I was, trying to reconcile that belief with his hurtful conduct. His contradictory behavior would become more prevalent throughout our marriage and would cause me to feel like I was in a constant swirl of uncertainty.

Eventually, Mike took my compliance with his bad behavior as permission to pile more on me. His subtle attitude shift was a way to test my boundaries. Since I gave him the benefit of the doubt and didn't call him out on it, he took that as an opportunity to encroach more on my easygoing personality. Even though his dark energy became prolonged and heightened, I was still digging into my belief that this was not the real person. I believed this behavior was just a manifestation of his work environment. I believed it would correct itself if I created a low-stress environment at home.

I was walking on eggshells, not sure what would set him off. I tried harder to create a sanctuary for him by making sure dinner was ready when he got home. I also made sure the house was tidy and the kids weren't under his feet. I would stock up on his favorite snacks and not ask for any favors when he walked in the door. I believed that if little was required of him when he got home, he would be able to relax and then interact with his family in a more positive and healthy way. It didn't work. The more I did for him, the more he acted like it wasn't enough.

Eventually, it became apparent that nothing I did made him happy. The more I gave, the more he took—and the more he expected. I was in a continued state of confusion with him. *What did I do?* It didn't dawn on me that he was emotionally manipulating me. I just knew that it didn't feel right. I knew that the way he was treating me was uncalled for. I tried to talk to him about his behavior toward me, but he just said I was making too big a deal out of nothing. I would end up questioning myself all over again. *Am I reading him wrong?* I would constantly second-guess myself and then keep quiet when he said or did something that caused me to think he wasn't treating me fairly. *Maybe I am being oversensitive.* The result of my confusion was that I started relying less and less on my own intuition.

I found myself pulling away from him—physically and emotionally. I cut back on how much of the day's events I would share with him, since he seemed annoyed when I did include him. He acted like he didn't want to be around us, so I tried to comply as best I could by giving him physical and emotional space.

Somewhere around mid-October, Mike came home with a fancy computerized sewing machine for me. It was an unexpected and extravagant gift. The sewing machine cost around $2,500 in 1992. I can only imagine what that same machine would cost in today's dollars. I wanted to know where he got the money for it. I had never indicated that I needed a new sewing machine, so I don't know why he felt compelled to buy it for me. Maybe it was a consolatory gift; maybe he felt bad about how he had been treating me lately.

He would do that—buy me things as a way to make up for his bad behavior, or he would do it to justify a major purchase for himself later. It was a nice sewing machine, but now I had to figure out how to pay for it.

I protested the gift due to the expense, and Mike lit into me, saying that he couldn't do anything right and that nothing he did seemed to make me happy. That was untrue. There's a lot that makes me happy. Simple things—like taking a walk together, holding hands, having deep, meaningful conversations. The gifts that light up my eyes the most are the gifts from the heart, the gift of self. I have never had a price tag on my happiness. Those were the simple, yet meaningful gifts I was looking for from him: just quality time.

What I discovered was that the price tag was more important to Mike than quality time with me. I believe it goes back to when his mom would buy him anything he wanted. He equated gifts—specifically expensive gifts— as validation for love. I had no choice but to keep the sewing machine and endure the burden of paying it off.

The sewing machine was amazing. It could do fancy embroidery with just the touch of a finger on the screen. I was able to elevate the quality of my sewing projects tremendously. It was such good quality that it lasted over thirty years before it wore out. I did eventually get my money's worth out of it, but it was a substantial purchase that he made without consulting me. I was worried that this extravagant gift would set a precedent for him to make more expensive purchases in the future without my knowledge. I would eventually be proven right.

There were a lot of writing assignments at AWS. Mike's writing and communication skills were weak, and it stressed him out whenever he had to write papers for his classes. He would beg me to help him write his technical responses to prompts and research papers. He knew writing was one of my strengths, so he begged me to help. I hated it. I didn't know the subject, and I didn't want him to hold me responsible in case he got a poor score on his paper. I could offer advice on sentence structure, but I didn't understand the material he was working on.

To offer meaningful feedback and suggestions, I had to ask clarifying questions. I wanted to make sure that my input was relevant to the topic and aligned with what he was trying to convey. With almost every question I asked, he would snap at me. He interpreted my questions as personal criticism. He would make me feel like I was trying to embarrass him. "I know I'm not as smart as you," he'd say. Then I would feel the need to defend myself or offer an apology to ease his tension.

Night after night, I found myself sitting on the stairs next to him at his word processor. I was already exhausted from a day of chasing three little ones around. Now I was trying to pull energy from a depleted well to help him. I was trying to understand what he was writing about, and at the same time, I was trying to gauge his mood so I wouldn't trigger him. I worked hard to offer suggestions in a way that wouldn't make him mad. I was in a no-win situation—he was going to get mad at me whether I helped or didn't.

This became an expected role from me several times a week during the entire nine months we were there. Helping your spouse is a given. Of course I would be there to help. Part of me thought *I could model how a spouse should support their partner when* they're *in need. Maybe he would learn to reciprocate and offer me consideration and support when I needed it.* Nope. Trying to lead by example never penetrated his skull. I kept hoping that if I just modeled the right behavior, he would follow suit. I kept giving him opportunities to show that he could return the favor. I was looking for that great guy I married to show up again.

I would stay up very late helping him, almost falling asleep on the stairs waiting for him to finish. He never thanked me. Instead, he would try to make me feel sorry for him by saying things like, "I know you think I'm stupid." That statement would make me feel responsible for bringing him back from his emotional cliff by assuring him I didn't think he was stupid.

It was a very exhausting routine: late nights, me carefully checking my comments to be sure he wouldn't be triggered, and then, receiving little appreciation from him. We needed a break from the pressures of his courses—and fortunately, the Marine Corps Birthday Ball was coming up. Fingers crossed it would do the trick.

Every year on Veterans Day, the Marine Corps would celebrate its birthday with a big ceremony. This year, the birthday ball was to be held in a grand hotel in Washington, D.C. Since the drive was almost an hour, we booked a room to spend the night and got our neighbor to watch the kids. I got busy making a beautiful navy velvet dress to wear. It turned out amazing, and I was so proud of the job I did on it.

Mike was starting to get into the celebratory spirit as well. He had his Desert Storm medals mounted and prepared his staff officer Mess Dress uniform. I was hopeful that we could have an intimate and romantic evening. It had been a while since he'd come home in a good mood, and it had certainly been a while since we'd had a romantic connection. His upbeat tone gave me a reason to hope that this night away would be an opportunity to reconnect emotionally.

The hotel was beautiful, and the ballroom was a spectacle, with so many tables set elegantly for hundreds of Marine officers and their wives. I was amazed at the precision of the wait staff as they placed food on the tables for hundreds of guests—seemingly all at once. We had our formal pictures taken and enjoyed the dinner and celebratory atmosphere. All seemed to be going well until they cleared the room for the band and dancing.

Mike never wanted to dance. He was always afraid that someone would laugh at him. I would try to convince him that nobody cared except him. It never made a difference. He wouldn't dance, and he didn't like me to dance. If I was dancing without him, he believed people would be wondering why he wasn't dancing with me. He thought others would judge him for not dancing with his wife. If I tried to dance—usually by myself—he would pull me aside and chastise me. The way he saw it, if he couldn't dance, then he didn't want me to dance.

One time, he came up to me while I was dancing and got close to my face so no one else would hear him. He grabbed and pinched a small part of the skin on my chest so that it hurt and then said very menacingly, "Stop dancing. Everyone is watching you." Then he let go of my skin, turned around, put a smile back on his face so no one would suspect that he had just intimidated me, and walked away. I was left with a smarting pain and the shock of his abusive behavior.

I knew Mike wouldn't be up for dancing at the ball, and I wasn't expecting him to dance. But the last thing I wanted was to stand around all night while he visited his Marine buddies, talking shop. Luckily, one of the other wives came over and asked me to wander around the ballroom with her. Since Mike was busy with his buddies, I went off with her and we visited other friends at the ball.

Almost every fifteen minutes, I made sure to return and check in with Mike to see if he needed me. Each time I did, he was busy visiting with colleagues. I would stand next to him for a bit, waiting for him to acknowledge me. He'd give me a quick look, but he was too absorbed in his conversations to give me any real attention, so off I went again.

I kept returning to check on him, and he was always busy with someone. At the end of the evening, he grabbed my hand and quickly guided me toward the elevator. He muttered angrily under his breath, "Where have you been? I've been looking for you all night." I was so confused. I had come back to check on him several times and even stood next to him while he chatted with his buddies. Now he was grumbling about me being absent all night. It made no sense. I tried to counter his claims, but he wouldn't listen. He just huffed onto the elevator and then into our room.

I was so confused. How could he say he had been looking for me all night when I had made my way back to him repeatedly? He saw me each time and acknowledged that I was there. So how could he claim I had left him stranded? It didn't matter if I reminded him that I had returned to him several times. It didn't suit his narrative of me. He wanted me to believe that I had abandoned him, even when he knew I hadn't. It suited him to play the victim once again—and I was cast as the perpetrator of his terrible evening.

What did he want me to do? Was I supposed to act like his obedient pet on a leash and stand by his side all night just because he was too insecure to dance?

Mike was trying to gaslight me. He was trying to rewrite the events of the evening to soothe his own emotional immaturity. I didn't bite. He failed to make me believe his twisted version of reality. I knew I hadn't abandoned him. But my reward for his insecurities was being treated like I had betrayed him by leaving him alone all night. He was hell-bent on teaching me a lesson. So, for the rest of the night and into the next day, Mike gave me the silent treatment. It was his passive-aggressive way of trying to exert power and control over me, to cause me to submit. It worked.

My poor brain was tired of trying to stay grounded in my version of reality. He made life so miserable that I gave in to his emotional abuse just to bring the barometer down in the house. After that, I went on high alert to watch his body language and gauge his mood. I started walking on eggshells again, trying to avoid triggering him. If he came home in a murderous mood, I simply got out of his way. I had no idea what caused his foul behavior—or why he would purposely take his tensions out on me. It wasn't fair. *I don't understand how he could be so callous and nasty.* This broody, moody behavior became a constant for the remainder of our time in Virginia. I had to endure six more months of his AWS-induced stress.

Mike continued punishing me by starting to do singular activities—no kids, no wife. He said he needed "downtime." Why is it that the man always thinks he's owed downtime from his family, but he never considers that the wife might need quality time alone as well? I got the pleasure of watching him come home from work in a grumpy mood, then leave to "do his thing," then come back and give me the silent treatment. I continued to make excuses for him and his behavior. *It has to be because of the academic load he's under,* I told myself. I couldn't comprehend that he was purposefully being cruel. That would have sent me to a deeper level of trauma—knowing that his behavior toward me was calculated.

I tried to rationalize his cruelty. My mind spun in so many directions at once. It became difficult for me to focus on daily tasks and remember simple obligations. My energy was focused on detecting any change in the emotional temperature of the house. Because I was continually on edge, waiting for his next explosion, my energy drained quickly. It affected my ability to reason through the day—even when he wasn't home. Just a foggy, incoherent brain.

Even with that brain fog, I was still able to confront him about money. He had expected me to find a way to pay all the bills while leaving me with little to work with. Those were tough conversations because I knew he would blow up at me. But I chose to go toe-to-toe with him on the finances because the consequences were too severe to ignore. Instead of accepting any responsibility, he berated me and pushed every emotional button.

One of these blowups went too far. I'd had enough. I was done listening to how I was the one being unfair. I just walked silently out of the room and left him by himself.

Mike knew he had gone too far. But instead of offering a sincere apology for his verbal takedown, he sent me a bouquet of yellow roses. I was so disgusted. It showed how totally disconnected he was from the real issue. He was driving us into debt, and instead of apologizing, he spent even more money on a dozen roses.

I felt like he was putting me in a double bind. If I thanked him for the flowers, he could accuse me of being a hypocrite—OK with him spending money on me, but not on himself. But if I chastised him for spending money on the flowers, then I was the ungrateful wife who couldn't accept an apology. I was going to be wrong no matter what I did. In that case, I chose to be the "ungrateful" wife, and I got after him for spending the money. *Why can't he just stop the crazy spending?*

He was such a child. His emotional maturity was so limited. He only saw what he wanted to see. He only did what he wanted to do. Just a little kid who acts like the world revolves around him and can't understand why he can't have what he wants, when he wants it.

How can I get him to evolve and become the life partner he promised to be? I had the noble idea that I could heal him and make him happy. After all, he was happy in the beginning—before we were married. Surely that person could return, right?

Spring was here, and Easter was approaching. Mike had missed Easter activities with the kids for the past three years, so I had hoped that this Easter he'd be excited to watch the kids hunt for eggs and go through their baskets. Maybe we could finally have a great day together as a family. Maybe...

I had my fingers crossed in my head.

I don't remember how Easter morning went. He may have hidden the eggs for the kids. But I do remember that after breakfast, he started making phone calls about going to look at a truck he was wanting to buy.

I was busy putting Easter dinner preparations in order when I overheard him on the phone. I was taken aback when I heard him tell the other person that he would come by around two o'clock to look at the truck. What was he doing? He knew it was Easter Sunday. He knew I was making a family dinner. I was about to say something when I heard him say, "Yeah, I know it's Easter. That doesn't bother me."

I knew he was pulling a power move on me. He wanted to hurt me by destroying Easter. He had already ruined the Marine Corps Birthday Ball—why not Easter, too? He was hoping to get a reaction out of me so he could tell me that *I* was the one being unreasonable for not letting him go on his "day off." Even if it was Easter.

I just stood in the doorway between the kitchen and the dining room and looked at him with a blank stare. I said nothing. That was all he needed from me. He glared back and said he didn't know when he'd be back.

Emptiness. Just total emptiness. That's how I felt. Void of emotions. Was I even surprised anymore? Was I even hurt? I don't know—because all I felt was empty. I felt totally discarded.

If your husband makes his own plans on a holiday *and* flashes you a look that says, I don't give a *sh*t* if you're upset,* you'll feel discarded too. I just remember feeling empty and shocked when I realized that family was not a priority for him. At a minimum, I recognized that he was willing to use his family as emotional pawns to get the reaction he got from me.

I felt the depth of his indifference to us. But I had a hard time believing that he could be so disconnected from his family that he could walk out on Easter to go look at a truck. I was so disgusted with him—and at the same time, so confused. *Who does this on Easter? How do you walk out on your little kids and your wife on Easter? I don't understand.*

All I could do was manage each moment the best I could without the kids being affected. Thank goodness they were so young that they didn't notice the tension rising around them.

The abuse toward me—and the total disregard for the kids and me—would only continue and get worse in the years ahead. I would end up staying in this high state of stress and vigilance for many more years to come. My brain was so altered that I couldn't see I deserved better. I couldn't see that I was worthy.

When your mind and body are flooded with stress hormones for a long period of time, your brain shuts down the logical part. All you see is what's right in front of you. All you have is brain fog.

It was the end of May 1992, and we had moved back to MCAS Cherry Point, where Mike joined VMA-542. A new squadron. A new start. Every time there's a new beginning, I always hope that things will change.

It took me many years to realize that hoping, wishing, and praying weren't going to bring about change. It took me many years to accept what my subconscious had known all along—that Mike was incapable of change.

Until then, I would continue to swim in my misery, constantly looking for a life raft that would miraculously pull me out. Not knowing that all I had to do was firmly plant my feet on the ground beneath me and walk to the shore.

It sounds metaphorically simple. Grappling with the hormonally poisoned brain I had made it impossible.

*　　*　　*　　*　　*　　*　　*　　*　　*　　*　　*

Having an abusive partner can look like…. **Monday:** he was a great listener today. I can really see the change in him. **Tuesday:** He called me a liar/slut for saying hello to a coworker. Rang my phone off the hook and I missed my meeting. **Wednesday:** He's acting like nothing even happened. He's back to nice again. **Thursday:** Came home with flowers "just because". **Friday:** I had plans with my friends but he said I need to prioritize the relationship right now, so I cancelled on them again. **Saturday:** Told me I can't do anything right and berated me verbally for an hour. I recorded some of it so that I can remember this. **Sunday:** Woke up like nothing even happened. Told me he didn't really mean it and that it will never happen again.

@GRACESTUART26

9. New Home, New Start?

The Universe will put you in the same situations over and over again until you learn, until you learn to react differently, until you learn to think differently, until you learn that enough is enough. Remember this, old habits do not open new doors. You must eliminate in order to evolve. -THE GLOW WAVE

Moving back to Cherry Point and joining a new squadron signified a fresh start. I was excited and energized. It was like putting new sheets on your bed—I got a burst of energy and felt confident about this next chapter. I was still clinging to the version of Mike that I had married, and I believed that, with just the right environment and enough patience from me, he would return to the wonderful person I had first met.

When we first moved back to Cherry Point, we returned to base housing. I was taken aback by how much we had outgrown the same space we had lived in just a year before. I really loved the close-knit relationships that came with living on base. You could leave your house unlocked, and the kids could roam safely. But we realized we needed a bigger house for our growing family of five. Unfortunately, the military didn't have anything larger to offer us, so we decided to buy a home.

The house was about ten miles outside of town. It had two stories, four bedrooms, three baths, a garage, and a screened-in back porch—sitting on one and a half acres. We moved in a couple of days before Christmas and hustled to put together a holiday, just like we had when we first moved to Cherry Point back in 1986. We made it through the holidays without any drama, and I was starting to let my anxiety go. I thought I could feel some real promise of a united partnership with him.

Mike was in his element with the house and the property. He was excited about having a garage where he could accumulate power tools and start new projects. He got busy acting like a lumberjack, cutting down trees. I was happy because he seemed to lighten up and smile more. Maybe this was just what we needed as a family. Maybe this would finally help him connect emotionally with us.

I realized that with a new house and mortgage, we'd need extra money. I had already started a direct sales business selling handwoven baskets and pottery soon after we returned from Virginia. I brought extra cash home after every show, which helped us pay down some existing debt. It also allowed me to catch up on personal items I had been putting off—like buying a new bra or new shoes. But this money still wasn't enough to offset the expenses of the new house.

So, I decided to try going back to work as a dental hygienist. It would mean putting all three kids in daycare and rearranging our lives to make the new routine work. I planned to continue my direct sales business, since I could set my own schedule. I figured I could work during the day at the dental office, then do home shows at night whenever it fit around the family. That was the idea, anyway.

Fortunately, I found a full-time hygiene position quickly with a local dentist. The job gave me a solid, consistent paycheck every two weeks. And with the evening shows, I had immediate cash in my pocket. I didn't have to wait for a paycheck—my customers paid when they placed their orders. Together, both jobs allowed me to contribute meaningfully to our household finances. That was an empowering feeling, and I was proud to help support our new home and family.

In addition to me going back to work, Mike was preparing to deploy again for another six months. His squadron was scheduled to leave in February and wouldn't return until late August. There wasn't much time to get everything ready in the new house—and for his deployment. We had projects we wanted to start, and we were still trying to unpack boxes. It was a whirlwind.

One of the projects was removing the numerous pine trees on our property. Pine trees dropped needles that altered the soil's pH, making it hard for grass to grow. And when a hurricane hit, it was usually pine trees that toppled, sometimes right through a house. So, on New Year's Day, Mike hired some men—who were already clearing a lot down the street—to cut down the trees on our property. They ended up cutting down eighteen pine trees but left the stumps and the tops. I couldn't really complain; they did it for free. All they wanted was the wood. I could live with that.

Another project we agreed on was expanding the kitchen. It was too small and tight when all five of us tried to sit down for dinner. We connected with a local contractor right away and quickly finalized the plans. The work would start in early March and was expected to take a couple of months. So much was happening, and Mike was counting on me to manage it all while he was deployed. The pieces were falling into place.

What I didn't account for was how exhausting it would be.

It was daunting. I was essentially working two jobs. I had three little kids to care for, a dog, a new house, all the yard work—and now, a major remodel to oversee while he was gone. I was bracing myself for the overload of obligations that I knew were coming.

I had a lot of confidence in myself. I knew I could do it. I had been working and earning my own money since I was in the third grade. I had paid my way through a private high school, and I paid for my own college and wedding. I was familiar with working hard and sacrificing. I knew I could manage it. But I also knew it would take a toll. I told myself it was only for a few months and that it would be worth it in the end.

You would think all of that would be enough to consume my mental load—but wait, there's more. Around that same time, we got our first computer. Mike wanted me to have a way to stay connected to him while he was on the boat, so he set up our first email and tried to show me how to use it.

This technology was all new to me. I was so worried that I'd click the wrong button and permanently delete something or mess up the settings. This was when America Online (AOL) was beginning to offer dial-up service for the internet. Remember the high-pitched wail of the computer trying to connect through the phone line? This would be the first deployment where I didn't send letters. Instead, we would communicate by email. It was supposed to be a more effective and efficient way to stay in touch.

Mike eventually left for his deployment, and it was now up to me to keep the engine of all my commitments well-oiled and running. I had a strict morning routine that got the kids up and out of bed so I could have them at daycare by 7 a.m. and be at the dental office on time. Jillian was in the first grade, so a school bus came by the daycare to pick her up for school and then drop her off again at the end of the day. I had to hustle to leave work on time since the daycare had zero tolerance for late pickups.

It was dark when I dropped the kids off, and it was dark when I picked them up. I was tired and hungry after a long day, and I still had to get home, make dinner, feed the kids, bathe them, try to have some quality time, and get them to bed—just to start the craziness all over again the next day. Somewhere in there, I had to take care of the dog and stay ahead of the never-ending laundry. Being a single-married mother was not fun. I gained so much empathy for single working moms and the load they were expected to carry.

In between the craziness of my day job, I was still booking shows at night. It was harder to get a babysitter now that we lived ten miles outside of town, so I had to minimize the number of shows I did. Everything was harder. Nothing was easy. The quick money I used to earn at each show was beginning to dry up because of how difficult it had become to find a sitter. I was exhausted and felt empty. I knew I needed help.

One day, I learned that one of my patients cleaned houses. After chatting with them about it, I decided to try it out. I would leave a key hidden for them, and they would come clean whatever I needed. I was excited at the idea of having some of my workload taken off my plate so I could find some relief. Unfortunately, it wasn't what I expected.

I needed help with laundry, sorting through clutter, and picking up the house. Those two things—laundry and clutter—just kept growing. The cleaners would start the laundry but not fold it. They'd pile up the clutter instead of sorting it. I'd come home to freshly vacuumed floors, but the laundry and the nicely organized piles of clutter still stared me down. It was costing a lot of money, and I didn't feel like my workload had eased up at all. After about a month, I ended it with the cleaners.

And then there was the kitchen remodel. It had officially started. We were being displaced in our own house at a time when I was already crazed with my daily routine. Once the new walls and roof were constructed, the old wall in the kitchen came down. There was plastic and construction debris everywhere. I had to constantly monitor the dog and the kids to keep them away from the potential dangers of the construction zone while still trying to use the kitchen. We worked around it, but it was just one more worry to manage.

I was only working four days a week at the dental office. That meant I had an extra day off. Yay. I needed that extra day. Spring was here, and the yard was begging for my attention. We had one and a half acres—and eighteen tree stumps and toppers that needed to be dealt with.

I gathered all the tops from the downed trees and tried to burn them on my day off when the kids weren't around. The grass was still brown and hadn't turned green yet. I didn't consider that the flames might ignite the dry grass and spread quickly. I had to run to get the garden hose to put out the fire that was creeping toward the house. It took forever just to burn a small part of the debris, and I still had to dig out all eighteen stumps. I was feeling overwhelmed.

I may have thought of myself as Wonder Woman, but I knew I couldn't do it all myself. I looked into hiring someone to remove the stumps, but it was going to be very expensive. Most businesses charged by the diameter to grind the stumps, and I had several large ones. That was going to cost close to two thousand dollars.

A random person stopped by one day and asked if I wanted him to pull the stumps out with his truck—for a fee, of course. I had to decline. As much as I wanted them gone, we had a septic system, and the truck was too heavy. It could collapse the drain field. Plus, with the ground still soft from winter and spring rains, the tire damage to the yard would've been another issue to fix.

So, I just kept plugging away. I focused on the many tasks in front of me that I could do something about. I took on one thing at a time and hoped I'd come up with an affordable solution for the stumps.

That solution came quickly—in the form of another random person who showed up at the door. He asked if I wanted him to grind the stumps down. He said he and a partner were starting a landscaping business and had driven by, saw the stumps, and decided to ask. I asked how much he would charge. He stood on the steps of the house, turned his head to look at the stumps dotted across the yard, then turned back to me and said he could grind all the stumps and burn the tops in two days—for five hundred dollars.

Whoop! Five hundred dollars? You know how many hours—and days—it would have taken me to do all that? I didn't know either, but I knew I couldn't do it in two days for that price. I quickly said yes! He and his buddy came out the next week, and true to his word, they had the tops burned and the stumps ground in two days! I happily paid them and kicked up my heels in joy. It took me a whole day just to rake up all the mulch from the stumps and pile it in the back. I even had the bonus of using that mulch in the flower beds around the house. What a score! I needed a big win like that. Thank you, Universe, for sending him to me.

Now that the stumps were gone, I could finally mow the lawn. We had a push mower, and I attempted to mow our massive lawn with it. I didn't get too far. I don't know what I was thinking—trying to mow an acre and a half in heat and humidity with a push mower. Are you kidding? Forget it. I worked for two hours and didn't even get halfway through the yard. I knew I needed a riding lawn mower. Off to Sears I went.

The benefit of working and doing in-home parties was that I had extra money to invest in the house. I paid cash for the riding mower and had it delivered. Mike wasn't around, so I learned how to use it myself. What would have taken me several hours with a push mower now took me one hour. That was money well spent. I may not have been able to get help with cleaning the house, but this mower lifted a tremendous burden. I took good care of it, and it lasted over eighteen years. I am still so grateful for having had the means to buy that mower and the enormous weight it took off my shoulders. Thank you, thank you.

I remained thick in obligations, chores, and commitments until the end of August. Getting the stumps ground, the tops burned, and the riding mower—those were huge wins. But I was still running on empty just trying to survive each workday and keep up with the kitchen remodel. Everything seemed to be moving along as well as it could—until...

Something happened to the computer, and I wasn't able to communicate via email anymore.

I was still receiving emails from Mike, but I couldn't send a reply. I tried reading the manual and troubleshooting, but I couldn't figure it out. So, I had to go back to writing him letters to let him know what was going on. At the same time, Mike started getting increasingly annoyed and upset with me. I'm sure he thought I was blowing him off.

Mike expected immediate responses from me now that we were using email—but that wasn't happening. His tone started to become accusatory and vicious. I tried going to the base library to use their computers, but I didn't know how to access our emails from a different machine. I'm sure there was a simple solution, but I couldn't figure it out. I was very intimidated by the technology and believed I might screw everything up if I hit the wrong button.

Eventually, my letters caught up to him. His tone softened a bit through the emails once he realized I was having computer problems, but I still felt stupid and incompetent for not being able to figure it out myself. The enormity of everything I was responsible for while he was gone was wearing me down. All I could do was keep putting one foot in front of the other until he came home in August.

Mike's number one concern while he was away was the kitchen remodel. He wanted updates constantly. He would write in his emails, "The kitchen is probably done by now." It wasn't. The whole process was moving slowly. The contractor we hired only had one worker on the job, and he was juggling multiple renovation projects. I only had so much mental bandwidth, so I just let the renovation roll along at its own pace.

As it turned out, the kitchen was barely finished before Mike got back in August. I worried that he would criticize me for the delay. I remembered how easily he had been triggered over little things when we were stationed in Quantico the year before. That fear of his explosive temper pushed me to another level of determination to get everything in order.

I got busy trying to perfect every corner of the house. I installed ceiling fans in every bedroom—yes, I installed the ceiling fans myself. I painted every room in the house, including all the doors. I bought new appliances and had them installed. I tried to get regular exercise to work off the stress. And all this while working two jobs, managing little kids, and maintaining the family finances. I was overwhelmed and felt like I was underwater, but I kept swimming through it all, hoping that he would come home and appreciate everything I had done for him and our family.

August finally arrived, and Mike returned. I felt a wave of relief from the heavy load I'd been carrying. He seemed eager to be helpful and engaged. That first week, everything was great. He had an endless smile, and he expressed appreciation for the transformation in the house. He seemed excited to spend time with the kids and be involved in their lives.

But happiness wasn't an emotion Mike could sustain.

Soon, he started coming home with a scowl and picking at small details around the house. Even though I prided myself on keeping up with the housework—on top of everything else—it wasn't enough for him.

He started complaining that the socks he wanted weren't in his drawer. There were plenty of other socks, but he focused on the one specific pair that was in the hamper. He expressed his disgust by slamming the dresser drawer. My old feelings of anxiety and emotional insecurity came back in an instant. Poof! The smiles were gone, replaced with scowls.

It didn't stop there. He got angry and slammed kitchen cabinets when he realized there was only enough Cheerios for one bowl. He did the same thing if we were low on milk or bread. He chastised me for not having "such a simple thing" in the house.

"My job is hard and dangerous enough. All I ask for is a simple breakfast of Cheerios in the morning. Is that too hard for you?"

I didn't eat bread, cereal, or milk, so I didn't know we were running low. I told him, "Let me know when it's low so I can get more."

That was the wrong thing to say.

He took it as a personal attack. "So, it's my fault? Because I didn't let you know? You're the one getting the groceries, not me. You need to check before you go to the store. It's your fault!"

I knew—subconsciously—it wasn't my fault. I knew he was overreacting. I knew he was being unreasonable. But he flexed his intimidation tactics in a way that left me shaking, unable to hear or trust my inner voice.

Slamming doors, pounding countertops—these were his way of showing me that I could be next. He didn't have to hit me to infuse fear. There was always the unspoken promise that he could.

All he had to do was show me how he treated the cabinet doors.

I was traumatized to think that someone who professed to love and protect me would purposefully intimidate me with the threat of physical harm. That's where cognitive brain damage begins—when love is laced with fear. How could he purposely sow fear into the mind of someone he claimed to love? How do I separate the two different personalities? It's a deep shock to your inner core. A betrayal that your mind can't rationalize.

My head was swimming in confusion and fear at his sudden switch in personality. What was going to set him off next? I had put so much energy into creating an environment where he couldn't find fault, and yet, he still did. He saw that I was hurt by his verbal abuse and the slamming of cabinets. Instead of apologizing, he doubled down.

"I wouldn't have gotten upset if the socks were in the drawer and we had cereal and milk in the house. You don't understand the stress I have to undergo every day when I leave this house. The least you can do for me is take care of the little things. It's not that hard!"

My poor, poisoned, clouded brain accepted his criticism. It was easier to believe I wasn't good enough than to accept that he was intentionally cruel. Why didn't I see that these little things were important to the success of his day? *If only the laundry were done. If only I had stocked more Cheerios. If only there were another gallon of milk. Then he could start his day happy. Then he could focus on work and flying.*

I accepted the blame. I was supposed to be in charge of the house, and I was failing.

From then on, I bought at least eight gallons of milk and no fewer than ten loaves of bread at a time. I stocked both in the garage freezer so they wouldn't spoil. I even bought his Cheerios by the case. He should be happy now—he had his milk, cereal, and bread whenever he wanted. *Mike shouldn't have any reason to get upset. Maybe now he will love me again.*

At the time, all I could think of was doing anything to put out his fire—to be sure that his explosions didn't reach the kids. I was in survival mode. I didn't allow myself to fully see his cruelty because of the trauma it induced. I simply accepted that I wasn't good enough to keep him happy.

It's crazy, but I see now that by allowing him to intimidate me, I was letting him step across another boundary of my self-worth. He was methodically challenging every boundary I had in place, and in turn, he gained more and more power over me.

Mike knew he was being an asshole. But he also knew that he had stripped me of the resolve to defend myself. He enjoyed the power it gave him, the elevation of his ego over mine. I was treated like I was nothing to him. And I felt like nothing. I blamed myself for not being the perfect wife he wanted.

It didn't matter that I was working two jobs and running the entire house by myself. I told myself: I should do better. I should be better.

I gathered the kids after that morning's emotional beatdown and dropped them off at daycare before heading to work. I was getting good at compartmentalizing my anxiety and trauma, putting on a smile for the world to see. Somehow, I got through my patient load that day. Then I picked up the kids and went home to get dinner ready. After that came cleanup, baths, and bedtime for the kids—all while Mike relaxed in front of the TV.

I was exhausted and still shell-shocked from the morning's verbal assault. My body had grown tense as we neared home, uncertain of what he might have in store for me. I rushed through the evening's chores, walking on eggshells. Even through my clouded, traumatized mind, I could still recognize the imbalance in our relationship.

I was hurt. Hurt that he didn't consider *my* long day— didn't even offer to help when I got home. It would have been a simple, loving gesture for him to start dinner. A moment of recognition. An acknowledgment of the daily sacrifices I was making. But it never came.

But that was not the dynamic in our marriage. Mike didn't see me as his partner in life. I was there to please him. Even if I didn't please him directly, he could still give himself a boost of ego and feel powerful through his threats and demeaning tactics. I was fuel for his ego either way.

He had grown up being catered to by his mom, and as a result, he became selfish, self-centered, and entitled. He knew I was a strong woman. He knew I had an empathetic and forgiving soul. His fragile ego needed someone to manipulate and control so he could feel superior. And I had just the personality that allowed him to do it—I was empathetic enough to keep making excuses for him, and forgiving enough not to hold him accountable. I was the perfect energy source for him. I just couldn't see—or believe—the extent of the intentional cruelty he laid out for me.

I couldn't get to bed fast enough that night. Eventually, Mike came up to bed and made his intentions clear that he wanted to have sex. I was not in the mood. How could he treat me with such vitriol and disgust—and then still expect sex? How could he think I would want to be intimate with him after the emotional beatdown I'd received that morning and the indifference he showed when I got home?

I'm not a robot. I'm not his possession. I'm not his servant. I'm a human being.

I want to feel respected and valued. I want to feel important and worthy to my husband. I want my feelings to be considered. I deserve to have my own needs validated.

How did I get here? *How did I end up becoming less of myself just so he could feel better about himself?*

It took me many years to realize that wanting sex after a verbal beatdown was another calculated power move on his part. He would abuse this intimate relationship again and again throughout our marriage. It was just one more tactic he used to maintain emotional control over me.

He used sex to feel powerful.

He used my emotions against me. He used my forgiving nature against me.

I was tired of being used. I just wanted to be loved—and to feel loved.

So much for a new home and a new start.

*   *   *   *   *   *   *   *   *   *   *

A narcissist doesn't want to discuss their actions, they want to provoke your reaction so they can then use your reactions as a distraction from them having to explain themselves.

Marcus Weaver weav_told_me

10. Sexual Abuse

"I deserve more" is a perfectly good reason to walk away. You don't need proof, closure, or permission. The fact that you weren't being loved and respected the way you deserve is enough.- evolvewith_sophie

I really did try to be the wife he wanted. I was so deep in a trauma bond with him that I rationalized his behavior most of the time and laid the fault at my own feet. I just vowed to try harder.

But when it came to sex, it was very hard for me to pretend that I felt an emotional connection with him after he had raked my soul over the coals for trivial things. He wanted me to passionately engage with him during every sexual encounter. I couldn't do it. I didn't know how to pretend that his demeaning behavior toward me didn't affect my ability to experience an emotionally connected sexual union.

Breaking news: It's a real sexual turnoff when your partner treats you like shit and then expects you to be a hungry call girl in the bedroom.

I could never understand how he could treat me so poorly and then wonder why I couldn't "give it all up" for him at night. That barrage of emotional abuse from the day was still clinging to me, and I had no interest in exchanging sexual favors.

From my perspective, it was even more demeaning that he expected sex after he had treated me so abusively. I felt used. I felt like I was his property—not a partner he respected and cherished. He demanded sex, and if I refused, he would say some of the most degrading things to me. That, of course, only made me want to withdraw more.

But I knew what he was capable of if I rebuked him. I also didn't want the kids to hear his anger directed at me. So most of the time, I gave in and complied.

He was never a considerate lover. His lovemaking was selfish. Everything was fine as long as he got what he wanted. The problem was, nothing ever made him happy. He always did what he wanted in bed, and then he'd lecture me afterward about how I didn't live up to his expectations. In a disgusted tone, he'd say, "I feel like you're only servicing me."

But that was exactly what it was.

He always made sure he had an orgasm. He never tried to bring me to one. It was always the same routine: grab my breasts, suck on them, then penetrate with his penis. Sometimes, he'd have me roll over so he could penetrate from behind—but it was always about his climax. When he was finished, he'd criticize me for not "being into it."

It didn't matter whether I refused to have sex or gave in. I was in a lose-lose situation.

If I refused, he would berate me and then give me the silent treatment. If I complied, he would chastise and lecture me because I didn't perform with passion. He turned what should have been an act of love between spouses into a detestable deed.

You just treated me with the utmost disrespect, and now you want to act like it didn't happen? And expect me to have a short memory too?

There was no authentic love or respect coming from him. He didn't make me feel emotionally safe. He didn't make me feel valued or worthy. I was just his property—to use and discard at his will.

When you have sex with someone who doesn't fill your emotional well but drains it, you feel used, disrespected, devalued. You aren't seen as a person with feelings who deserves to be treated with love, compassion, and empathy. You're just an object—used when they want you, discarded when they're done. This kind of mental abuse, mixed with sexual coercion, is evil. It leaves you emotionally empty inside.

There were times when he would bring up my ex-boyfriend, Jack, while he was penetrating me. He was so disgusting. He would say, "Am I as big as Jack? Huh? Am I? Does he do it as hard as this? Should I go harder? I bet you wish I was Jack. If I were Jack, I know you would give him a blow job. Wouldn't you? Wouldn't you?"

Even now, it still makes me sick to my stomach.

What was I supposed to say while he was screwing me and saying those disgusting things about an ex? Did he think that verbal humiliation would turn me on and inspire me to give him the best sex of his life? He knew what he was doing. He was reminding me—again—that he had power and control over me, and there was nothing I could do about it.

He was a bully. He elevated his weak ego by cutting me into a million little pieces with his tongue. And somehow, I was supposed to be motivated to perform my best sexual moves for him. It makes me sick to recall those times. It makes my stomach hurt to think of how he betrayed our marriage vows with no remorse—and how long I stayed trapped in that living hell.

This sexual abuse was interspersed throughout our entire marriage. The only orgasms I ever had were with Jack. Mike never tried to give me one. But he'd still get angry at me for not having one. I thought if I told him what I needed, he would appreciate it. No. He took it as criticism.

"Oh, so you're saying I suck? You're saying I'm not good enough."

Holy cow. Always the victim. He wanted me to have an orgasm but didn't want me to tell him what to do to get me there. How was he supposed to know unless I told him? He wasn't. Once again, I couldn't win with him. He always set me up to be the bad guy—and him the victim.

One time, Mike came home from work and walked straight into the kitchen, where I was sitting at the table paying bills. He stood with his left hand resting on the counter and his right on his hip and said, "I told the guys at the squadron that you don't have orgasms, and they said some women *just* don't. So it's not my fault. *It's* yours." Then he turned and walked away.

WHAT DID HE JUST SAY??

There wasn't even a greeting when he got home. He just dropped that humiliating detail of his day in my lap like it was nothing. Thank you very much for humiliating me in front of your squadron buddies. Thank you for making "my not having an orgasm with you" into pillow talk for the pilots and their wives. Thank you so very much for coming in, planting your victory flag at my feet, and declaring—once again—that I was the problem, not you.

And, oh, by the way, I'm *really* feeling turned on by you right now and can't wait to go upstairs and have wild, passionate sex with you.

He just pulled the pin on the grenade—and walked away.

Not every sexual encounter between us was an extreme, but it was always centered on him. And he always made me feel like I wasn't good enough. There was no romance. There was no foreplay. No cuddling on the sofa at night while watching a show. He couldn't—or wouldn't—put in the effort during the day to make me feel like I had a loving, considerate partner. And without that, how could I possibly feel a deep, romantic, intimate connection in bed?

I tried.

I missed having a loving touch. I missed kind words. I missed having an intimate connection with someone I could share my dreams, my fears, my future goals with. I missed having someone who supported and loved me unconditionally. I was married—but I was very much alone.

I would often look for him after finishing my chores, hoping to connect. I missed adult conversation. I wanted to share the events of the day. Usually, I'd find him in the garage working on some project. I would sit on the steps leading to the kitchen and try to engage him.

"What are you working on?" I'd ask.

"Just organizing," he'd say.

I'd ask how his day went, and he'd offer a short answer. He never—not once in our entire marriage—asked how *my* day was. Still, I sat there, hoping, waiting for him to reciprocate my effort to connect.

I would usually sit in silence for quite a while. Most of the time, I would just get up and go back into the house because he showed no interest in communicating with me. One time he asked, "Why are you out here?" and I said, "Because I want to be with you." He replied with a smirk, "You're weird." So, I just got up and walked back into the house.

He showed me time and again that I was not important to him. He was so self-centered that he couldn't detect that I needed and wanted his attention—that I needed an emotional and intimate connection with him. Even when I came right out and said, "I just want to be with you," he still couldn't see my pleas for connection. He just said I was weird.

So how was I supposed to suddenly want to roll around with him in the most intimate of ways in bed? Discard, discard, discard. I was just a thing—not a person with the emotional needs our creator granted us. My needs weren't even secondary. I was nothing unless I could do something for him.

Can you even fathom the depth of emptiness that comes from being disregarded by the one who has pledged to love, care for, and protect you?

Many times, when I was at a low point and feeling unworthy as a woman, I would go into my closet and pull out the old photo album I had of Jack. There weren't many pictures—film was expensive, and so was having it developed. But the photos I did have reminded me that I had once lived a beautiful life. That I had once been loved unconditionally by a man who would have cut off his own arm before cutting me with a thousand shards of cruel words.

I would stand in my closet and remember his love for me. I would remember how close we came to making it forever. It was a reminder that I was worthy to someone. But then my present reality would come crashing back, and I would return the album to the back of the closet.

So many times, I would go back to that photo album and allow myself to be pulled into a happier, more beautiful time. So many times, that memory would allow me to refill my emotional well. It was one of the few ways I had to ground myself in a time when I felt valued, loved, and cherished. It gave me the strength to keep going and hope that, one day, I could experience that same connection again—with someone who would truly see me the way Jack once did.

Many of you may say that my account of our sexual discourse is not an example of sexual abuse. Maybe you're right. Maybe it wouldn't hold up in a court of law. But I do know that I was traumatized and humiliated during sex with him. I do know that he emotionally abused me during sex. I do know that I felt intimidated to comply—or suffer the consequences.

For me, it was abuse.

He abused the sacred union between two people. He would often bring up his displeasure about my performance at random times, outside the bedroom. He made me feel "less than." It was abuse centered around sex. So, for me, it was sexual abuse.

To protect my mental wellness, I wouldn't allow myself to react emotionally. I would wear mental armor made of stone. I would pack up the defeating experience in a tight little box and store it deep in my brain—hoping to forget it existed and never open it again.

Eventually, all those little boxes started to leak and spill over into my seemingly controlled reality. Little by little, the belittling memories would seep out and demand my attention. Even if it was just to pick them up and shove them back into their box.

There were many random times when these episodes would rise back into my awareness and cause me to cry. If I was around people, I'd have to excuse myself and hide in the bathroom until I could force the memory back into its box—or until it passed, leaving behind a dull ache in my stomach. If I was alone, I would allow myself to feel it and cry as much as I needed.

I usually had no warning. It just bubbled up—and broke loose.

Later in our marriage, he wanted to go a step further and have me "watch him" as he dressed up in women's clothes. He wanted me to see him in all his splendor—dressed like a woman—and then have sex. I absolutely would not. I absolutely would never. I told him unequivocally: *No.* Just thinking about it now still makes me sick.

This is not a rebuke of gay or lesbian people. If that is who they are, and it makes them happy and whole, then who cares what consenting adults do behind closed doors? They deserve dignity, freedom, and respect. And I should have been given the same respect. I should be free not to be part of an act of intimacy that makes me feel unsafe or disconnected from myself.

I could never have sex with him dressed as a woman. I would feel as though I were having sex with a woman— and that would repulse me. This was a hard *no*. I reminded him that if I didn't know about it, he could do what he wanted—but I did not want to see him dressed like a woman. I gave him permission to be who he wanted *only* if he reciprocated by respecting my right not to be involved in it.

He backed off and never asked me again. One small battle I had won.

Reflecting on it now, I can see how my emphatic resolve—my hard line—took him by surprise. He most likely thought I would roll over like I had in so many other areas. But this time, he found a boundary I would not let him cross. A hard line for myself.

If only I had been able to hold that same hard line in all the other victories he claimed—those times he plundered my personal space and took it for his own.

We had been married for about ten years at that point, and I still wasn't sure how I had made it this far and still had a heartbeat. The years had been a blur of moving moment to moment, living on high alert, and tending to the needs of three vulnerable and innocent children.

This couldn't be all there was to my life. I wasn't meant to go through this much continued hell—and to do it alone. I couldn't see too far beyond each day, so I was surprised to realize how much time had already passed. I would have expected myself to fall into depression, but I didn't have the luxury. I had three little ones who needed me to be their protector—even if they didn't know they needed protecting.

Ironically, not long into 1993, *he* was the one who claimed to be depressed.

I celebrated quietly to myself.

Finally—finally—there was *a reason for his cruelty.*

*   *   *   *   *   *   *   *   *   *   *

They don't have to hit you, choke you or slam your head into the wall for it to be domestic violence. They can degrade you, humiliate you, blame you, scream at you, cheat on you, withhold finances and even just try to control you and it still is domestic violence.

@understandingthenarc

11. Suicide and Depression

Speak positive words into your life every single morning. Think big, Think healing. Think success. Think peace. Think happiness. Think growth mindset. Always start the day with positive energy. You deserve it. - universe.guidance

At the time, I really didn't understand how he felt his life was so bad that he had to come home from work and give me the worst of it. Somehow, he was able to put on a smile for everyone else when he walked out the door, but when he came home, he turned into the darkest rain cloud. I noticed that his dark moods were becoming more consistent, and I tried hard not to have any expectations of chores placed on him—just so he could have an opportunity to unwind when he got home and not explode.

I did all the chores outside: mowing, trimming, raking, weeding, cleaning up after the dogs. I painted the outside of the house several times over the nineteen years we lived there, and I even built a large stone patio outside the kitchen in the back. Inside, I did everything I could to avoid asking for help. Beyond the usual household chores, I repaired the walls with spackle and paint, replaced air filters, fixed molding, changed lightbulbs, and cleaned out the fireplace.

All he had to do was relax. I thought I could do all this and barter for a happy marriage.

He loved bragging to his colleagues about how his wife did all the yard work and how I relieved him of extra responsibilities. I was a trophy—something he could hold up to the world. I made him look good. I gave him social credibility. He thought people would look at him and think, Wow! He must be some wonderful guy to have such an amazing wife *who's* willing to take on so much so her husband can come home and relax.

To others, he talked like we had the perfect marriage. But at home, he held me in contempt.

He rarely thanked me for doing the chores. He never offered to give me a break or even considered the toll it was taking on me. I hoped I could make the emotional barometer in the house go down by taking on the extra work. But I was wrong. He came to take me for granted and expected me to maintain the load—if not take on even more. I wanted to make our life better. Instead, only his life improved. Mine got worse.

He never took advantage of the low-stress environment I created to become calmer or more relaxed. Instead, he became even more unpredictable with his outbursts.

One time, after putting the kids to bed, I came downstairs and found him in the living room, watching TV in the recliner. The lights were off, except for the glow of the television and the lights in the kitchen. He seemed relaxed. I don't remember what I said—it wasn't anything critical or provocative—but he suddenly blew up. He took his right fist and slammed it down on the extended footrest of the La-Z-Boy recliner, breaking it in two. He shouted something after breaking the chair and then glared at me—as if I had broken it.

I remember recoiling and turning around quickly to go back upstairs. I wasn't about to get any closer to that erupting volcano. I quickly got into bed and pretended to be asleep by the time he came up. I didn't want to engage with him any more than necessary.

We had that broken recliner for another twenty years. It was always a reminder of his unpredictable potential for damage—to property and to people.

He also exhibited his explosive nature on many occasions while driving, especially when I was helping him with directions. He'd have me read the road map and serve as his "co-pilot." I thought his assigning me that label meant he saw me as a partner in the adventure. It's silly, but something so small can make you feel important—especially when you've been dismissed by your spouse for so long. I embraced every little crumb he threw my way.

I took the mission seriously. I was excited to feel like I was being seen as an equal. Unfortunately, that feeling didn't last long.

If I missed a turn and he had to double back, he would resurrect his temper immediately. He'd swear at me and make a violent U-turn, causing my body to be flung side to side, front to back. This was his way of punishing me. He got to watch me jerk in my seat and see his intended result—causing me physical and emotional distress—without ever laying a hand on me.

He could tell himself he never hit me, yet he still inflicted harm. He watched me crouch down in the seat, flinching from his reckless driving, and *that* gave him power.

He never apologized. If he said anything at all, it would be something like, *"Well, I* wouldn't have had to do it if *you* hadn't missed the turn in the first place." The message was always the same: *It's your fault.*

He inflicted emotional and physical distress, then blamed me for it.

A classic narcissistic ploy.

It was a win for him.

Early in our marriage, when we were stationed at Quantico in Northern Virginia, we were driving around Washington, D.C., trying to find some landmark. I was tasked with using the map to give him directions. Somehow, we managed to end up in a part of D.C. where the cars were stripped and plenty of struggling people stood on the corners, staring at us—the obvious outsiders who were lost.

He never let me forget it. Whenever I was navigating, he'd say, *"You better not get us into the ghetto like you did in D.C."*

He loved telling that story to his friends—turning it into a joke, making them all laugh at how I couldn't read a map. He brought it up time and time again over a span of more than twenty years.

He knew exactly what he was doing.

He'd flash me a certain look—one that only I recognized. It was a challenge, daring me to push back in front of everyone. He knew I wouldn't. He *counted* on that. And he telegraphed that acknowledgment with his look. He could intimidate me even in a crowd, and I wouldn't—or couldn't—do anything about it.

Any opportunity to embarrass me was one he seized. It made him feel superior. It fed his fragile ego. He didn't like himself, and deep down, he didn't think he was worthy. So, to manufacture confidence and a sense of self-worth, he used belittling and humiliation— especially if he could get away with doing it under the guise of humor.

In this case, it was a "joke" at my expense, told in front of others, with the added benefit of knowing I wouldn't say anything. Because if *I*, the victim, pushed back, then suddenly I'd be the one who looked unhinged. I'd look like the one out of line. And the narcissist gains supporters—people who will unknowingly become witnesses to his narrative and future "evidence" that

I was the problem. That *I* was the perpetrator, not the victim.

So, there I was, standing at a squadron function with everyone's eyes on me after he told his "joke." They were all laughing, looking at me. I always managed to put on a smile, but inside, it made me feel completely alone. It reinforced the belief that I had no one I could confide in about his treatment of me. Everyone viewed it as a non-issue—especially since I smiled along with the crowd.

Who would take me seriously if I complained or shared how he made me feel stupid and incompetent? Who would recognize this as a serious breach of trust between spouses—one that merited counseling or deeper concern?

No one.

This was yet another example of why I felt so alone. I convinced myself I had to carry the burden of his abuse silently and alone—because no one would believe me.

There were many, many times when we had a social function to attend that Mike would give me the rundown beforehand. He made it clear he didn't want to go and that we were only staying for an hour. He was adamant that I watch the clock and come find him at the one-hour mark so we could leave.

When we arrived, I would tell people that we wouldn't be staying long—making up an excuse so our quick departure wouldn't catch anyone off guard. I kept a close eye on the time, and when the hour was up, I would go find Mike to let him know it was time to go.

I'd find him in a group of guys, laughing and drinking, having a great time with a beer in his hand. When I interrupted to remind him it was time to leave, he'd look at me like I was crazy. Then he'd shrug me off and say something to the guys like, "I have no idea why she wants to leave so soon."

And just like that, I looked like I was the one who didn't want to be there.

He threw me under the bus every time.

It took me many years of going through this routine with him before I stopped reacting to it. At first, I was intimidated—afraid of what he would do if I didn't come find him like he asked. Later, I started taking my power back. I would silently roll my eyes when he declared we'd only stay for one hour. Eventually, I quit listening to his declarations altogether and let him come find me when he was ready to go.

During the early 1990s, Mike would have massive meltdowns—always out of the blue, always when no one else was around, and always after the kids were in bed. A common theme in these eruptions was the threat of leaving me and the kids—and taking all the money. After all, in *his* words, *"It's my God-damned money."*

The threat of him taking our investments and abandoning me with the kids would rattle me every time. It threw my logical reasoning off balance.

My poor brain would start racing, trying to figure out how I would manage with three innocent children if he took everything. This should have been my way out—my moment of clarity—but remember: you can't think logically when your brain is poisoned with stress hormones. If I were a robot, emotionally unaffected by his constant yanking of the floor out from under me, I could have created a rational plan to ensure I got half the money—for me and the kids. But I wasn't a robot. I was alone. I had only myself to confer with.

After his tirades, he needed to put an exclamation point on the beatdown. He would say, "I'm leaving," and storm out of the house, driving away in a rage. Every time, I was left in a state of panic—not knowing where he went, when he'd return, or what form of punishment he'd have in store for me when he did.

I'd stand vigil at the upstairs bedroom window, watching the street, anticipating his return. I didn't want to be caught off guard. I wanted to be mentally and physically prepared for whatever version of him walked through the door. Sometimes I sat at that window for twenty minutes. Other times, it was hours.

When I saw him turn down the street, I would quickly run downstairs to meet him at the door. I'd rather he yelled downstairs than risk waking the kids. When he entered the house, he'd slam the doors and give me the silent treatment. His eyes held that familiar intimidating glare, and his body language—his menacing lunge as he passed by me—was calculated. It said everything without a word.

Somehow, even though I was afraid of him, I still climbed into bed next to him—lying there for hours, unable to sleep, on constant alert for my safety.

If his sudden outbursts weren't enough to shake me to my core, he began threatening suicide.

He would look at me—eyes full of fire, his body tense—and say, "I know I'm not a good person. I know God hates me. I want to kill myself. You know how many times I've thought about taking a gun and killing myself? The only reason I haven't is because you wouldn't get any life insurance."

In other words: *I'm staying in this hell of a marriage for you and the kids.*

He made sure I understood the magnitude of his "sacrifice."

When he threatened suicide, my entire body would ignite with panic. Every nerve was on high alert. My survival instincts would kick in, and my mind would spin with dreaded possibilities. How would he do it? Shoot himself? Hang himself? Where would I find *his* body? In the garage? In the bedroom? Would the kids see *it*? How could I protect *them* from *that kind of* trauma at such a young age?

All this played out in my head while I tried to stay present, trying to listen for any cues in his words—

any signs that might tell me what to say next. At the same time, I was desperately searching for the magic words that would pull him back from the ledge without pushing him over it.

He kept coming at me with venom, raging about how miserable his life was, how he thought we had a great marriage but now he didn't. He accused me of not living up to his ideals, of not loving him, of not caring about what happened to him.

I kept waiting for a pause so I could offer a word—*any* word—of comfort. But each time he paused and I tried to speak, he'd interrupt me and talk right over me. He only wanted his voice to be heard.

And yet, he was laying accusations at my feet, daring me to respond—but never letting me.

Each pause felt like a trap. He'd fix me with those dagger eyes, catch his breath, and wait for me to speak. And when I did, he'd cut me off. Drown me out. Dismiss me.

Crazy, but he actually said this to me after I tried to take advantage of a pause in his tirade: "You're always interrupting me and won't let me talk." It was so absurd—almost comical. I would have laughed out loud if I hadn't been afraid he might come after me. It was clear: only one voice was allowed to be heard—his.

He wanted the moment to be all about him. He wanted to put me in my place and manipulate me into feeling sorry for him, all while blaming me for his mental meltdown.

Even though my brain was so f'd up from the constant barrage of emotional and psychological abuse, I knew deep down I wasn't responsible for his mental instability. But when you're simultaneously afraid he might take his own life—and possibly take yours—then rational thought is a million miles away.

I was not the cause of his suicidal thoughts. That, I never owned. I knew I had been sacrificing myself, doing everything I could think of to make him happy. What I did believe was that if I were to leave him—if I turned my back on him while he was "in need"—he might use that as motivation to follow through and kill himself. And then I would be left to pick up the shattered pieces for our children.

I wouldn't take responsibility for his death, but the pain it would inflict on the kids—that thought alone propelled me to stay. It kept me from actively seeking a way out. In that way, he succeeded in coercing me into obedience.

When he finally wore down enough to let me speak, I'd say something like, "God doesn't hate you. You're a good person" (choking on those words). And he'd reply, "Yes, he does. God hates me. You hate me."

Now he was challenging me to profess my love—after he had just emotionally bludgeoned me. If I didn't respond quickly enough with a reassurance of love, it would be all the evidence he needed to escalate his abuse again. Of course, I told him I loved him. Mostly because I was afraid. I was afraid of what he would do. I would say almost anything to calm the fiery demon in front of me.

These outbursts—these suicidal threats—began happening more frequently. And I was mentally rocked to my core.

What do I do now?

How do I protect the kids from this possibility?

I would lie in bed next to him, unable to sleep. My head spun with the absurd, out-of-the-blue declarations he hurled at me. He wasn't crying for help—he was lashing out. And there's a difference.

The lashing out was meant to intimidate me with his rage and make me believe he might take me with him on his suicide mission. I don't think I had any coherent thoughts during those nights. I was so traumatized that all I could do was lie awake, monitoring his every move, his breathing—watching for signs of danger.

What I couldn't understand was how he could fall asleep so easily after a storm like that. Meanwhile, I lay awake in a constant state of vigilance. Eventually, I'd fall asleep, but when I woke, the fight-or-flight anxiety would still be coursing through my veins.

I look back now and wonder: How did I survive this hell? How did I stay with him for another twenty years?

I was so f'd up. My brain was so, so f'd up.

I needed a lifeline.

Who would have thought that lifeline would come from him?

At some point, Mike came to me and admitted he believed he was clinically depressed. I was relieved. Secretly, I cheered inside. *Finally—this is the reason. This is why he's been so cruel and unstable.* I had held on to the belief that there had to be an explanation. I couldn't believe someone could be this heartless on purpose.

Now, here it was: he was depressed.

The stigma around depression still exists—but it was especially pervasive in certain professions. And being a fighter pilot? It was almost intolerable. The military needs to know their pilots are mentally stable. A pilot can't afford to have thoughts of self-harm while in control of an aircraft. The risk is too great. The military wouldn't hesitate to ground someone over it—and Mike knew that.

I went with him to the base hospital to see a psychiatric doctor. It was clear the military treated psychiatric visits with the utmost discretion. The psych wing was tucked away in the back of the hospital. Curtains were drawn over every window. Each waiting room doubled as an exam room, and only one patient at a time was allowed inside. The rooms had windows, but every one of them was covered.

We waited alone in our assigned room for the doctor. I never saw another patient.

Eventually, the doctor joined us and began asking Mike questions to determine whether he needed depression medication. Mike sanitized the details of his breakdowns, carefully feeling out the doctor's intent before revealing too much.

He had told me ahead of time: if he was diagnosed, he could be grounded. They could take his wings away. That terrified him—his whole identity was tied to being a military pilot. So he held back, fearful of what a diagnosis might cost him.

Then the doctor turned to me.

He asked, "Do you feel unsafe around Mike?"

Of course, I felt unsafe. There was hardly a day that went by when I didn't feel anxious and unsure of what he would bring home to me. I was always on guard—for my physical, mental, and emotional well-being. But do you think I was going to tell the doctor that? With Mike sitting right next to me? Are you kidding?

If military doctors are going to ask that kind of question, they need to do it privately, without the mentally unstable partner in the room. So, I answered, "No, I don't feel unsafe."

This whole experience was another confirmation for me that I had no one to turn to in the military. Even the doctors didn't provide a safe environment where I could be honest.

The meeting with the psychiatric doctor didn't take long. He cautioned Mike that if he prescribed depression medication, Mike would be grounded—he wouldn't be able to fly. He urged Mike to be absolutely certain before pursuing a formal diagnosis and treatment plan.

Mike got quiet. He thanked the doctor and got up to leave. I could feel his tension rising with every step we took out of that hospital and back to the car.

That walk felt extraordinarily long. No words were spoken—just thick, choking tension. I dreaded getting into the car, knowing it was a confined space where he would feel safe unloading on me. It's amazing how much energy we absorb from those around us, and I could feel his negativity spiking fast.

In response, I began building my mental wall. I needed to deflect as much of his inevitable storm as possible. My body tensed. I started to emotionally detach, preparing myself for what I believed was coming.

But surprisingly, he said nothing. All the way home: silence.

And that silence, paired with his pulsing, toxic energy, was terrifying. He usually didn't hold back. So now I was left unsure: *When would the fallout come? In what form? How much?* I wanted to say something to break the tension, but I knew better and stayed quiet.

We got home, and he went upstairs immediately. I didn't follow. I wasn't going to go looking for trouble. It would find me soon enough.

I busied myself with some menial task—anything to distract my mind. After a while, he came back downstairs. In that slow, dark, menacing tone of his, he said:

"Well, you obviously don't care about me since you didn't say anything all the way home or come up to see how I was doing. Don't worry. If I kill myself, it won't be in the plane."

And then he walked away.

He had decided not to seek treatment. He was more afraid of what would happen if he lost his wings. Flying was his only identity. He had nothing else. He was a Marine Fighter/Attack Pilot—and if you took that away, he was no one.

I could understand his fear. But for me? I was deflated. I had hoped this would be the beginning of him getting help—that we could finally return to the guy I met in the beginning. That our marriage might finally turn around.

To this day, I still don't know if he was truly clinically depressed. Maybe it was all part of a gambit—a tactic to extract more sympathy and attention. Maybe he was hoping to get a diagnosis without consequence, still be allowed to fly, and have me feel sorry for him in the process.

He thrived on being the victim in his own story. So I can't completely rule it out. He wasn't above fabricating an elaborate ruse just to keep me tethered to him.

And he succeeded.

I made more excuses for his behavior because of his "depression," and I erased any immediate plans I had for leaving him. After all, how *could* you abandon your spouse if *they're* ill? That's what I told myself. That's how I convinced myself to stay. That's how I kept my own mental and emotional unraveling in check.

I was so alone. I was trying to be the rock for everyone, but no one was there for me. I had so much to hide from the outside world, and yet I desperately wanted it to all come to light—just so I could finally be free.

But I didn't know how to make that happen. All I could do was survive moment to moment. I had hoped that his depression would be the lifeline I needed, but instead, it became just one more weight for me to carry—for almost twenty more years.

*   *   *   *   *   *   *   *   *   *   *

As a narcissist gets meaner and meaner, they get convinced that you're not going to leave them. They see your tolerance as your permission to keep taking more of their abuse. They think you are stupid and a fool that you keep giving them chances because you are totally invested in the relationship. They do not recognize your compassion, and they don't care. The longer you stay, the darker they become.

Danish Bashir, narcabusecoach.

12. 1994 Hurricane Gordon

Never feel guilty for protecting yourself from people who never felt guilty for hurting you.

-turtlebreeze

It was Friday, November 18, 1994. The kids were home from school, and Mike was home from work due to Hurricane Gordon hitting our area the night before. We had prepared several days in advance by getting nonperishable food, bottled water, batteries, candles, getting the laundry done, and making sure our cars had a full tank of gas. All the loose items outside were secured. All of us were emotionally on edge, bracing for the unknown that Hurricane Gordon had in mind for us.

We all slept downstairs in the living room the night before, and eventually the hurricane had passed us by with little destruction. Now we were just trying to find things to do without any electricity.

The morning after the hurricane passed, the two youngest—Claire and Craig—were playing in the family room. Jillian was doing homework at the kitchen table, and Mike was in the garage organizing. I went outside to survey the debris and destruction from the hurricane. The damage was minimal—mostly debris from the trees: large limbs, small twigs, leaves. We had a small shed that housed rakes and shovels, and it had been blown over by the storm.

I cleaned the garden tools out of the shed and tried to put the shed back up by myself, but it was too heavy. I found Mike in the garage and told him about the manageable damage that had been done.

In a quick second, he exploded. He started yelling at me with his fists clenched by his side and his shoulders tightening up. I had no idea what brought it on. All I did was tell him that the little shed blew over. My body tightened up, and I could feel my heart start to race. He was acting scary and seemed to be taking out the hurricane damage on me. I was not going to stay there and take whatever abuse he was going to dish out, so I took a page from his playbook and said I was going to leave. I think I said something like, "You know what? I'm leaving." I was going to get in the car and drive somewhere—anywhere—just to not be in the presence of his anger.

He quickly leapt over the pile he had on the garage floor and came at me with intent to harm. He said to me as he came toward me, "Oh, no you are not." I quickly opened the kitchen door and ran in, trying to shut the door behind me, but he caught it as he was bursting into the house. I was trying to figure out very quickly where to go to get away from him. Jillian was at the kitchen table with her back to me, so I instinctively decided to go away from her so she wouldn't be caught up in his fury.

I turned left and ran down the short hall, then another left to go up the stairs. He was right behind me. In my mind I thought, "If I take two stairs at a time, I can get away from him faster." So I tried taking two steps at a time to get away. It didn't work. Taking two stairs at once only slowed me down. He came up the stairs right behind me and lunged, grabbing my legs. I fell face down on the stairs as he pulled me back down to him.

At the same time, our dog—a Boxer named Briggs—was barking loudly and came after Mike to protect me. Mike kicked the dog and threatened to shoot it. "I'm going to kill that goddamned dog. Where's my gun?"

Mike let go of me and stormed off toward the living room, where I heard him open his gun cabinet. My heart was beating fast, and my head was spinning with fear and adrenaline. It was hard to comprehend what was happening, let alone try to figure out what to do at that moment. My first thought was to get away fast. Then I realized I couldn't leave the kids alone with him and a gun, so I turned and ran into the kitchen, standing between the kitchen and the living room, watching him load his gun.

Claire and Craig had come out of the family room, most likely to see what all the noise and commotion was. I saw them standing next to their dad, crying loudly in fear, not understanding what was going on but screaming for their dad to stop. He said something about wanting to kill the dog and then himself. Briggs continued to bark and stayed close to me, and I saw out of the corner of my eye Jillian, still with her head down, looking at her schoolwork. I quickly put Briggs outside so he wouldn't get hurt and turned my attention back to their dad.

Mike had a pistol loaded, and he was glaring right at me. His blue eyes were dark, and he looked possessed. I flinched and took a step back when I saw the gun and the look in his eyes. My first thought was to get away, but what about the kids? If I turned to get away, he might shoot me in the back. Would he turn the gun on our screaming children next? Or kill himself right in front of the kids? If not, then what about the trauma of seeing their mom shot by their dad? I couldn't leave them. I had to stay and put the gun between myself and their dad.

So, I went toward him, and I put my hands on the gun. Claire and Craig continued screaming and sobbing. Mike was breathing heavily and had the look of someone who was unhinged. My heart was pounding, but I wasn't going to let go of the gun. He was going to have to shoot me before I let go.

I had my hands on that gun for at least fifteen minutes, with the two youngest screaming and crying, before he finally let go. It is so exhausting to endure all that adrenaline running through you and trying to anticipate what he is going to do next with the gun. I could see the toll it took on him. He dropped both the gun and his shoulders. His madness was now given over to self-pity and shame.

The kids saw that I took the gun and that his mood had lightened a bit, so they ran forward and put their arms around him. I made him give me the key to the gun cabinet; I secured the gun and eventually hid the key.

He made his way out to the back porch and sat in silence with a deflated look on his face. The two youngest would not let him go. They hung on to him for the next hour or so, still crying. I sat out on the porch with them, trying to get my nervous system under control while I carefully monitored him for any change in mood that might signal danger again.

Interestingly, Jillian never came out on the porch with the rest of us. She just stayed at the kitchen table doing homework. I thought, "Is it possible that she was so focused on her studies that she didn't see what just happened?" I wasn't going to ask her about it; I was just going to monitor her and her behavior to see what kind of assistance she was going to need from me.

Years later, she told me she saw and heard everything but just stayed at the table—her way of protecting herself.

Looking back, this would have been a good time to leave him. He was a real danger to himself and the rest of us. It was so hard to think straight and know what to do. I had many scenarios rushing through my mind. How do I leave without triggering him to hurt us or himself?

If we left and he killed himself, the children would be forever devastated and traumatized by his suicide.

My nervous system was on overdrive. He may have started to calm down, but I was still very much on high alert, and I had to come across as being calm for the kids' sake. I didn't have the luxury of taking care of my own emotional needs; I felt responsible for everyone else's.

I was so angry with him. How dare he do that to me, to us? How dare he explode with so much rage and then leave me to clean up the emotional mess that all of us were feeling. I tried to understand where his rage came from so I could avoid doing whatever I thought I did to provoke him. If he could turn from Jekyll to Hyde so quickly, then at any moment on any given day it could happen again.

How does anyone stay prepared for danger every waking moment and still be able to function? How do I get through each day and not let the kids or anyone else know that I am falling apart?

Is this part of his untreated depression or something else? Aren't I supposed to stay by his side and support him—as in "for better or for worse"?

I felt alone in this. Who could I confide in? This was such a horrendous and traumatic event that it would leave anyone with their jaw on the floor. You tell the wrong person, and it will come back to me and the kids in spades. I couldn't tell his commander or anyone connected to the base. I know they have resources on base for things like this, but I wasn't prepared to go there yet. I didn't know what the military would do. If it was anything short of him still coming home to us every day, then I couldn't take the chance. There would be a real fear of him taking revenge on me because I "betrayed" him to his superiors. I felt like I couldn't tell anyone without putting my and the kids' lives in jeopardy, so I kept it to myself.

I didn't have an exit plan—a complete and total exit plan where the kids and I could get away and never fear him finding us. If I had a clear path where I knew we would be safe, I would have taken it. Number one, I needed money, lots of it. But he kept our checking and savings accounts near zero every payday. We had money in our investments, but I was under the impression that he would have to agree to my withdrawing it. I later realized I could withdraw without his permission, but I didn't dare call the investment company to find out. I was worried that they would contact him to let him know of my inquiry. Real paranoia sets in when you are under intense and prolonged trauma, and it totally skews your judgment.

I was on the East Coast, isolated from my family on the West Coast in Washington State. I felt isolated from my peers in the squadron. I felt so alone. I vowed to put more money aside each pay period in my little checking account so I could eventually have the funds to leave with the kids and not fear that he would find us. In the meanwhile, I put on my armor and moved forward with a fake smile on my face for the world to see. I kept a constant vigil for his changing moods, all the while wondering if I would make it through the night. How do I climb into bed with my back to him every night? How?

After this episode with the gun, I was on high alert. Every radical mood change and behavior caused me to think, Is this when he does it? Is this when I come home and find that he has blown his brains out? I had taken the key to the gun cabinet and hid it. I taped it under the drawer of one of the cabinets in the living room. I couldn't dispose of the guns, but at least he didn't have a key to gain quick access to them.

I started to get into the habit of distracting the kids when I brought them home from school. I would say as we got out of the car, "Craig, can you let the dogs out? Claire, can you get the mail?" and "Jillian, can you get the garbage cans and bring them around to the back?" I wanted to be the first one in the house and make sure he hadn't hung himself—or worse. I wanted to make sure the kids were protected. If need be, I would just hustle them all back into the car and pretend that I forgot we needed something at the store, and then I could call the police to come while we weren't there. Somehow, I would gently inform the kids that their dad took his life. That was the best scenario I could come up with to protect them from seeing anything so traumatic.

It was so exhausting coming home constantly on edge, constantly having your heart race a mile a minute while you quickly scan the house, thinking that I would find him dead. I hated him for that. I hated him for the darkness that he brought to the family—more specifically, to me. Because of me, the kids saw very little of his dark moods. I did my best to shield them. They were the innocents, and they deserved to have a childhood where they felt emotionally safe. I was determined to do what I could to protect them.

Many of you will be saying, "This is exactly why you should have left." I get that. But you must understand that with all the trauma I was dealing with—and dealing with alone—I only had my own disjointed, cloudy, hormonally poisoned brain to confer with. I was in constant fight-or-flight mode. I was constantly on edge, surveilling my environment so I would know which armor to wear in each situation. All I could do was survive each moment. Part of that was also knowing that leaving him without a foolproof plan was not an option.

I started secretly wishing that he would die in a plane crash. At least that way I could escape this prison with his dark secrets. The kids could mourn for their dad as a hero rather than someone who was unhinged, hateful, and evil. I would then be able to have control of the investments and, with his life insurance, be able to start over and put my energies into my children's mental health—which would most certainly be compromised if their dad passed away while they were young.

My dad used to say, "Only worry about the things that you can control. Everything else is a waste of energy." I would use that reminder over and over again throughout my marriage to help me manage the mental and emotional load I was carrying. Since I couldn't control his outbursts or when they would happen, I could at least have a plan in place.

I tried to have coherent and logical thoughts on what to do. It was really hard since my head was swimming in chaos and wouldn't calm down enough for me to think straight. I already had a plan for when we came home and I wasn't sure if he had committed suicide in the house somewhere. I had already locked up his guns and hid the key. I needed a plan to escape. That was the part I had a hard time figuring out. I would need people I could trust. I would need a car ready to go. I would need money. A lot of it. I would need faith.

Faith—I didn't have. I was so lost in how to reconcile the different people that were locked inside of him. Where was the "family is everything" person? Where was the guy who promised to love and protect me? Who is this unstable person? Who is this guy who is willing to torment and torture his family with no remorse? I couldn't tell from moment to moment which version of him would show up. How do you draw from faith when you can't even see through to the next hour?

Even though my dad was right—not to worry about things that you can't control—it was almost an impossible task for me to do. My nerves were raw, and his eruptions would come from nowhere. I couldn't help but worry when I tried to make contingency plans. The two went together. I would have to imagine different scenarios in order to make a plan. Each scenario that I imagined was traumatizing. It was like being in a fight-or-flight emotional and mental state twenty-four/seven.

Trying to manage these emotions is overwhelming. I am appalled at the depth of his torture. I am appalled that he had no real remorse. I am appalled that I was expected to just get over it. I am appalled at the depths of his hatred toward me. And I am so, so sorry that I didn't have the clarity or the courage to leave him.

When I first looked back, I was so angry with myself for not leaving. But I have to remember that when a victim blames themselves for what their partner did, it is just the trauma speaking. No one can be expected to think and act logically when their brain is so chemically altered. I hate him for that. I hate him for destroying this beautiful light inside of me. *Why didn't he just let me go if he hated me so much?* Why?

*   *   *   *   *   *   *   *   *   *   *

Emotional blackmail: The narcissist uses fear, obligation, and guilt to create a sense of responsibility and dependence in you. The goal is to maintain power and control by making you feel you must comply with the narcissist's demands to avoid negative consequences. They will use threats and ultimatums such as threatening to leave the relationship, harming themselves or revealing personal secrets if you don't comply with their wishes. Ultimatums can be direct or implied. But they always create a sense of urgency and fear.

@SHELLEY.WHITWELL

13. 1995 WAS A F'D UP YEAR

To hurt someone deeply and act like you're the victim is not how normal people behave, but how abusers manipulate.

happilyeverafter -the_traumacoach

I came into 1995 limping. My nerves were still ready to blow at any time, trying to monitor the mood swings that Mike would manufacture. I had been rocked by how quickly he was able to get to his gun and have it loaded. Even though I had the key to the gun cabinet hidden, I would check often to make sure it was still there. I couldn't really let myself relax; I had to be vigilant to his mood changes so I could see which way I had to jump.

If I had hoped for a lull in the emotional, mental, and psychological storm that he produced, it surely didn't happen for 1995. It was a totally F'd up year.

There were four major events that come to mind, and the first starts in April over Easter week. We took a camping trip to Grandfather Mountain in the western North Carolina Appalachian Mountains. I remember the date because it was also the same time that the Oklahoma City bombing occurred. As usual, Mike was focused on spending money instead of enjoying the quiet time together with the family. He wanted to check out some power tools someone had listed in the local classified circular. It was only $400. "A great deal." I told him we didn't have the money, and he got pissed and stormed off into the camper, slamming the door.

I hated being the keeper of the purse. I continuously felt like I was the parent and he was the child. I had quit my dental hygiene position because daycare for three kids ate up all but $10 of my pay each week. Our money was finite, and I had to bear the responsibility of reminding him about that.

There were many times I believed that he purposely would push the financial boundaries just so he could have another reason to show his anger toward me. He knew I wasn't going to approve because we literally didn't have the money. We were constantly living paycheck to paycheck because every time he would see any money in the checking account, he figured it was his to spend on himself. He never took into consideration that there were bills to pay with that money.

At some point, I had to make a grocery run into town, and he stayed behind with the kids. Everything seemed fine when I left. The kids were sharing the rocks they found on their recent scavenger hunt around the campsite, and Mike seemed to be engaged with their finds. When I got back, it was dark, and the kids were roasting marshmallows. I found him disengaged with a stone face. His eyes were blank. He didn't greet me, and he didn't turn his head to look at me. The only look on his face was that of disgust. I could feel the dark energy he was putting out, and I immediately guarded my emotions. I knew something was going to blow.

Then he said, very steadily and clearly so I wouldn't misunderstand him, "I don't like our kids. I never have."

What the heck kind of crap is that coming from his mouth? I know he says he is depressed, but where do you go with that? What kind of response do you give? I was shocked that those words came out of his mouth without any hesitation. His comment, backed by his withdrawn and menacing demeanor, triggered my survival anxiety and sent me into an emotional cyclone. How can a parent say that about their children and not blink?

If he was looking for a reaction from me or an argument, he wasn't getting it. I had learned not to react. I had to. He was hoping I would push back so he could let loose on me. What he did was succeed in triggering a swirl of emotions that kept me on edge, waiting for the complete fallout from this comment. He was so emotionally manipulative and selfish. I resolved, again, to protect the kids and myself. Not sure how I was going to get it done. Somehow, I had to make it through the rest of the camping trip—sleeping next to him.

The next event was in June. I left him at home with the kids for five days while I drove to a convention in Ohio for my direct sales business. I may have quit the dental office, but doing these parties at night was easier on me financially since I could get a babysitter to watch the kids if Mike wasn't willing or able to. Not having to pay daycare for three kids meant I was able to bring in some extra money for the family.

This convention was planned months in advance, and Mike had said he was on board with the plans. He took time off from work to stay home with the kids and was looking forward to getting some projects completed.

I came back all excited and energized for my business. I had been recognized as a top performer for 1994 and won some furniture and a cruise to the Bahamas. It felt great to be recognized for my accomplishments. I knew I could be amazing at whatever I put my mind to, and this recognition was a fulfilling affirmation that left me flying high with a new sense of excitement for this next year.

I pulled into the driveway and saw the kids outside playing. They came running over to me to give me a big hug. This was the first time I had been away from the kids, and it was the first time Mike ever watched them solely on his own. I gave the kids big hugs back and told them I had a surprise I would give them later. They left me all excited and continued their games.

The garage door was open, and I could see Mike working in the garage. I was smiling from ear to ear, so eager to share with him my awards and accomplishments. He didn't greet me with open arms or a smile or congratulations. He barely acknowledged my presence.

My smile left my face when I sensed his sour mood, and when I asked what was wrong, he just gave me a dirty look and the silent treatment. It was a message from him that he would not tolerate me leaving the kids with him again. He was punishing me for some reason—maybe because I was wanting to have my own ambitions and succeeding at them. I got no support from him, and once again, I was sent into emotional whiplash. One moment I was floating high on the happiness cloud, and the next I was sinking into a dark pool of his loathing.

Where did this come from? Did he have problems with the kids while I was gone? I asked him to tell me what the problem was, but all he gave me was cold, dark silence. I could not understand how someone who is supposed to be your partner—your chief supporter—could be so cold and angry just because I left for a couple of days celebrating my business success. My accomplishments were not celebrated or valued by him. He turned the attention from my success toward his own loathing, sulking mood. He did that a lot—destroying any good times if they weren't about him.

In July, his parents drove the Ford Bronco that he had purchased from Seattle all the way to North Carolina. They ended up staying for a month before they flew back. One Sunday, after his mom, the kids, and I finished with church services, the priest asked if I could take a group of visiting parishioners to the church's beach retreat on Emerald Isle. It was an hour and a half round trip, and the Volkswagen van I had could carry everyone at once. There wasn't room for the kids, my mother-in-law, and everyone else, so I called Mike to have him come and pick up his mom and the kids to take them home.

I should have known he would not be pleased with doing this task. When he picked them up, he was visibly angry; he gave me daggers with his eyes and took off driving recklessly. He wanted everyone to know he wasn't happy with me. I watched him drive away and was shocked as he sped up, then braked hard, then turned quickly so everyone inside the vehicle was thrown around. I was shocked that he could be that brazen with his mom in the seat next to him. This display of disregard, even for his mother's well-being, shook me deeply. This was whole new territory—showing his true colors to someone other than just me. I was so concerned about this escalation in his abusive behavior. I couldn't even imagine what his mom must have thought about it.

I knew then he was going to be in a punitive mood and take it out on me. I just wanted to make sure he didn't do anything to the kids. So, holding back tears, I told my priest I couldn't drive the guests to Emerald Isle. I went home with my nerves on high alert. I found him throwing things around as he feigned organizing the garage. He turned to give me the ugliest, most disgusting look. I went up to the bedroom to change, and I overheard his mom in the nearby room speaking to a friend on the phone. She said, "It's not good. I don't know what is going on, but it is not good."

He made it easy for her to pick up on his dark mood by the way he drove them home. I can only imagine how the entire ride must have been. I remember feeling so much sadness and shame. I also remember feeling trapped. I knew he was toxic. I knew he was suffering from untreated depression, but I could only think about how to protect the kids and how not to further trigger him. I was constantly walking on eggshells and looking around every corner. And now, his mother was caught up in the "friendly fire" between Mike and me.

The summer eventually passed, his parents went back to Seattle, and we ended up getting a new van since our VW van finally gave out. School started again, and I was busy trying to get through each day without setting him off.

Then, in early November, our oldest daughter, Jillian, was having intense migraines and had to stay home from school for the week. At first, I treated her with Tylenol in hopes she would get better. I had her rest and tried to give her fluids. Nothing seemed to give her any sustained relief.

On Wednesday evening, I took her to the ER on base to be evaluated. The attending doctor couldn't find anything, so he just sent us home, prescribing more Tylenol or something like that. I kept a close watch on Jillian. I put her in my bed and used that time to clean out my drawers and closet. Still, she got no sustaining relief.

That following Saturday, with Jillian still in intermittent pain, I was in the kitchen fixing dinner. I had her on the sofa in the living room so I could keep an eye on her.

Twice I heard her moaning, and twice I went into the living room to check on her. Both times she had fallen on the floor and was writhing about. I picked her up and scolded her for falling off the sofa. The second time I picked her up, I decided to take her to bed.

As I was carrying her upstairs, I happened to notice that her pupils were uneven, dilated, and fixed. Oh my God. An image I will never forget. Her eyes were open, but they were eerily vacant—no recognition of her surroundings at all. What was happening to my little girl?

I quickly carried her back downstairs, screaming for everyone to get into the car. We left so fast that we left the lights on along with the oven and the TV. It didn't matter—everyone sensed this was serious. We jumped into the car, with our poor dog left behind, most likely feeling very anxious and scared, not understanding what just happened.

Six-year-old Craig was sitting in the back seat next to eight-year-old Claire and asked, "Is Jillian going to die?" I had no answer for him. I was holding my ten-year-old Jillian on my lap, monitoring her breathing and thinking that the car was barely moving, even though Mike was racing as quickly as he could.

We rushed through the front gate of the base and raced into the ER. I don't remember how Claire and Craig got out of the car and into the hospital, since I was running, carrying Jillian inside.

Once in, I immediately handed her over to the attending doctors and nurses. They quickly took her to the examination room, and I think Mike followed them, but I can't remember. My mind was so numb, and I was having trouble focusing. The front desk was trying to get me to give them basic information, and I couldn't come up with it. My mind couldn't focus. I gave them my military ID. Fortunately, it had a lot of pertinent information already on it, and somehow they got what they needed out of me.

I knew it was serious, and I knew we would be there a long time. I had to get someone to come get Claire and Craig and take them home. I also needed someone to turn off the oven and take care of the dog. I had a neighbor I could call, but I couldn't get my brain to calm down enough to remember their phone number. I tried looking it up in the phone book, and everything was a blur. The woman at the front desk somehow got the name out of me, and they found the number and dialed on my behalf. Our neighbor came quickly and took Claire and Craig with them. I was a total mess. I could barely see or hear anything going on around me. Everything was fuzzy.

Eventually, I made my way back to the examination room with Mike and Jillian. The attending doctor told me he thought it was viral meningitis. He was very concerned and wanted me to be prepared for the worst. They quickly determined that they couldn't handle her condition, so they arranged to have her transported by ambulance to the university hospital in Greenville, North

Carolina—one and a half hours away. They wanted to airlift her, but there were tornadoes in the area, so we were left with the long ambulance ride to the hospital. I rode in the back of the ambulance while Mike followed behind in the car.

The university hospital emergency room was waiting for us and took Jillian back immediately. They diagnosed her with a brain abscess and quickly got her into surgery. Mike and I were inundated with hospital personnel and different social representatives informing us of what was going on as they escorted us to a private waiting room. Somehow, somewhere, Mike and I were able to call our parents and let them know, and they made immediate plans to fly out.

It was such an emotionally charged and chaotic experience. I lost track of time and waited for the doctors to come and fill us in on her treatment and progress. The surgeons informed us that they tapped into her skull just above her right eyebrow to try to drain the abscess, but they realized that the infection was much deeper into her ventricles. In the second surgery, they drilled directly through her skull on the top of her head and inserted a tube, reaching deep into the brain. The doctors told us that we were fortunate—she didn't have much more time. If the infection had gone much deeper, there would not have been anything they could have done.

We were up for over twenty-four hours straight. So many emotions were raging through us. Mike was sobbing, and I was numb. Later, nurses and doctors said they were impressed with how strong I was during the crisis. That's when Mike got pissed. They didn't make the comment directly to him, so he assumed it was only meant for me. When we were alone, he let me have it. He was so angry he was spitting saliva as he berated me for being "strong" while he must be the "weak" one.

Even in that moment of extreme crisis that our daughter was going through, he was focused on himself and saw me as his competition for attention and validation from others.

No, I did not cry. Yes, he did cry. Why didn't I cry? I believe I didn't melt down because I was used to being under extremely heightened anxiety for the past ten-plus years just being married to him. For my body, it was another stressful event in a long list of stressful events. Even though it was the worst event up to that point that I had gone through, my body had become accustomed to the high stress. I had a lot of practice in how to push my anxieties aside and put on a fake face for the world to see.

Not crying was most likely a survival instinct for me. I had learned early in our marriage that he would not tolerate me crying. It wasn't conscious behavior. I didn't have to tell myself not to cry. My body was just familiar with this level of anxiety, and it adjusted as needed. Only now, I had to monitor how my behavior was going to be received by him. I couldn't just react to the stress—I now had to calculate how I was going to show my emotions so it wouldn't trigger him. That is very difficult to do and is extremely exhausting to your nervous system—to try to analyze and filter your emotions.

It was going to be a long road for our daughter's recovery. I was able to stay at the Ronald McDonald House near the hospital while Mike had to go back home. His mom flew in from Seattle to help him out with the kids. I spent my day at the hospital monitoring every little improvement. Jillian did not come out of her coma for two weeks, and even then, she still had another four weeks of physical and occupational therapy. It was clear that I was going to have to cancel my Bahamas cruise that I had won earlier that year as I settled into a daily routine of monitoring Jillian and following her around for her therapy sessions.

Eventually, she was released on Christmas Eve, 1995.

Jillian came home with a patch on her right eye and a port placed in her clavicle artery for antibiotics to be delivered by a home nurse. She was going to need some outpatient therapy and a lot of rest. Besides trying to create a magical Christmas for the younger two kids and taking care of Jillian's needs, I also had to tread lightly around Mike and monitor his mood swings. It helped that his parents were there, but whatever I could do to try to keep him from dispensing dark energy during the holidays, I tried. I was so grateful that Jillian was going to recover and that our family was whole again.

But not everyone escaped this trauma without lasting scars.

When I returned home, it became apparent that our poor Boxer, Briggs, had felt the anxiety and stress of Jillian's and my absence. In just a few weeks, his coat became white and his face pale. He had lost a lot of weight and was moving slowly. I could see the sadness lurking behind his eyes, and I tried to make it up to him for my quick departure in November and my prolonged absence by sitting on the floor, putting his head in my lap, and stroking him for a very long time.

My poor, beautiful boy had always been there for me for the last twelve years. He and I spent so many hours together during some very lonely times. Briggs could always count on me to be by his side, and I could always count on him being there for me with a wagging tail to let me know everything would be all right. Now he was fading away.

He would only have another month with us, and then we would have to put him down. I know in my heart that this difficult period for the family was also difficult for him, and it was the reason his health declined so fast.

1995 was a hell year. It was a dark year. Thank goodness it was over.

*   *   *   *   *   *   *   *   *   *   *

The one predictable thing that covert narcissists always do is play the victim card. They'll play victim in particular to circumstances that they themselves have created and perpetuate. They are in fact, the poster child for the perpetual victim, always. No matter what has gone on, you can count on it, predict it, with 100% accuracy just like clockwork.

tamiemjoyce

14. Toxic Decade

You can tell how much someone loves themselves with the partner they have chosen. Is this a compliment or a criticism? Does it make you proud of the treatment you have accepted? ~Anonymous

The '90s was such a toxic decade. It seemed that one traumatic event after another just kept coming, and I had nowhere to go and no one to turn to: his betrayal of me when I was sexually assaulted by his friend, his irrational response to the Hurricane Gordon incident in 1994 when he threatened suicide with a loaded gun, all of 1995 with his destructive and traumatizing antics, his threats to leave and take all the money. How do I continue and stay strong for the kids? How does anyone negotiate this sh*tload of suffering and come out whole?

All I could do was navigate moment to moment, day to day. Every night I went to bed, I congratulated myself for making it through another day. I thought I was dealing with it masterfully. Nobody on the outside knew or suspected anything was wrong. I kept up with all the motions of the day—planning meals, getting groceries, going to dental appointments, taking the kids to and from Girl Scout and Boy Scout meetings, helping with church activities. I volunteered wherever I could to feel like I was making a difference somewhere. To everyone else, I had it all together.

But my body knew differently.

My body was steadily building up high levels of cortisol and adrenaline due to the prolonged and consistently toxic marriage I was in. While I was congratulating myself for making it through each day with all my assigned tasks completed, my body was silently falling apart. My eyes would twitch uncontrollably. I started putting on weight, even though I shouldn't have been. I got a bad case of impetigo on my face. My stomach was getting bloated, and I would have severe cramps in my abdomen that were not related to my monthly period.

The worst of these cramps landed me in the back of an ambulance, with a neighbor running over to take care of the kids and the dog.

The doctor in the ER couldn't find any cause, even though I would pull my legs into my stomach and guard against his probing. I wasn't pregnant, and my blood work didn't indicate any active infection. He recommended exploratory surgery to see what was causing the pain.

At about that same time, Mike finally showed up at the ER after he got home from running his errands and the neighbor told him what happened. I wasn't going to jump into any unnecessary surgery, so I decided to just go home and lie down to see if it would ease up. It took the rest of the evening and through the next morning before I felt better.

Mike took what happened to me and used it to his advantage. He got to tell his mom and everyone else how he "watched the kids the whole day and made them dinner" while I was in bed. Oh yes, he was the hero! Here I was, with my body turning against me because of the trauma he had been inflicting on me, and he wanted to take the credit for being the hero. Even during this traumatic, physical emergency that I had gone through, he was able to make it be about himself. He was able to get the attention and validation from everyone who heard his story—that he was such a great husband and father.

Sick. He made me sick—figuratively and physically, sick.

I remember being at the hairdresser's getting my haircut when the stylist abruptly swung my chair around. She was face-to-face with me, hands on the arms of the chair and leaning into me as she very seriously said, "Okay. Tell me what's going on. What happened six months ago?"

I had no idea what she was talking about. This was strange and alarming behavior by my hairdresser. I just sat and looked at her, my brows furrowed with confusion. She wouldn't take her gaze from mine. She looked straight into my eyes with so much concern for me that I was taken aback.

What could she have detected in me that got her so worried in such a short time after I sat in her chair? She waited a moment for me to respond, still not breaking eye contact. I must have said something like, "What do you mean?"

She said very sharply, but with much concern, "You have two large bald spots of missing hair. That only happens when you're under a lot of stress—and it usually shows up six months after the event. So, what happened six months ago?"

Holy cats! Bald spots?

She showed me with a hand mirror the two spots on the back of my head. Fortunately, they were concealed by a top layer of hair, but I could see two very shiny spots of my scalp right behind my right ear.

Holy crap! How did that happen? Stress? Six months ago?

My mind raced back to March of that year. What was going on at that time? Ah, yes. I remember.

That March was when Mike was extremely intimidating and unhinged. He had a tirade where he accused me of not caring about him, not caring whether he lived or died, and he threatened that I would find him dead when I got home from picking the kids up from wherever they were.

I remember the look in his eyes, the tenseness of his body, and the hate he had for me. I remembered that I was in such a foggy and highly traumatized state that I had a hard time focusing on the road when I was driving.

Somehow, I put on the appropriate face for the kids when I picked them up, and I tried to make myself have the usual banter with them on the way home—

but I couldn't. Only incoherent words mumbled out. I remember being shocked that I couldn't come up with a simple sentence. What was happening to me? Why couldn't I make any sense talking?

As we got closer to home, I put up another level of armor, and my mind raced with what I would do if Mike kept his promise to kill himself. When we turned down our street, I quickly scanned the yard for any signs of his demise. I then distracted the kids with some quick tasks outside while I went into the house to investigate before they came in.

I quickly and carefully looked around the corners of every room downstairs and in the garage to see if he had done himself in. I had to be quick, since the kids would soon be coming in, and I didn't want any of them to be the ones to find him dead. The big ball of stress that knots up in my stomach was so intense as I braced myself for the worst.

I climbed the stairs, my legs feeling like bricks, taking one stair at a time, wondering if he did it in the bathroom or bedroom. As I walked down the hall closer to our bedroom, I could hear noises coming from the computer in the office. I slowly opened the door to the office—just off our bedroom—and braced myself for what I might find.

That son of a bitch was there, alive, and on the computer playing a video game!

He acted like nothing was wrong, like it was just another great day to indulge in a favorite pastime. No hint of the grenade he had just detonated thirty minutes earlier. How dare he put me through so much emotional and mental hell. How dare he place real fear in my heart and head. How dare he have no consideration for my mental state. How dare he.

I was discarded. I was nothing to him. Nothing! I felt like nothing. I was disposable.

I remember that I had a hard time hiding my disdain for his presence, and he responded with, "What's your problem?" I just turned and walked away, trying to hold back the tears and trying to keep this fragmented body of mine from breaking apart. He had no clue—nor did he care to understand—how much I was hurting inside.

I felt like I had been cut a million times. Like I had been crawling through barbed wire, and with every inch I crawled forward, I would be cut again—all the while trying to protect my kids by holding them high above the barbs. I had been carrying the weight for all of us, and no one knew the toll it took on my body—except my own body. I thought I was making it through each day, tucking every stressful event into its own box and shoving it somewhere deep inside of me. But my body was keeping score—and here I was, six months later, with my hair falling out.

All of this passed through my thoughts in a quick moment as I prepared to respond to my hairdresser. I just shrugged my shoulders and said I had no clue what could have caused the hair loss. She turned me around again and started to cut my hair.

She was so awesome. I was so grateful that somebody finally "saw" me—saw my pain—and recognized that I must be going through an extremely hard time, even though I didn't feel it was safe for me to confirm it to her. I now think of her as a messenger from my spirit guide or one of my angels, trying to get me to see the big picture: that Mike was never going to change, and that my body was breaking down unless I changed my environment—both because of his abuse and because of my failure to see a way out of it.

The toxic '90s kept rolling along, and I kept my head down and tried not to trigger him. I would let him play his computer games as much as he wanted. At least he was happy, which kept him from spreading his negative energy my way. Or so I thought.

There were many times he would come downstairs to the kitchen where I was working and would just blow past me with a dark scowl on his face, slamming the door to the garage behind him. I would follow and ask, "What's wrong?" I knew it couldn't have been anything I did because I hadn't even been around him much that day. He wouldn't answer me. He just blew right past me again, this time storming back into the kitchen and marching toward the family room. I continued to follow him and kept asking, "What's wrong? What's going on?" He wouldn't answer me. He just gave me the silent treatment.

I understood that his silent treatment was simultaneously showing me that I was the problem—and that he was going to punish me for it.

What did I do to tick him off? I had purposely been keeping myself busy doing house chores while he was upstairs, seemingly having fun playing his computer game. Why now? Why come downstairs now to show me you're mad at me—when nothing has happened?

He did this many, many times over the course of our marriage. And I usually would chase him around, pleading for him to talk to me, to tell me what was wrong, and what I did wrong. He would never say a word. He wouldn't even look at me. This form of cruelty was so unsettling. It left me imagining all the horrible possibilities of how this might explode on me later. I would, once again, have a hard time going to sleep—not knowing what his state of mind was, and what he might do to me while I was asleep and couldn't protect myself.

Eventually, I got so emotionally drained by these antics that I stopped chasing him down. When he would blow past me with obvious contempt, I would ask him what was wrong. And when he didn't answer me, I just let him be. When I quit chasing him down to beg for a response, it caused him some discomfort.

He would come back into the house and stand in front of me with his hands on his hips, his face all wrinkled up, and say in a hostile tone, "You obviously don't care about me. You haven't asked me what is wrong." He was trying to bait me so I would respond emotionally—and he would then have some more fuel to burn me with.

I simply replied in a stone-cold manner, with no emotion, "I did ask you what was wrong, but you wouldn't tell me, so I left you alone."

He would just stand there, staring at me, not knowing what to say. Then he would turn around and go back out to the garage.

If there was really something wrong that he wanted me to know about, then you would think he would have used that time—while standing in front of me—to tell me what was bothering him. But he didn't. This told me there was really nothing wrong. He was just trying to emotionally manipulate me.

I was beginning to understand how to handle his toxic abuse: indifference. He hated it. He wasn't getting the emotional response from me that he had expected, and it was throwing him off. For the longest time, he had kept changing the goalpost on me. I could never quite anticipate what was going to happen or when. He liked to keep me off balance. I was starting to realize that I could take some of this power back by not giving him any more fuel to work with.

In addition to indifference, I started to use passive-aggressive techniques. I rarely ever called him out on his abuse directly—for fear of his reprisal. But I was so tired of being his punching bag. So, instead of coming right out and pushing back, I would say or do things to camouflage my real intent of getting back at him.

For example, after he finished lashing out at me for something ridiculous—most likely that he was out of Cheerios or milk or something like that—I might throw something down on the countertop and make a low growl. He would say in an accusing tone, "So you're mad at me now? Why are you mad at me when you're the one who didn't buy the Cheerios?"

And I would look at him and say, "Why is it always about you? Why can't it be about me? Why can't I be upset about something else besides you?"

This would cause him to stand still with a blank look on his face and no response. He would just turn and walk out to the garage.

It had been a long time since I had put a smile back on my face, but one was slowly forming as he turned to go out to the garage. I was able to show my frustration to him and, at the same time, claim it was for something else. He didn't know how to respond, and I put a silent little check in a box somewhere in my brain.

I will never understand why he felt like he had to constantly pull the ground out from under me with no causal reasoning. There was no way to forecast it. He could be in a great mood, laughing and telling funny jokes—then suddenly turn on you and destroy the good times. He developed a history of dropping bombshells when the mood was light, and then would just walk away, leaving me totally dumbstruck and searching for the cause of his actions.

I could never find a logical answer.

It seemed like every grenade he detonated, I was in the kitchen doing chores. No one else was around to witness his display—just me and him.

There was the: "You don't love me, and you don't need me. I'm going to leave you and the kids and take all the money. After all, it's my money."

Then another: "I used to think we had an ideal marriage, but not anymore."

And then: "I'm not happy. I haven't been happy for a long time. You don't care about me."

All these outbursts would play out pretty much the same way: he would turn and walk away and leave me to figure out what was going on. Sometimes I would chase him down to find out what the real problem was, but he would often just give me the silent treatment and leave me to my own conclusions.

I mentioned earlier how he completely humiliated me by telling the pilots in the squadron that I don't have orgasms. Now came one of the biggest detonations he had ever dropped up to that point.

He came home from work one weeknight and stood by the kitchen counter with his arm resting on it and said—very casually, yet sinisterly—"I told Mike Bellows (a fellow pilot in the squadron) that I was leaving you and the kids. And I'm taking my money with me."

I didn't even get to say, "Welcome home. How was work?" Nope. No greeting—just this declaration that he was leaving me and the kids and taking the money.

The embarrassing part was that he told someone at work, which meant everyone in the squadron would know about this before I did. And to top it all off, we were supposed to be going to a squadron function that evening, where I would be face-to-face with everyone there who now knew that Mike was leaving me and the kids.

What a great guy. What a considerate man. *Thanks for feeding me to the wolves with no warning.*

I probably shouldn't have gone to the function, but I didn't have a lot of time to process this emotional dump. Do I not go and have it be a silent confirmation that he is, in fact, leaving me? Or do I go and put on the appearance that there is nothing wrong with our marriage? I was caught off guard and paralyzed by my thoughts.

I recognize now that this would have been a great opportunity for me to take him up on it and leave him. In hindsight—which is always clearer than in the present—I should have shocked him and said, "Good riddance." But this threat was a big one. He was threatening to leave me without any money for the kids. And worse, he had now made it public knowledge.

How can anyone use their kids as leverage in a psychological mind game? How could anyone purposely say they will abandon their innocent children?

My scrambled brain couldn't see that I would be just fine without him when all I saw was being homeless and destitute with three innocent kids.

We left for the squadron event, and I don't really recall what happened on the drive. I'm sure it was the same gut-wrenching turmoil I had been through so many times. I do remember that I was an excellent actress. I didn't overdo it with my "happy-go-lucky" mood I projected to everyone at the event. I visited with everyone the same way I usually did and laughed at all the right jokes, at all the right times—not too loud and not too long.

I know I was putting on a good front, but then the commanding officer's wife of VMAT-203, Patty Thumb, took me aside. She placed her hand on my arm, looked me in the eyes, and asked with a concerned tone, "Is it true that Mike is leaving you?"

I looked at her with confusion (what an Oscar-worthy performance I put on) and told her no. Then I asked, "Why would you think that?"

She went on to tell me that Mike Bellows had told her husband—who was the CO of the squadron, also named Mike—that my Mike had told him he was leaving me.

I hated to do this to Mike Bellows, but I had to throw him under the bus and deny the whole thing. As far as I knew, my Mike may very well follow through and leave us, but I wasn't going to discuss something I hadn't even had time to process yet. I wasn't going to stand there shrugging and saying, "I don't know why he's leaving me," or stammer with incoherent remarks about the threat.

I was still in shock from the bomb he dropped on me right before we came.

Patty turned around and said something to her husband like, "You see. I told you not to believe Bellows."

Poor Mike Bellows.

I don't know how I made it through the evening. I don't remember what was said—if anything—by Mike on the way home or after we got home. It was just another heartless maneuver by him that left me reeling and numb. Just another long night of listening to his snoring before I could finally fall asleep.

When do I get to stop blaming his cruelty on his untreated depression? When do I get to say, *enough,* and walk away without any guilt or shame? When will I finally break?

I had put up with so much for so long. I watched as every boundary I had in place was removed by him. I was ceding my personal territory to him, and he took every inch without blinking. He treated me like I was his property to use and abuse at his will. He hated me because I had all the qualities he lacked. I was like a mirror being held up to him of what he wanted to be but wasn't—and he hated me for it.

We had recently gone to our yearly portfolio review with our financial advisor, and Mike sat there with a scowl on his face and said nothing. He anticipated the advisor was going to chastise him on his spending habits, and he didn't want to hear it, so he just sat there with contempt written all over his face.

I was the total opposite. I could feel the dark energy that Mike was bringing to this meeting and how he was directing it toward our advisor. I purposely put extra positive energy into high gear to mitigate what Mike was manifesting. I remained engaged during the review, smiled, and asked questions.

At the end of the session, our financial advisor asked me if I would like a job working for him. He said I was a "match light" person. When I asked what that meant, he said, "The room lights up when you walk in."

Wow. What a nice compliment. No one had ever said anything like that to me before. It had been a long time since I'd received any positive affirmations from anyone— and most certainly not from Mike. I didn't realize how starved my soul was to have someone recognize my good qualities, and here it came from someone I only see once a year.

That little bucket of positive affirmations that we all carry inside of us had become depleted. I was so grateful for his beautiful words that I could almost hear the plunk as I deposited them into my empty bucket. I thanked him generously for the compliment and the job offer, but I declined.

When we got into Mike's truck after the meeting, he laid into me. "So, you're a match light person. What does that make me?"

He could have said something like, "Wasn't that nice of him to say that about you?" He could have been proud that someone gave his wife a distinctive compliment—but that would have put the attention on me and not on him.

It was always a competition for him. There were no words of confirmation from him for my beautiful qualities. He negated such a wonderful gift that was given to me because all he could see reflecting back in his mirror was what he lacked.

He was so flawed. He was so, so flawed. He hated himself. He hated that I knew the secret of his cross-dressing. He hated that I would get compliments instead of him. He put out so much negative energy into the universe that all he looked for in return was more negative energy to validate his victimhood.

He had become the master at playing the victim and trying to make me feel sorry for him. I had given over so much of myself to him in hopes that I could help him heal and change. But it was becoming too exhausting for me, and it was coming at such a high physical and mental cost.

I wasn't ready to physically leave him because I still didn't have an ironclad plan that would guarantee our safety. But I was starting to emotionally leave him. I started to disengage from the emotional whiplash that he doled out, and I began to build a strong wall of resolve to keep his manipulations from reaching my soul anymore.

What I needed now was a very clear plan and a path to my independence.

I got busy and put my focus and energy into making it happen.

*   *   *   *   *   *   *   *   *   *   *

EMOTIONAL ABUSE: By withdrawing affection, communication, or support, the narcissist creates anxiety and desperation. You feel compelled to do whatever it takes to regain their approval and avoid the painful silent treatment.

@SHELLEY.WHITWELL

Part Three:
The Shift

15. Working Towards Independence

There are people in this world whose faces light up when they see you. And that is not because of what you can do. Or what you can provide. Or how they can benefit from you. It's just because of who you are. -THINK LIKE A BOSS

It seems like I've always been working. Growing up in a family of eight, with three boys and three girls—all of whom my mom had before she was twenty-five—money always seemed to be the topic and the stressor around every corner I turned. My mom had learned to economize from her mom and older sisters by sewing clothes and canning fresh produce when it was in season. She tried to teach us girls the same skills at a very early age.

I was in the third grade when my mom gave us girls a sewing kit for Christmas. It was made from an empty plastic ice cream container, which she had decorated for us. Inside were scissors, a thimble, measuring tape, thread, and other sewing notions needed for starting out. I had always been a very artistically creative child and was super excited to learn a new way to express my creativity while simultaneously creating something practical.

Mom's primary intent wasn't necessarily to stoke our creativity but rather to help us develop a skill that would teach us how to economize—a skill that would also help take the load off her from having to sew clothes for six kids. I dove right in and loved it.

Over my lifetime, I've used that skill to make some spectacular clothes for myself and my own children. I made coats, dresses, suits, pantsuits, curtains, and bedding. I learned to knit and made scarves and blankets. I taught myself how to quilt, and I even made my own wedding dress to save money. I took a lot of pride in my sewing skills, and I got many compliments from friends and strangers who were surprised I was able to create such beautiful necessities with my two hands and a sewing machine.

The reality is that fabric and sewing supplies cost money. So, my mom volunteered me to babysit for a neighbor when I was only nine and a half years old.

That first babysitting experience was scary. I was looking after an infant, and I was alone in the house with the baby until late into the evening—much later than my regular bedtime. I remember standing over the baby's crib, looking at it and hoping it wouldn't wake up because I had no clue what I was supposed to do if it did. I didn't know how to change diapers or give a baby a bottle, and here I was, in charge of this little being.

I remember my mom negotiated for me to earn fifty cents an hour. When I came home with the two dollars I had earned, she told me, "Now that you're earning your own money, you can start paying for your own things. We'll provide for the things you need, but anything extra you want, you'll have to pay for yourself."

I want you to imagine being that young and then being told you had to start contributing to your own existence. I was only nine and a half years old. This was the beginning of my working career.

I babysat for money all through high school, but I also took on a second job serving at Baskin-Robbins when I was fourteen. It was an easy walk down the road from our house in Yakima, and I was making $2.30 an hour—which was way more than the fifty cents my mom said I should charge for babysitting. I stayed there for about a year and then went to The Royal Fork Buffet, an all-you-can-eat restaurant located off 40th and Summitview. I worked there as a server, then a cashier, and eventually moved to the kitchen to help prep food for the cooks.

I needed all the money I could make at that time. I had to—since my mom and dad couldn't be counted on to help. There were a couple of times when Mom and Dad had me believe they were going to pay for something. They walked me up to the register with the item, paid for it, and then surprised me with, "You can pay me back with your next paycheck." I felt so betrayed at that time. I didn't have the money to buy the items and only gave in to getting them because of Mom and Dad's insistence, which made me think they were paying for it. After I got burned too many times in this manner,

I never *ever* took them up on "buying" me something again.

I was a unique teenager. When other teens were working to pay for their car or their car insurance, I was working to pay my way through high school. Four years at a private high school where I paid my own tuition, books, and supplies. Crazy, right? A teenager working just to pay for high school?

You say, "Why? High school is free." Yes, public schools are free—but I was extremely intimidated by the large schools in the Yakima School District. The population at Franklin Junior High was three times that of the elementary school I had just come from. I was afraid I wouldn't be seen or noticed in a much larger school.

The idea of shouldering the financial load for high school seemed easier on me than getting lost at the mega public high school down the street. Because of that, I decided to go to the much smaller Catholic school, Carroll High School, where my dad was teaching and coaching.

You would have thought that I would have gotten a break in the tuition since my dad worked there, but I didn't. If I wanted to go to Carroll, then I would have to pay the entire tuition—no discounts. This was in addition to any personal items I was already paying for myself. It was an extreme ask of myself. But my lack of self-confidence in a larger school was much greater than the thought of paying for high school on my own.

When I applied to college, I never thought of anything other than me paying for it—and so, I did. I devised a plan to financially get through the next four years of college. Since I had worked all through high school while trying to keep up with my grades and extracurricular activities, I made a promise to myself that I wasn't going to work while I was in college. I would work hard during the summer and make as much money as possible. Then I would take out a student loan for the rest and make the cash I earned in the summer last the nine months of college.

It seemed that I had always been working, and that I had always been taking care of my own financial needs. I wasn't comfortable asking for—or expecting—any financial help from anyone. I had always been financially independent, and I knew how to budget and save. But being married to someone who always had money handed to him and who had no self-discipline with finances meant that my budgeting skills would no longer have the same positive outcome. If there was any money in the checking or savings account, Mike found a way to spend it. It didn't matter if he agreed we would save money to buy airline tickets home—he didn't have the discipline to wait for a financial goal to pan out. If the money was there, he spent it.

Here I am, in 1996, married for almost thirteen years, and I have no ready cash in case of an emergency. It had been hard for me to get work since we moved around a lot, and then I had three kids in three and a half years. I didn't have access to my own money stream. I opened my own checking account when I started my direct sales business back in 1992. I kept it strictly for business. It was the smart thing to do. I also knew this ensured Mike didn't have access to it and couldn't compromise my business.

When he started getting erratic and cruel in his behavior, I knew I had to plan for an eventual exit. So, I decided that I was going to use that account to put money away so that I could eventually have enough to leave him.

I had weaned my direct sales business down to a trickle after Jillian's brain abscess in November of 1995. I knew if I wanted to make money to leave him, I needed to get a traditional job. So, I eventually quit my direct sales business sometime in 1996 and enrolled in a class at H&R Block to become a tax preparer. My goal was to make some good money and put it away in my own account. I was hoping this would mean I could leave Mike much sooner rather than later.

Mike was excited that I was working as well. He started making plans for repairs and updates to the house, including calculating how much supplies would cost. I was caught off guard by his automatic assumption that he would have access to my money.

Two different things crossed my mind at the same time:

1. If he expects and gets access to my money, then I will never be able to have the money to leave.

2. Wow. He's making plans to spend money on our house instead of on himself. Has he changed?

I knew he hadn't changed, but I also realized I hadn't considered that he would assume I would deposit the money in our joint account. I understood his assumption—I had access to the money he made, so why wouldn't he have access to the money I made?

I realized that I wouldn't be able to put my entire paycheck into my own account, which meant it would take me longer to save the money I needed to leave.

The first item on Mike's list was to put gutters on the house. We needed them to protect the house and property, so my paycheck was transformed into gutters. Next, he decided to replace some siding on the house and update the aging shutters. Again, I recognized that this was needed, so I didn't resist when my money— once again—went somewhere other than my savings account. It continued like that until tax season was over and I had no more money to give. The house did need updating, but my checking and savings account had grown very little.

I realized I needed to reach higher in my professional aspirations to achieve my freedom, so I re-assessed my options.

Working as a dental hygienist had not panned out like I thought it would. The hours were inflexible with children. If the kids had an early release day at school and I was still working, I would have to scramble to get daycare or take time off from work—which is a big no-no in a dental office. If the kids were sick, I was encouraged by the dentist to bring them to work and have them lie down in the back so the office wouldn't have to reschedule my patients.

There was one episode in the winter where the kids were put on the wrong school bus. Instead of going to the after-school daycare down the street from my office, they were sent on a bus home—way outside of town in the country where neighbors were far apart. When I was alerted by the school about the mistake, I had to leave work immediately, racing home and trying to beat the bus, worried about what the kids would do if they couldn't get in the house on a cold winter afternoon.

Besides the inflexible work hours, there were also no health or dental benefits that came with the profession at that time. Dental offices are considered small businesses, and small businesses rarely offer benefits to their employees. I was going to need a profession with benefits—in addition to flexibility for raising children. I had to take all of this into consideration before I could successfully leave this marriage and guarantee that I could support the children.

If I'd been in a clearer state of mind, I would have recognized that Mike would be legally required to help support the kids when I left. But I had felt so alone for so long in the marriage, I believed I could only count on me. I didn't even think about the fact that he would have an obligation to contribute. I had been emotionally alone for such a long time that all my plans reflected the idea that I had to do it all by myself.

I immediately turned my thoughts toward teaching. My dad was a high school teacher, and my mom worked as a secretary in the school district. When I was young, I assumed everyone's parents were home for Christmas break and the summer. Teaching seemed like a great profession for raising kids on my own. If the school had a surprise snow day or early release, then I would have one too—and the kids would always have a parent (me) nearby.

I remembered that I preferred the high school level when I worked as a substitute teacher while we lived in Texas. I started looking at college course requirements for earning my Science Education degree. I discovered it was going to take me a minimum of three years to get my degree.

What gave me the most concern was the math requirement: Algebra II, Pre-Calculus, Physics I, and Physics II. I hadn't taken a math class since I was a sophomore in high school—and that was twenty years ago. I didn't want to waste time taking a remedial course, so in December 1997, I went to the local community college library and "borrowed" a teacher's edition algebra book from their resource section. I brought it home and studied it all through the kids' Christmas break.

I made a detailed "rule book" so I could quickly look up examples on how to solve different algebra problems. I loved that rule book. It came in handy for so many years to come—and I only lost it when Craig borrowed it in high school. Nonetheless, I studied, worked out practice problems, and took practice tests. When I finally felt confident, I returned to the community college, took the Algebra placement test, and scored nearly perfect. I was able to bypass the remedial course and enroll directly into Algebra II!

Yippie, yippie! I was so excited. This was not only going to save me time—it was also going to save me money. One less course I had to pay for! Now I had to figure out how I was going to pay for the next three years.

I knew I couldn't use money from our joint account—Mike would have a fit if money was being diverted from him. So I had to get creative.

Fortunately, I found an educational scholarship that the state of North Carolina was offering at the time to any math, science, and special education prospective teachers. It was very generous and free—North Carolina would pay for my education if I agreed to teach for four years after graduation in the state. I had to maintain a C in every class, or the scholarship would go away. This was almost a perfect solution.

It did solve my dilemma of how to pay for school, but the scholarship would also require that I stay and teach in a North Carolina public school for four years after graduation to honor the loan. This hit my heart hard. I didn't have the money to pay off the loan, so that meant I had to stay and teach. That meant I couldn't leave him for at least seven more years—three years of college and four more to repay the loan. I was looking for a full financial break, a miracle. I was hoping they would pay my tuition and I wouldn't have to pay them back. Very *Pollyanna* of me.

There is always a cost to a benefit. I wanted both. But I was grateful that I didn't have to pay upfront. I could always pay on the back end when I had my own money. I figured I would concentrate on the positive—that I was going to get my Science Education degree for free, and I would then have a profession that worked around my kids' schedules and offered benefits at the same time. I was just going to plow forward and deal with the future when it came.

My first semester back in college since I graduated from dental hygiene school in 1983 was the spring of 1998. I took a couple of undergraduate courses at the local community college and worked another year as a tax preparer for H&R Block. I had to regularly clock out of work for a couple of hours each day to attend classes, and my employer wasn't too keen on my leaving—but it was what needed to be done. Mike was busy planning how he would spend the extra money I was earning, and I was hoping to keep putting money aside for myself. I couldn't save much, but I kept my eyes on the long goal—my eventual freedom—and I kept moving forward.

That fall semester, I took a ferry across the Neuse River to Pamlico Community College to complete more of my undergraduate requirements. I made good use of the twenty-five-minute ferry ride—catching up on sleep, reviewing for a test, making grocery lists, etc. The school was just four miles from the ferry dock on the north side of the river, and our house was just a couple hundred yards on the south side. It was an easy on-and-off trip. There may have been a few times when the ferry wasn't running due to weather, and I had to drive an hour around—but usually, it was a simple, reliable commute.

During this time, Jillian was in seventh grade, now a middle school student, and Claire and Craig were in fifth and fourth grade. They were very capable of coming home from school and taking care of themselves for a short while. This made it a bit easier for me to be gone all day and not have to worry so much about their well-being.

Mike was getting ready to deploy again, so I would eventually have six months without his dark cloud hanging over me. I was enjoying my daily academic routine, knowing I was getting closer to my goal of independence.

Even with Mike at home every day, he didn't really provide me with much relief. I was still taking on most of the home responsibilities, and I was the one primarily responsible for getting the kids to and from their activities. I wanted the kids' lives to move on with as little disruption as possible, so I made sure my class schedule worked around their sports and scout activities.

I was doing a lot, but I also started to ask more of the kids. They were old enough to take on more responsibilities, so they began helping with laundry, vacuuming, dusting, cleaning bathrooms, and baseboards. It was good for them—and it also freed me up when I got home, so I could put dinner together and study.

One day blended into the next. Eventually, I was able to enroll at East Carolina University, where I expected to get my diploma in two more years. The drive to ECU was approximately ninety minutes. I had to leave the house no later than 5:45 a.m. so I wouldn't get stuck behind the school buses that eventually filled my long route. I found that if I left the house even five minutes later, the traffic lights would all work against me, and the buses would be out.

The extra five minutes meant it would add another twenty-five minutes to my drive. So, 5:45 a.m. it is.

Early in the semester, Mike was still around but getting ready to deploy. He made sure the kids got up and on their bus. When he deployed, it was up to the kids to do it themselves. Jillian was in the eighth grade, Claire in the sixth, and Craig in the fifth. They were doing super— getting up and out the door on their own. Fortunately, I was able to get back home in time to pick them up from school. We were making it work as a team.

When it became apparent that Craig wouldn't be able to play Fall Ball due to a lack of coaches, I volunteered to be the coach. Crazy—but somehow, I did it. And I even coached his Little League team the next spring. I was Superwoman. I was proving to myself that I could take on and do anything if I set my mind to accomplishing it.

I was gaining a lot of confidence in myself—proof that I could be the sole provider for our kids if I needed to be.

One semester after another, I kept it going. I even had to take summer classes if I expected to graduate on time. This was a tough time for the kids, since they would be tethered close to home in the summer without seeing their friends while I was in class. They started getting into fights with each other as they jockeyed to be in charge of themselves, so I came up with a solution.

I would give them a very specific, out-of-the-usual chore to complete, then pay them for getting it done. I also offered to take them with me to the university on Fridays—when my class load was light—and treat them to the university's student center where they could play all kinds of sports, swim, and have fun.

One chore I gave them was to remove all the wallpaper in the living room. I assigned them each a wall and showed them how to take the wallpaper off. They surprised me when they had it all completed on the first day. I was so proud of the kids. I promptly paid them their well-earned money, then treated them to a summer evening at our HOA's pool and dinner out.

The kids were really stepping up to help me out and, in turn, they were gaining some much-needed realization that we were all part of a family—and that we all needed to contribute to make the family function for all of us. They were so excited to come with me to my Friday class, knowing they'd get to play all they wanted at the student center on campus. They were so excited, they didn't even mind the 5:45 a.m. departure.

I was working so hard on so many levels, and I needed the kids to step up and help. They were super. I was so proud of them. That was a great time. I look back now and realize the best times I had were when the kids and I were alone—without their dad. I also realize that most women would not consider being on their own with this mental and physical load a "great time," but I didn't have to deal with his mood swings, his intimidation, or his changing and ruining our family plans. He was a negative variable in my life that had been removed for six months—and I was very happy.

Please keep in mind, just because I haven't included any of his meltdowns, tirades, dark mood swings, or his mental cruelty doesn't mean it wasn't there. I would be navigating all that for the rest of my marriage. It's just that I no longer believed he was going to change, and I had a very clear goal I was working toward—to ensure my freedom.

After years and years of abuse, I eventually fell into the habit of not responding or reacting to his mental torture. I would let him blow up at me, try to intimidate me— but I refused to allow any more darkness to penetrate the already poisoned brain I carried. It was a natural progression toward survival. I had to preserve the little bit of mental and emotional energy I had just to get through each day.

So, I stopped reacting to his provocations. I've now learned the term for this is "grey rocking." Be as impenetrable as a rock, give no response like a rock, and just move on. This didn't mean I stopped believing he could harm me. No—I was still vigilant. It's just that I had been at such a high cortisol level for so long that my body had adjusted to this elevated amount of hormone as the "normal" of my daily life.

I intuitively knew that the only way to protect myself was not to give him any more emotional ammunition.

He would come into the living room and yell at me because I was watching sports. He hated the athletes. He felt they made too much money and all they did was just "play a game." So, I would simply turn the channel or turn the TV off when he came into the room. I tried to avoid triggering any emotional outburst from him. He would feel superior because he got me to change the channel. I didn't care if he felt like he won. I just walked away. I took myself out of his line of fire. If he chose to follow me and continue his verbal accosting, I would pretend he wasn't there and just continue doing what I was doing—not stopping to even look at him while he was exploding.

Grey rocking.

Yes, he started to hate sports. He said it was because one of the pilots in his squadron had played football for the FSU Seminoles, and Mike felt like this pilot received preferential treatment because he was a jock. The only thing Mike's venom accomplished was exposing the fact that he was jealous of his fellow pilot's college life—that Mike, himself, didn't get the preferential treatment he believed he deserved.

What he neglected to recognize was that he had his own kind of preferential treatment all his life from his mom. Remember, she paid for everything he wanted and needed all through college. He had nothing to want for. But a narcissist isn't happy if they perceive others to have more. They are never satisfied and are always blaming others for their unhappiness.

I just refused to follow him down his rabbit hole anymore. I was too busy keeping my goal of getting my degree—and then being able to leave him—at the forefront of my thoughts. I tried not to put any more energy than absolutely necessary into his antics.

I put in many long days, nights, and weekends studying. It was not unusual for me to sit down at the kitchen table on Saturday and Sunday by 9:00 a.m. and not be done until after nine o'clock at night. When the kids came in and asked what was for dinner, I would simply point toward the kitchen counter, where I'd set out a can of ravioli, a can opener, and a bowl for them to microwave their own meals.

I worked hard. The kids and I sacrificed a lot during that time, but it was all worth it. I had to have a career where I could take care of them if I needed to.

Eventually, I found myself at the end of my goal. My time had finally come to graduate. May of 2001 was the end of one chapter and the beginning of another. I was so proud of myself. This degree meant so much more to me than my dental hygiene accomplishment back in 1983 because I had so many more obstacles to overcome. I felt the stakes—for both me and the kids—were much higher.

I even bought myself a college class ring to commemorate my accomplishment. I never got a class ring when I graduated high school because I didn't have the money to pay for it. But I was surely going to get this one. I may have taken off my wedding ring once I finally left him, but my college ring has remained firmly planted on my finger.

Now that I had graduated, it was time to figure out my next step. I finally had my degree, but I still didn't have enough money saved to leave. Plus, I now had to figure out how to repay the state of North Carolina, since they required me to teach for at least four years to release the loan obligation. I wasn't sure which way to jump. I wanted out of the marriage, but paying the money back became a blocker for me.

The biggest dilemma, however, eventually revealed itself to be something other than how I would repay the loan if I left.

By the time I got my Science Education degree, the kids were getting older. Jillian was going into tenth grade, Claire into eighth, and Craig into seventh. If I worked for four more years to pay back the loan, then Jillian would be in college, Claire would be a senior, and Craig a junior. These were not good years to be moving kids in and out of schools.

Besides the issues of the kids having to build new social groups—at an age when their identity is so deeply wrapped up in peer connection—there was also the concern that not all credits would transfer to a new school. And then, what about their mental and emotional state? They would want to know why I was leaving—and I would have to tell them.

I wrestled with that decision for a long time.

The biggest problem that I saw was that the kids rarely witnessed the abuse their dad inflicted on me. He was very selective about when and where he unleashed his fury. He usually waited until I was alone before thrashing me. There were a couple of scenarios I kept playing over in my head. If I left, the kids would have to move away with me. There was no way they could stay with their dad due to his constant deployments and unpredictable schedule. If that was the case, they were now old enough to ask questions that I would have to answer.

It wouldn't be the same as when they were very little and I could just say, "Daddy is busy fighting to protect people, so we need to let him do his job." Or maybe something like, "Daddy is sick and needs to stay here to get better." When kids are young, you can get away with a simple explanation like that—and then slowly tell them more when they get older and start to ask. But when they are older, like my kids were at the time, you have to give them pretty much the whole truth. They won't let you get away with anything less than that.

Since my story of trauma and pain was pretty much only observed by me, how would they believe me if they didn't see it? And what about his cross-dressing? It would devastate them to learn that their dad was a cross-dresser and that he had been torturing me in so many ways all this time.

The best-case scenario would look something like this: I tell them the truth, and now they have their family foundation pulled out from under them without any warning. They would suffer for years in their own emotional turmoil as they tried to make sense of what their dad purportedly did to their mom—and then somehow try to regain trust in any intimate relationships they develop in their own lives. This would almost certainly be accompanied by a lot of therapy to help them navigate the new reality I had unleashed upon them.

The worst-case scenario would include all of the above—and also bring about personal rebellion. They might get caught up in the wrong crowd at school, trying to fill the void left by the blindsided trauma that had come their way. Many times, this kind of trauma manifests in teenagers through experimenting with drugs.

These were very heavy thoughts swirling through my head. Remember, I was alone on my journey of domestic abuse. I had no one to confide in, no one to ask for advice.

Many of you will look at this and say I wasn't doing the kids any favors by staying in this abusive relationship. You'll also say that I wasn't portraying a healthy, married relationship by staying—and that I was doing a disservice to both my son and daughters by letting them believe this was what a marriage looked like.

I understand your thoughts.

But you must remember this: the kids didn't see the abuse. In their eyes, we had a great marriage. They never saw or heard us fight. Any revelation from me would have their entire world crashing down.

Now they were burgeoning on their adult lives, and I had a decision to make: do I leave their dad because of the ongoing abuse and risk traumatizing the kids? Or do I stay, wait for a time when they're more emotionally equipped to handle the revelation—and continue taking the abuse?

I had spent so many days and nights—morphed into years—worried about protecting them from this monster. And now, I was on the verge of blowing the top off their reality.

The choice became clear.

I would have to stay and continue to protect them until they were all strong enough to handle the truth.

*   *   *   *   *   *   *   *   *   *   *

Narcissistic abuse is not just that someone dumped you or who you had a little tiff with. NA is psychological abuse and brainwashing using intermittent reward and punishment, coercive control and withholding normal empathetic, emotional reactions to lower your self-esteem.

ALICE LITTLE, *Narcissistic Abuse Truths*

16. 9-11

*More time with the wrong person = less time with the right one.
Every second spent doubting, hoping, or trying to fix them is time
stolen from your healing, happiness, and the life you actually
deserve.* -evolvewith_sophie

I had just completed my science education degree and
was fortunate enough to be offered a teaching position
at the kids' high school. I was so eager to get started as
a professional, and I took that summer of 2001 to get
myself ready for the school year by tackling a project I
had wanted to do for a long time.

We had access to the backyard through the kitchen,
but when you walked down the steps, you ended up in
the mucky grass. I had wanted to create a patio back
there, but Mike didn't want to do the work. He was more
interested in spending his time and money on singular
activities. In the past, I would just let him have his way,
since putting up resistance only created more hardship
for me. But this time, I was putting my wants first—and
I got busy designing and building the patio without his
knowledge.

After researching the project, I started measuring and
laying out the parameters of the patio. I decided to make
it round and out of stone. First, I had to dig up the yard.
It was hard because of all the clay in the soil, so I waited

for the next rain to soften the ground. Then I jumped outside—while it was raining—to dig. I enlisted Jillian to help. There we were, outside in the rain, digging up the yard.

I needed to work quickly to get to a point of no return in case Mike came home and discovered what I was doing. I knew I had a couple of days of digging before he would find out, since he rarely took notice of anything around the house.

I was right. A couple of days later, he looked out the kitchen door and said, "What's going on?"

I told him I was building a patio, and he said, with a bit of disgust in his voice, "I was going to do blah, blah, blah with the money. Now there won't be enough to do both."

I replied, very matter-of-factly, "I've been wanting to do this patio for a long time, but you've been too busy to do it. So, I'm going to do it."

He replied dismissively, "You're on your own."

I didn't mind. I didn't expect him to help. I was actually very excited about doing it on my own.

I really had no clue how big this project was going to be. I just took it one step at a time. I made several trips to Lowe's in my little car, carrying as many retaining blocks as possible. I had a truckload of sand delivered and got busy tamping it down—by simply walking on it. I had three tons of stone pavers delivered, and I spent the entire summer laying down those three tons of stone myself.

I was on my hands and knees with thick knee pads, working from 7:00 a.m. until 9:00 p.m. The heat and humidity in North Carolina are ridiculous, so I had to work around the shifting sun and take several water breaks. I was so exhausted and dirty every night—and for once, I slept hard.

The most physically challenging part of the project was placing grout around each stone. The grout would set up fast because of the heat, so I had to place it and smooth it with my fingers very quickly. The skin on my fingertips was raw from smoothing out the grout, and my protected knees were red, bruised, and still peeling for several months after the project was finished. My back was sore, and my arms were tired from being on my hands and knees all day.

When I first started, I was sure it would only take me a month to complete. Instead, I found myself racing to get it done before school started.

But—I did it! It turned out beautifully. I even built steps off the back end of the patio due to the yard sloping away.

What a great accomplishment. I did get a little help, but 98 percent of it was me. I was feeling very proud of myself. Besides finishing three long years of college, I had just completed a huge and beautiful patio practically by myself. I knew I had it in me to do anything I set my mind to. I knew I was strong-willed and determined. I knew I could make my dreams a reality—and here were two major accomplishments I could lay claim to.

Besides lifting my soul, the project left my body toned and buffed from hoisting tons of rock all summer. I was starting my professional career feeling my power, and I was determined to hang on to that image of myself and not let anyone or anything bring me back down.

It was now September 2001, and I was diving into my teaching career. Craig was in seventh grade, Claire in eighth, and Jillian was now a sophomore and in her second year of being in the marching band at the high school. Mike and I were volunteers as band parents. Since he was handy with construction, he volunteered to help make props for this year's marching band competitions. That included cutting down some of the boxes they had used for last year's competition so they could remake them into new props for this season.

It was September 12, 2001—the day after the terrorist attacks on the World Trade Center. All airspace had been shut down in the United States, and only essential military personnel were to report for duty. Mike was not essential personnel, so he was home alone, cutting down the boxes when the worst happened.

I was teaching when I was contacted by the front office to take an important phone call. Someone from NADEP, where Mike was currently assigned, was on the other end of the line. They told me that Mike had fallen from a ladder at work and was being taken to the hospital.

Did I hear that right? I thought he was home—not at work.

Whoever it was on the phone assured me that he was all right. I just shrugged it off and made arrangements for someone to cover my class so I could go to him.

Then I received another call—this time from the Fire Chief, Rick Zaccardelli, an acquaintance of mine. Apparently, Mike was not okay. He hadn't fallen from a ladder, and he wasn't at work. He had been at home, as non-essential personnel, and was cutting down those boxes for the band director when he hit a nail that was hidden in the construction of one of the boxes.

The nail had been kicked out by his table saw and penetrated his chest, creating a tiny little hole with a tiny droplet of blood. That tiny nail caused him to lose blood pressure. He was feeling faint when he called for the ambulance. Rick told me the ambulance was taking him to the city park, where they were going to try to get a helicopter to transport him to the university hospital.

He offered to pick up Claire and Craig from the middle school and meet me with Jillian at the city park.

I had to put a mental break on my emotions as I reprocessed the emergency. First, I thought he had fallen off a ladder and was okay. Now I had to shift to him being airlifted to the university hospital. I quickly let my science colleagues know what was happening and got Jillian out of school as we raced to meet the ambulance at the park.

Mike was there—pale and sweating. He was very scared, and I offered reassurance as I tried not to look concerned. I could see the puncture wound in his chest; it looked like a small pinprick. How could something so small create a life-or-death scenario so quickly?

I was informed after I arrived that, due to airspace being shut down because of the terrorist attacks, they would have to drive him to the county hospital thirty minutes away.

Almost immediately, Rick showed up with Claire and Craig, followed soon after by a fellow pilot friend, Tony Elliott, who volunteered to drive me and the kids to the hospital. I could see the kids' expressions in the back seat as they sat quietly, not knowing what was going on. I knew very little myself, so I wasn't able to offer much to them—except checking in from time to time on our ride.

Once at the hospital, I rushed to the ER, where they already had Mike prepped for surgery. He was whiter than pale, and they had him nearly upside down so the blood would drain toward his head. He looked at me, clearly scared, and said, "I love you," as they wheeled him away.

My colleagues from the Science Department seemed to arrive almost immediately to support me. It was very sweet of them to come and wait with me. A big part of me wanted to be alone with the kids, but it was so important for them to be there for me that I couldn't complain.

I surprised my friends by not being overly emotional about the seriousness of his injuries. I can only explain that I was so used to high-stress situations that this was just one more to manage. My dad used to tell me, "Only worry about the things you can control. Everything else, let it go." And here I was again, having to apply that sage wisdom to maneuver a tragic event.

While I was waiting for the results of the surgery, I surprised myself when the thought of him dying didn't bother me. I had spent all these years emotionally alone—and many years physically alone due to his deployments. Being without him didn't scare me. I knew I could take care of the kids myself.

What had kept me from leaving up to this point were four things: lack of money, fear of retaliation, hope that he would change, and not wanting to traumatize the kids.

If he passed away, I would have the money to start over with the kids. I wouldn't have to worry about retaliation. And I believed the kids would be able to accept their dad's passing easier than discovering his abuse toward me. They could hold him in their memories with only love. And even though their hearts would break from his death, their world wouldn't completely crumble.

They could accept that a freak accident took their dad away from them instead of feeling the shame, anger, and betrayal of knowing he had been a narcissistic abuser. Like my dad always said, "Only worry about the things you have control over." I didn't have control over whether Mike lived or died—but I could put my energy toward the worst-case scenario and make mental plans just in case.

Eventually, the doctors came out and updated me on the surgery. It was a success. Apparently, the small finishing nail had penetrated his chest and lodged next to his heart. With every heartbeat, the heart bumped into the tip of the nail, and the nail would make a small tear in the pericardium surrounding the heart. Slowly, the space between the pericardium and the heart began to fill with blood. That pressure kept the heart from fully beating. In other words, it was slowly strangling the heart.

The doctor said he barely made it to surgery in time—and that if they had airlifted him to the university hospital in Greenville, he wouldn't have survived.

Lucky for Mike, the airspace was shut down.

I was very neutral in my emotions. I had trained myself well over the years to moderate my emotional reactions. It was a survival mechanism—you don't let yourself feel too much because there is so much to "feel" all the time. And now, all the mental plans I had just made in case he passed away were dumped from my brain. I began planning for what it would look like when he came home.

He was alive after a close call. That meant I would need to take some time off from work when he got home from the hospital to care for him. I wasn't looking forward to this, because he had always treated me like his servant.

And now, he would really dive into that role and use it to control me on another level, trying to squeeze as much sympathy and guilt from me as possible.

He would soak up all the pity and attention he could get from friends, family, and colleagues, while I would just be the utility person—not his wife. Not that I expected grandiose gratitude from him; he had never shown that in the past. But I knew he would treat this accident as his permission slip to play the victim at a whole new level.

Mike came home after five days and wasn't allowed to take the stairs, so I set him up in the family room downstairs, where he would hang out all day and night for the next ten days. It went pretty much as I had expected. I took care of whatever he needed, whenever he needed it. I helped him to the bathroom and back. He would say over and over again how much he wanted to live, how he didn't want to die. He promised to change as a person. He vowed to get back into better shape.

I took his promise to change with a grain of salt. I nodded and smiled, kissed him on the forehead, and treated him lovingly—but inside, I wasn't giving in to the "new" him. I had created a thick wall that kept his energy at bay. Even if he came across as genuine, I didn't buy it. I went through the daily motions and said and did whatever I needed to get to the next moment, and the next day, with some mental peace.

He had made promises to change before, but always went back to being the same hateful person within a week.

For better or for worse. Yes, that's what I promised. But my faithfulness in our marriage was based on fear and intimidation. There had been very little "better," and a whole lot of "worse." I had already started separating myself emotionally from the marriage, and his tragic accident didn't change that.

I had been through so many ups and downs, lefts and rights, and had been yanked back and forth by him so often that I was now on remote control to protect myself. The thick wall of armor was up consistently now, and it would be a while before I let it down again.

Mike was getting close to twenty years in the Marine Corps and was considering retiring in January 2003. Even though he was medically cleared to fly again, he decided it was time to get out. With the time he had remaining, he began considering his next step.

He could have flown for a commercial airline, but he talked himself out of it. That path would have required promoting himself in interviews in the civilian world— something he had never done during his time in the Corps.

He had such low self-esteem that he paralyzed himself when it came to applying for jobs. He couldn't imagine anyone wanting to hire him because he believed they would see right through the mask he wore every day.

So, he took the first position that fell into his lap: a subject matter expert (SME) with a contractor to the Marine Corps, writing training manuals for the AV-8B Harrier community. The first month working for the contractor, he was still technically in the Marine Corps on terminal leave, so he was proud to "double dip" for a month.

His retirement ceremony was held at his last duty assignment at NADEP at MCAS Cherry Point, North Carolina. I took the kids out of school for the day, and we got to meet some of the people Mike worked with. I got to hear what a great guy he was, how considerate he had been to the men he had managed. We ate a delicious catered meal in his honor.

And I got to endure one more humiliating act of dismissal by him.

At every squadron we had been associated with, there were many opportunities for spouses to get involved and help make the constant deployment of the servicemen easier on the families left behind. There are many young women who are married to a serviceman and then left alone for long periods while their husbands are on deployment. Sometimes their pay gets messed up, or a financial emergency arises, and these women need help to get through to the next pay period. I had always been a part of the squadron organizations that helped support our own, and I most certainly had done a stellar job of holding our family, finances, and home together while Mike was gone.

When the men came back from deployment, or when they received orders to a new squadron or duty station and were leaving—or were new to our squadron— the squadron wives would always put on a "Hail and Farewell" gathering. There was much socializing around the food and drink that the wives provided, and everyone generally had a fun time until it came time to give out the awards and the farewell plaques.

One by one, each pilot, when called up to get his award, would give a little speech of gratitude and parting words. And one by one, each pilot would stand up in front of the entire squadron and thank everyone who helped them along their path. Every pilot—*every* pilot— thanked their wife for her sacrifice at home so that he could achieve professional success. Except Mike. He never, never, ever thanked me. *Never.* I sat through every pilot's moving speech as they placed their highest gratitude on their wife's contribution to their success, thinking this time Mike will do the same. He never did.

When it came time for his retirement after twenty years of service—six duty station changes, seven deployments, the Gulf War, the sacrifice of my own career for his—I was certain he would finally include me in his farewell speech. I was wrong. He stood up there, in front of everyone, and spoke about how much the Marine Corps meant to him and how he was going to miss it. But not one word about how I made this journey with him. I put on a smile and pretended not to be devastated. The five of us gathered for a happy family photo, but I was empty inside.

I shouldn't have been surprised. This was who he was. Did he not understand how such a simple act of recognizing his wife's contribution would have gone a long way in repairing the damage done to our marriage? Since I was wearing my thicker coat of armor, I didn't let this seep too far inside my soul. It was a disappointment, but it was usual for him. I called him out for it when we got home. I said, "This was your last opportunity to publicly acknowledge the support that I have given you all these years, and you didn't say anything." This was his response: "I didn't say anything because I didn't think it mattered."

There you go, folks. It didn't matter. I didn't matter. All twenty years of his military service, I had been with him—and I just didn't matter. Someone who has an ounce of empathy or compassion would see all the others give public praise to their wives and, you would think, be inspired to do the same. Even if the impulse to praise their wife was not genuinely of their own making, at least they would recognize the importance of making sure they included her in their speech. Not Mike. No empathy. No compassion. He could see others exhibit it, but it never resonated with him. It didn't matter how many times public praise of the wives was modeled by other pilots—Mike never, ever internalized it as something that was worthy for me to hear from him.

Invalidation is one of the worst forms of abuse. When your partner dismisses you over and over again—your feelings, opinions, wants and needs, your dreams— they are telling you that you don't matter. You are insignificant and have no value to them. The only value I had to him was to give him social credibility, to put on a show to the world that he must be a great guy since he has such a great wife and family. I was just an accessory in his life.

I would wonder after every squadron Hail and Farewell that Mike had to give a speech at, how many others noticed that he never acknowledged me in his gratitude. I would wear my fake smile and purposely not look around the room to make eye contact with anyone, for fear I would see the knowing in someone's eyes. That would hurt me even more. I didn't want anyone to magnify the emotions that I was already feeling.

I had married a self-centered asshole, and he showed his disdain for me one last time by not publicly acknowledging my support for him at his retirement ceremony. I should have wept, but my thick wall of armor was protecting me from internalizing the pain. I had placed that pain in a small box and pushed it deep inside of me. It would eventually find its way out several years later, but for now, I just placed a Band-Aid on it and left it alone.

I knew his almost-near-death experience with the nail in the chest wouldn't change him. It didn't take long for him to prove to me again that he was incapable of change. I had already accepted that. I was committing myself to more of his hell just so the kids would be spared from the realization of who their father really was. I was just sailing along, trying not to get in his way while simultaneously looking forward to the time when the kids would be secure enough in their own lives for me to be able to leave. It couldn't come fast enough.

*   *   *   *   *   *   *   *   *   *   *

Narcissists love to play "happy family" or "loyal friend", but only with the people who cater to them. If you speak up or see through them, you're out. And honestly... That's a blessing in disguise.

E.S.

17. Planting a Flag

Loving yourself isn't just about affirmations and self-care Sundays. It's about choosing yourself even when it hurts, even when you care deeply, even when walking away feels like the hardest thing in the world. You are not meant to beg for love, respect or recognition. The right people, the right places, the right opportunities, they will see your worth without you having to prove it. Let this be the season you refuse to shrink for those who cannot see your light. You are not too much. They are simply not enough for you. -THE GLOW WAVE

It was the early 2000s, and Mike was now out of the Marine Corps and working for a contractor supporting the AV-8B fleet. The two girls were in marching band, and Craig was an eighth grader at the middle school involved in sports. I was teaching science at the high school. It was a busy period—when you work full time and have three active kids you want to support in their interests.

Mike and I were still band parents and supported the girls' marching band competitions practically every weekend. Then we would switch up to catch Craig's football games and wrestling matches during the week. If you have active kids, then you know that you are always on the go and have to become a master of logistics. You also have to work extra hard to make sure the kids keep up with their homework responsibilities. The two girls were self-starters and didn't need much oversight, but Craig was more of an easygoing kid who enjoyed being distracted from time to time.

Since I worked at the high school, it was easy for me to stay on top of what the girls were doing. Their teachers would often stop by to casually give me an update on how they were progressing in their classes. They were both academically gifted and curious students, so their reports were always favorable. With Craig being at the middle school, it wasn't so easy to keep informed. I had to wait for the progress report to come out to see where he was academically.

Everything seemed to be fine for Craig during football season, but then there were signs of trouble during the wrestling season. He was coming home very upset and disturbed by some girl at school who was bullying him. It's very demoralizing for a guy to get bullied by a girl, knowing he would get into a lot of trouble if he tried to stick up for himself. Craig would try to ignore her because he knew he couldn't hit a girl. She knew he wouldn't hit her, and that just gave her more freedom to expand her bullying.

I was very concerned about Craig since I understood his dilemma. He is such a great guy, and I couldn't understand why this girl started to emotionally beat him down every day. I had gone to the middle school to talk to the principal and guidance counselors about it, but I wasn't encouraged that they would follow up. Craig finally had enough and pushed her—or hit her, or something like that. I was happy he did it, and I supported him. I had placed my trust in the school's leadership to mitigate the drama, and when they failed, I was pleased that my son said "enough" and reclaimed some of his personal boundaries.

One day, I went to pick Craig up from wrestling practice. I waited outside the wrestling room door when I heard his coach go off on him for hitting a girl. He continued his verbal assault on my son for quite some time and then gave him some punishment pushups to complete before he was allowed to leave.

How dare the coach humiliate my son in front of the team. It was bad enough that Craig was already struggling with low self-esteem from this girl's bullying, but to have my son feel like he was the abuser—when in fact, he was justified in standing up for himself—was beyond the pale. I was even more sensitive to the situation since I had been living a secret life of abuse, and I knew how damaging this was for him. So I was obviously not pleased with what I heard. I knocked on the wrestling room door and requested that my son leave with me right away.

I talked with Craig on the way home and told him what I had heard the coach say. I told my son that I was proud of him for standing up for himself. I remember how Craig's shoulders were hunched over as he sat in the front seat of the car, once again feeling the shame of this bullying drama. But I also remember him sitting a little taller when I told him I was proud of him, and that he didn't need to worry about his coach—because his coach was totally out of line.

The next day, I went into the principal's office after work and had a thorough conversation about the inappropriateness of the coach's words and actions. I reminded the principal that I had been seeking a resolution to the bullying and now it had escalated to my son having to take it into his own hands.

The principal agreed that the school had let my son down. Craig told me that the coach apologized to him later that day in front of the team. *You're darn right you're going to apologize. How dare you browbeat and humiliate a twelve-year-old boy when you don't even know the whole story.* I felt vindicated, but I still had to keep a close eye on Craig for a while after that.

I don't recall that Mike had any input in this matter. You'd think he would love the opportunity to flex his muscles and put on an outward show of intimidation, but I remember handling it alone. That wasn't unusual. Mike was only sporadically involved in the kids' upbringing. I did most of the counseling and disciplining, mostly because Mike was gone a lot. But even when he was home, he abdicated most of the parenting to me. When Mike did get involved, it was usually an over-the-top demonstration of how he was the boss of the family and everyone else had better get in line.

There was an incident where Craig's progress report came back with a failing grade. It showed that he had not turned in all his homework and that his grade had suffered. When his dad found out, he went ballistic and told Craig he had to quit wrestling.

Now, I understand the importance of earning your right to participate in sports by maintaining good grades, but this was just a progress report—not a report card with a final grade. Craig's teacher was simply asking that he turn in the missing work so his grade would rebound. I pointed this out to his dad, but Mike didn't care. He wanted Craig to quit wrestling. In fact, he said in a very intimidating tone, "I forbid him to wrestle." Mike was trying to flex his clout as the "man of the house" and expected me to bow down to him. I refused.

Craig was very upset at his dad's insistence that he quit wrestling. He ran upstairs to his room in tears. I knew Mike hated any athlete's perceived privileges because of his past interactions with one of his fellow pilots in the squadron years ago. He was trying to plant his "integrity" flag and wanted to show his toughness by taking a stand on this issue. But this stand was based on Mike being purely jealous of athletes.

It made him feel powerful to give his ultimatum. I'm sure he felt that this was his opportunity to stick it to all the athletes who had more perceived privileges than he did. Mike didn't stop to consider that the bullying incident Craig had been dealing with played a large part in his lapse in homework.

Craig was a good student. He always had good grades. I knew this was just a blip for him, and he deserved compassion and empathy for all he had been going through. But his dad was capable of neither.

I knew Mike could go completely unhinged, but I was not going to back down on this issue. I stood toe to toe with him and told him that Craig was going to continue to wrestle. After all, he was only twelve years old, and he was trying to navigate some tough personal issues. Mike tried to shout me down, but I wouldn't let him. I stood firm, even though my heart was racing and my head was spinning with the anticipation that Mike would escalate this to something worse. I eventually won out on Craig's behalf, and Mike was furious. It was one of the few times I ever stood up to him, but I would be damned before I let him take out his own insecurities on Craig.

This escalation of Mike's hostilities directed toward the kids was relatively new. Most of the time, he didn't get involved with any discipline and left it up to me. But now that Mike was no longer in the Marines and was around the house and the kids more, he was starting to make up for his lack of input in their lives. He was trying to assert his authority by flexing his testosterone. There was never any calm inquiry as to Craig's side of the story. Mike just wanted to take the opportunity to lay the hammer down and prove he was in charge.

Mike had flipped out on Craig a couple of years before. I can't remember exactly what happened, but Mike had a short fuse and decided to take it out on our son. I remember hearing Mike shout something fierce at Craig and then saw him chasing Craig up the stairs—much like he chased me back in November of 1994, when he grabbed my leg and caused me to fall face down on the stairs.

I heard Craig screaming in terror as he ran to his room and quickly shut the door behind him. His dad followed, shouting terrible things, and began pounding and trying to kick the door in. I was just a few steps behind Mike on the stairs and saw the fury in his body as he drove his right leg repeatedly into the bedroom door, trying to break it down—all while Craig screamed in terror on the other side.

I didn't hesitate. I ran toward Mike and placed myself in the door frame just as he kicked the door open to a frightened ten-year-old. I stood there with my arms and legs sprawled wide against the frame, and I dared Mike to go through me. I was shaking all over, and I knew he could seriously hurt me if he wanted to, but I was not going to leave my son to the fate of this unhinged maniac. Mike burned his eyes right through me—and finally backed down.

Now I had to turn my attention to my traumatized son and his broken bedroom door.

What an asshole. How dare he terrorize his own kids. Whatever Craig did didn't warrant that kind of explosive response from his dad. He was just a ten-year-old boy with such a good heart. How f'n dare he do that to him. Mike never apologized to me or to Craig. He just turned and walked away, with smoke billowing from his eyes and ears.

Years later, I read something that brought me right back to terrible times like this. It said something like: *Would you want your kids to marry someone like their dad?* The answer is—*HELL NO*.

I tried so hard to protect the kids from his fury. Somehow, I had failed to interrupt this fallout before it escalated to this traumatic level. Now, I found myself once again standing toe to toe with Mike, as he tried to exert his dominance over Craig by insisting that he quit wrestling. When I needed to be there for the kids—and stand fast and hard for them—I was. There was never a second thought. I would do whatever I could to stand between Mike's erratic behavior and his potential abuse of our kids.

He was mentally sick. He hated himself, and he was now taking his personal shortcomings out on the kids. So much for his promise to change after surviving the nail to the heart.

As for Craig, he went on to be an honor roll student all through high school—a three-sport athlete—and was even awarded the top two prestigious athletic honors the high school had: Male Senior Athlete of the Year and the Joe Hailey Award for the most exemplary athlete of the year. I was so proud of him. That little blip in middle school was just that—a blip.

Sports were so important to him. They made him a better student. I know that if he had quit wrestling like his dad wanted him to, his motivation for school would've taken a hit, and his grades would surely have suffered. One of his teachers in high school once told me that Craig would have done much better in her chemistry class if he wasn't in sports. I told her, "He did as well as he did because he was in sports."

Don't ever underestimate the importance of extracurricular activities. They provide the flavor in life and make following through on our primary obligations more palatable.

Mike was up and down when it came to sports. He didn't like me watching it and would rant and rant about how athletes made too much money and were privileged. He got so mad about Craig not quitting wrestling that he declared he would not go to any of his matches.

Eventually, as the next four years rolled on, Mike started to ease up a bit on his sports moratorium. He began attending Craig's wrestling matches and even came to the volleyball games and track meets that I was coaching. It looked like there might be some softening of his hatred for sports when he started coming around to the games.

It helped to take the edge off at home, since sports were important to both Craig and me. It was also a strong topic of conversation between us.

There were a few times when Mike would watch sports on TV, and it was usually when the Seattle Seahawks were on. He would allow himself to get emotional and cheer them on—as long as the Seahawks were playing well. When they weren't—when the Seahawks had a turnover or the other team was scoring on them—then Mike would go full-out mental.

Besides yelling at the team, he would get up out of his seat and pace back and forth somewhere just out of sight of the TV, but where he could still position himself to catch a glimpse of the game. He would get furious, send me dagger looks with his eyes, and rant about how "God doesn't like me. *They're* losing because God hates me." He would take the loss personally and let it reinforce the notion that the Universe was against him. *Yes, Mike, that's right—the Seattle Seahawks and the Universe purposely lost the game because they hate you. Let's all feel sorry for Mike because the Seahawks and God hate him.*

The best I could do was just ignore him. I felt fortunate that I was at least able to watch the game, and I intended to keep watching—regardless of whether he was upset at God and the team. His constant yelling and swearing made me work extra hard at ignoring him. He hated that I didn't pay him much attention during his rants. He would come back into the living room where I was watching and stand between me and the TV while yelling.

He was forcing me to acknowledge him. I would just look at him with no expression on my face, so I didn't feed into his hysterics. Then I would try to maneuver my gaze around him so I could watch the game. He was ruining the viewing experience for me, so my little piece of joy came from causing him more frustration by ignoring him. Put another check in the box for me!

The back and forth—hating sports, then being okay with them—was so annoying. He tried to make a case against athletes and their privileges and money. He would plant his little flag of integrity with his angry assertions and then later remove the flag when it benefited him. Just like moving the emotional goalposts on me to keep me off balance, this posturing about athletes would shift when it suited him. He lost credibility when he went back and forth with his opinions.

I believed he just lashed out at anyone he thought had more advantages than he did. It wasn't because they were athletes—it was because they had more money. He felt that he was more deserving of the big money than the athletes were because he was a fighter pilot and his job was dangerous. He was always operating from a perspective of lack instead of looking at all the abundance he already had. Because of that, he was never happy. He always wanted more, and he hated it if someone else had the "more" instead of him.

I still had to be vigilant when he would have his tirades directed toward the TV. I knew he was capable of snapping and then physically taking his frustrations out on me because I wasn't joining in on his meltdown. I had to constantly be aware of his proximity to me—and the real possibility that he would physically come after me. I may have looked calm, but my nerves were on high alert as I constantly monitored for any unexpected movement toward me.

Watching any television with him was not fun. He would often shout at the news or any sitcom that he thought was making fun of the men in the family. He would go off on a verbal assault about what was wrong with the world and how sitcoms were unfair to men, always making the woman look like the reasonable and smart one in the marriage.

I was trying to listen to the news or the TV show, and I couldn't follow along due to his loud rants. He would then turn to me and say, "What did they just say?" I couldn't hear anything with his yelling, so I would simply reply, "I don't know. I couldn't hear." Then he'd get upset again because I couldn't answer his question. Most of the time, I would just silently get up and walk away. This would prompt him to get mad at me again—how dare I reject him and walk away.

He had been the King of Rejection in our marriage, and he did not like that I took some of his power away by simply removing myself. I think back to all those times he would shut me down with his silent treatment and how I felt dismissed and devalued. Now he was getting a small portion of it from me, and he didn't like it.

The difference between me and him was that I actually had a reason to get up and leave—his constant yelling. He never had a reason to shut me out with his silence, except to keep me emotionally off balance.

He loved watching me chase him around the house, trying to get him to tell me what was wrong. He loved seeing me get upset. It was a power move. He never had a reason for his silence—it was always pure emotional manipulation and personal satisfaction that he could continue to exert some control over my emotional well-being.

But the times were slowly changing in my favor. He was starting to see that I was taking some of my power back, simply by removing myself from his presence—and he didn't like it. I was no longer chasing him down, begging him to tell me what was wrong. I was getting better at grey rocking, and it flustered him.

I may have ceded most of my boundaries to him earlier in our marriage, but I found myself creating new internal boundaries—boundaries where I refused to let his abusive antics penetrate me any more than they already had. Unbeknownst to him, I was gathering more of my energy back to me and getting stronger. Somewhere, deep inside, I saw myself planting my own flag—and I knew it was there to stay.

*   *   *   *   *   *   *   *   *   *   *

You've never been truly hated until you've been "loved" by a covert narcissist.   silenceofthenarcs

18. Ambitions and Old Girlfriends

I make myself a priority. I love and accept all of me. Everything works in my favor. I am enough exactly as I am. I deserve good things. I am whole and complete as I am. I am confident in my ability to create the life I want. My strength is greater than my challenges. The journey I'm on has a purpose. I am a treasure, and I treat myself as such. -DailyOM

Mike was forging his way through a new work reality—one where he now had to wear dress slacks instead of a flight suit. He was sitting behind a computer all day instead of being behind the controls of a fighter jet. Everything always seems fine during the honeymoon stage of a new job, but now that a year had passed, he was starting to come home on edge and was quick to start an argument.

Personalities in his office were starting to clash. His boss was asking more of Mike than what Mike felt his job description dictated. He would come home every night and loudly complain about the day's events, and I would sit quietly, letting him blow off steam. I tried to offer some words of encouragement, but he would just beat me down. He preferred to stay upset because it suited him to be the victim in his story.

One day after work, he came home and loudly declared that he was going to start drinking because work was so stressful. So, he pulled out a bottle of Gentleman Jack whiskey he had just bought, poured himself a drink, and slugged it back dramatically so I could see the show. When Mike came home from work, I would ask how his day was, and instead of answering me, he'd give me a dirty look and go directly to his bottle of whiskey and pour a drink. I wouldn't even comment. I just looked back down at my own work on the kitchen table as he walked silently into the family room to be alone.

Fine by me. Go be alone. I asked how work was, and he refused to answer. I had learned from many past experiences that chasing after him to talk was futile—it just gave him more power. I offered him the opportunity to vent, but he declined, so I didn't feel bad about just letting him walk away. Sometimes he would silently return, putting his glass down heavily so it made a sharp sound, and pour himself another drink, all the while looking to see if I would react. I usually kept my head down and ignored his dramatic display. Grey rocking was coming easier to me.

Eventually, Mike started talking about wanting to change professions. He had no self-confidence to go through traditional interviews, so he was looking for a way to work for himself. He asked me what I thought about him becoming a crop duster. He missed flying and thought he could make a living doing it. I had no confidence in this new profession, but I didn't share that with Mike. I learned a long time ago that he didn't respond well to difficult conversations. He had repeatedly shouted me down in the past if I dared to offer anything that might sound like criticism. His unhinged reactions had created an unsafe place for challenging conversations. So when he asked what I thought, I just said something like, "If that's what you want to do."

He proceeded to make the necessary arrangements to get his license, but I didn't realize it would cost $25K. He neglected to tell me that part. He took the money out of our investments and paid the guy for the lessons, then spent several weeks after work studying and flying with this old guy who made big promises to Mike.

I was always skeptical. Mike liked to have money to spend, and I didn't see how this profession would provide him with the income he would be happy with. But I just kept quiet. Mike had to find out one way or another for himself.

Mike eventually got to the point where he took the state exam and passed. Now it was time to try to find a job. The old guy who took our money had promised it would be easy. But that was not the case. Mike was very dejected when he realized the crop-dusting training was just a way for the old guy to make money. There wasn't anything legally Mike could do about it. He got his training, passed his exam, and the old guy could say Mike got his money's worth. Mike just didn't do enough research to realize crop-dusting wasn't going to be the answer.

I wasn't happy to see him fail, and I wasn't happy that $25K was lost on a foolish venture. It was the norm for him to find a way to waste our hard-earned money, but $25K lost with nothing to show except a license and no opportunity to recover the investment was foolish and reckless. I had been skeptical from the beginning, but if I had voiced my doubts, he would've used that against me when the plan failed. It was best that he found out on his own—even though it cost us $25K. At least Mike could believe I was supportive, and he couldn't blame me for this dead end.

Almost immediately, he pivoted to the idea of owning and operating his own welding business. He looked into courses at the community college and enrolled shortly after. Once again, he kept busy after work with classes at night and practiced welding at home. He always liked working with his hands and was very good at it, so this new focus kept him happy and gave him a positive outlet from the stress of his daily job.

I do give him credit for recognizing he needed a change and having the courage to pursue something else that might make him happier. But I had no confidence that it would pan out, because I knew he didn't have the discipline to own his own business. At least this distraction didn't cost as much as the crop-dusting fiasco.

Mike moved forward with the intention of making the welding business successful. He bought himself a work truck with storage panels on the side and came up with signage for advertisement that he placed on the outside of the truck. He applied for and received an LLC for his new business and started advertising his talents. He got a little bit of business right away, which made him happy—but he was already starting to run into the common issues faced when launching a small business.

He needed to get insurance to be bonded so he could have some financial protection in case a client sued him. He needed to set rates to make it profitable, but first, he had to sit down and figure out all the costs he needed to cover to turn a profit. I tried to stay out of any of his decisions. I knew that if it didn't work out, he could blame me for the failure of his business.

I did offer one point of view to consider when he was trying to come up with a competitive rate: he needed to be sure he was able to match his current income so he could keep living the life he was accustomed to.

This advice caused Mike to pause and think. He was not good at the details. He just wanted the emotions of what he thought owning his own business could bring. I knew he didn't have it in him to run a business and give up his primary job. But Mike was too obsessed with wanting people to like him, which meant he would give his services away for cheap just to manufacture a happy client. Of course, this meant he would bankrupt his business in no time. I knew this venture was another dead end, but I didn't stand in his way. I let him find out for himself that this wasn't going to solve his problems at work.

Mike eventually realized he wasn't cut out for it when he completed a welding job for a guy who complained that the sparks had flown over to his vehicle and left black marks on the paint. Mike was flustered by how to handle the complaints and the fact that the guy wouldn't pay for the job he'd performed. This was just par for the course when you own your own business. There will always be people who try to take advantage of you, and you have to have a plan in place. Mike didn't have a plan, and he left without getting paid.

I felt bad for him, but I saw it coming. I knew Mike didn't have the personality for owning his own business—but again, he had to find that out for himself.

I knew Mike was feeling poorly about himself, and I wasn't so cruel as to add salt to the wound. I'm sure I gave him a hug and told him it would be okay. Whatever I did in response allowed Mike to still maintain some self-respect. Instead of seeking work from unknown people, Mike kept his welding talents for those he knew. He picked up a little bit of money here and there welding hitches on trailers for a local guy who had a trailer business. That side diversion helped him manage the stress he was bringing home from work, so eventually his whiskey drinking started to ease up.

As Mike settled into a healthier rhythm at work, he started coming home in a good mood, telling me stories about his day and his new colleague, Laura. It was, "Laura this," and "Laura that." "You should see her high heels. She always has great heels."

I suppose if I were emotionally invested in our marriage, I might have become jealous with all the attention he was giving her. But I really didn't care. I was just going through the motions of being married until the kids were old enough to deal with the fallout. Besides, he was coming home in a good mood and not bothering me.

I thought back to when I found out he had contacted his high school girlfriend. I know that a person only does that when they're unhappy in the relationship they already have. I wasn't living up to Mike's expectations for a wife. He had repeatedly said he wanted me to dress up like Donna Reed from the 1950s—in a dress and heels while I did the housework. He was such a misogynistic asshole to want to put any woman in that demeaning position. Early television programming did a huge disservice to women's rights, and it perpetuated the idea that women had value only when serving their husbands.

Again, I should have been jealous when he told me he looked up his old girlfriend online. But I was already gone. She could have him. I'm sure he took my indifference as permission to do whatever he wanted, as proof that he owned me and that I wouldn't have the courage to stand against him.

What he didn't know was that I was continuing to take my power back—little by little—by not caring what he did.

My indifference gave Mike more incentive to continue his interactions with his "work wife." He would spend hours chatting with her on Facebook in the evening and even text back and forth with her while they were watching Dancing with the Stars together—in their own living rooms. I found it humorous to watch him interact with her so much. I marveled at how blatantly he gave the best of himself to someone else when he never had any of that same energy for me.

This is a form of emotional abandonment. When one person gives their best energy and effort to others and not to their spouse or partner, they are abandoning you on an emotional level. I had spent over twenty years believing he would change and become more loving to me. I had allowed myself to believe I was in love with him, when in truth I was only in love with the potential of who he could be.

And here he was, showing that loving potential to someone else—because she didn't know his truth. He could put on a show for her like he did with me before we were married, and she would think he was the most wonderful guy. He was getting fuel from her. He was getting a woman to laugh at his jokes and smile at him when he walked into the room.

I didn't care. She could have him. But another thought entered my mind—if the tables were turned, he would never tolerate me giving this kind of emotional attention to another man. He was so hypocritical. But narcissists only see how a situation benefits them. He had no empathy. He didn't have the capacity to put himself in my position and see how I might feel about the extra attention he was giving someone else.

I knew he would never have sex with her. He didn't have the guts or the self-confidence to promote himself to another woman in that way. But even if he did, I wouldn't care. In fact, if he did follow through with physical infidelity, it would give me what I needed to leave. I could tell the kids why I left—and they would understand.

It wasn't concern for his marriage vows that kept him from cheating. Hell, no. He broke those years ago when he didn't tell me about his cross-dressing and when he unleashed a barrage of abusive tactics on me. No, our marriage vows were not what kept him from having a full-on affair. What held him back was fear—fear that he wouldn't live up to the lovemaking part, and that the other woman would see through him. He was afraid of being humiliated and discarded.

His continued after-work interactions with Laura were becoming more brazen. I only discovered the extent of it because Mike was confident enough in my indifference to tell me. Apparently, Laura's brother had been watching their chats on Facebook and realized how inappropriate they were. Mike came down the stairs after chatting with her and proudly told me that her brother had chastised him, saying, *"Your* wife would not be happy with *this."*

Mike just laughed at the accusation and, with pride and smugness, told me that he'd replied, "My wife knows—and she doesn't care."

Yes, he was so proud of the fact that I didn't say anything about his extra attention to her—and he bragged about it to Laura's brother. Of course, I knew. And ultimately, I didn't care—because I didn't love him anymore. I also knew Mike was incapable of understanding that maybe his *own* wife would like the loving attention he was giving someone else.

A healthy marriage would never entertain this kind of emotional relationship with someone outside the marriage. But ours wasn't healthy—and he wasn't capable of seeing anyone's needs except his own, or unless it benefited him in some way. His after-work interactions with Laura fed his weak ego, and he was feeling on top of the world.

His relationship with Laura kept evolving into deeper layers as he continued to fill me in on all things related to her: how she was training for a marathon, working on her master's, her endless supply of gorgeous high heels. How her husband was lazy and inept with repairs around the house. How her parents lost all their money to some fraudulent investment scheme.

Yes, he was comfortable telling me all about Laura and her family. And again—I wasn't jealous. I was just continually amused by how, if the tables were turned, he would not tolerate *any* of it.

Sometime around 2010, Laura and I found ourselves at the same baby shower for a friend. Mike found out about it before the event and kept urging me to get to know her. "You should meet. I've told her about you and how you painted the entry and the kitchen." The baby shower happened to be up the street, and Mike wanted me to take her to the house so she could see the updates. I was rolling my eyes in my head. I had no desire to get to know her. I had nothing in common with her—except Mike—and that didn't say much.

At the baby shower, I quickly introduced myself and then sat with other friends. I could see her out of the corner of my eye, looking at me—and looking often. I knew what was going on in her head. She wanted to know what kind of person Mike was married to. He had been courting Laura outside of work, and she enjoyed his attention.

Even I enjoyed his attention way back before we were married. I'm sure she had gone to bed many nights with fantasies of Mike, and now here we were, in the same room for the first time—and she couldn't stop looking in my direction. Mike had already told Laura that I would bring her by the house after the baby shower, so I reluctantly arranged for her to follow me on the short drive home. After quickly showing her the entryway and kitchen I had just painted, I indicated that I was ready to go to bed—so she left.

It was a weird meeting between the two of us. Mike loved the fact that we met. I'm sure he thought it would help pave the way for us all to get together sometime in the future so he could sanitize his relationship with her by having me there. Yippee. I'm so excited. I'm so excited at the prospect of hanging out with his "work wife" and getting to know her. I was so excited to be put in a situation that Mike would never tolerate if I did that to him.

I realized that Mike looking up his old girlfriend on the internet—and then having a casual affair with a colleague from work—was the obvious result of me reacting less and less to his outrageous behavior and distancing myself from him more and more. Mike wasn't getting the same attention from me, whether in the positive form of adulation or the negative form of reacting to his abuse. I was slowing the flow of any attention given to him, and he was trying to get his supply from somewhere else.

Fine with me. I had nothing left to give. The wall I had built inside me from years of mental, emotional, and psychological trauma was holding firm. I had given way too much of myself over the years and had gotten very little back from him. This wall allowed me to protect what I had left and gave me the strength to stay in this hell until I knew the kids would be okay.

I was having a relatively easy life with Mike's female distractions, and I enjoyed that someone else was filling in for me. But Mike wouldn't tolerate my indifference much longer. He always found a way to shake things up if he suspected I was pulling away. And it didn't take long for Mike to manufacture his storm cloud and demand the attention he craved from me.

How did it happen?

The usual way—by dropping a grenade and then walking away.

*   *   *   *   *   *   *   *   *   *   *

If you have to hurt other people in order to feel powerful, you are an extremely weak individual.

11.eleven.eleven.11

19. Sleeping at the High School

I am proud of all the hard days that I survived. I have faith that I will feel like myself again. I am confident in the face of adversity. Very soon, I'll smile and say, "This is even greater than I ever prayed for." -universe.guidance

It was the end of October 2010. I was near the end of volleyball season, where I was the head coach, and we were heading to the state playoffs. Coaching and teaching high school science at the same time is exhausting. I only know one way to operate when I make a commitment—and that's 110%. I had to get to school early every morning to have both my science lessons and labs ready, to fold the volleyball laundry, and to plan for the day's practice—or get the bus ready to drive the team to their next match. Many mornings, I would be at school by 6 a.m. or earlier, and I wouldn't get home until around 10 p.m., especially on days with away matches. I would then sit at the kitchen table grading papers and reviewing game film to prepare for the next day.

That particular volleyball season, I didn't have a JV coach, and the principal expected me to coach both squads. It was exhausting to prepare for two separate team practices, drive the bus to events, and then stand on my feet for the duration of both the JV and varsity matches. I knew this wasn't ideal for me—or for the girls who were counting on their coach to show up 100% for them every day. But I made it work, even though I came home completely drained.

Even though Mike said he hated sports, he would sometimes come to the volleyball matches to watch. If not for that, we would have seen very little of each other. That was okay with me—I didn't have to be exposed to Mike's ever-changing mood swings. The stress of my schedule was predictable, and I could manage it. Mike was the one who was unpredictable. I never knew which way the wind would blow. Even after walking on eggshells for the past twenty-some years trying not to trigger him, he would always find a way to inject his dark energy into my life, causing my emotions to spin out of control.

It was always easier for me to deal with the stress I had manufactured than to stay on constant alert for the debris field that would rain down on me whenever Mike decided I wasn't giving him enough attention.

It was after eight in the evening, and I was at home in the kitchen, going over the last volleyball game film when he came down the stairs. He stood in his usual spot—whenever he decided to pull the pin on a grenade—leaning against the kitchen counter, right hand on his hip. He said, very clearly and with a tone of disgust: "I don't love you anymore. I haven't loved you for a long time. You wonder why I don't even want to touch you."

And then he just left. He walked through the kitchen, past me, into the living room, and back around the other side to head straight back upstairs.

Kaboom.

I was stunned. You'd think I would have said to myself, "*Good* riddance," but years of trauma burn a path of familiar tracks in your brain, and I found myself on autopilot as my fight-or-flight emotions took hold of me again. I got up from my chair in the kitchen and followed him through the living room and toward the stairs, calling after him—something like, "I know you still love me."

Now my mind was racing. Where do I go from here? How do I sleep next to someone who has just declared—through both words and tone—that I disgust him? I was done with his emotional bombshells that ripped me apart. I wasn't going to spend the night in the house with him, so I started packing.

After I cleared my coaching materials from the kitchen table, I went upstairs to grab a few things. Mike was busy playing computer games in the office just off the bedroom, and I knew he wouldn't see me packing. I was slightly amused by how he could drop such a huge bombshell and then casually start playing games as if nothing had happened. He was a master at that. Clearly, he wasn't bothered by the sentiment he'd just delivered.

I grabbed a bag and stuffed it with some clothes and my makeup for the night. I quietly went back downstairs, grabbed my coat, purse, and school backpack, and prepared to leave.

Our beautiful dog, Xena, was by my side, looking confused. I decided to take her with me—because I feared that, once Mike realized I was gone, he might take it out on the dog, as he had threatened to do many times before.

Out to the car we went—Xena thinking it was a grand adventure, and me not sure where I was headed. I decided to call Mike and let him know I'd left. I could have just let him discover it on his own, but something told me to give Turd Head the courtesy of knowing I was gone.

When Mike answered the phone, I said, *"I just wanted you to know that I've left—and I took the dog with me."*

Mike's tone immediately shifted from the disgust he'd shown earlier to a contrite, apologetic one. "Why? You know I don't mean what I say. You know that I'm all wind—I didn't mean it. Don't go."

I calmly replied, "I don't know when I'll be back. You should be happier now that I'm gone."

And then I hung up—and kept driving toward town.

I left so fast that I didn't take my hairdryer, so I decided to go to the local Walmart to pick up any needed supplies. As I drove into town, I went right past the high school, and it dawned on me that I could sleep there. The science department had a kitchen with a microwave and a small refrigerator, so I knew I could have an easy breakfast if I needed it. Also, one of the science teachers, John, had a sofa in his office, and I could sleep there—but I'd need a blanket and a pillow. John was also someone who got to school early, like I did, so I knew I'd have to be up super early and out of his office before he arrived.

My list for Walmart grew as I walked through the store and started looking for what I needed. I found a blanket, a pillow, a hairdryer, and a small rug for Xena to sleep on. I remember running into some of my old students while I was shopping and thinking how crazy it was to pretend that all was well in my world while I was buying survival items. I stopped by the deli and picked up a couple of chicken tenders for dinner—and made sure to get an extra one for Xena.

It was now getting close to 9:30 in the evening as Xena and I arrived at the school. Fortunately, because I was a coach, I had a master key that let me into the building. Xena and I walked down the long, dark hallway toward the science department, where I would be sleeping for the next few days. It was very quiet, as it should be, with only the sound of Xena's nails clicking against the floor as we made our way to the sofa in John's office.

I put the rug down for Xena, placed the pillow on the sofa, and pulled the blanket over my fully clothed body. I set the alarm on my phone for 5:00 a.m. so I'd be up and out of the office before John arrived. I could see

Xena in the glow of my phone, looking up at me with a question on her face—wondering why we were sleeping here. I reached down and stroked her head, trying to comfort both her and myself as I attempted to make sense of what had just happened.

I was so glad I left. Even though I was a refugee from my own home, I knew it was the right thing to do. I was so fed up with his crap, and he needed to be alone in the stew he made for himself.

Fortunately, the kids were out of the house. Jillian was in grad school in Wilmington. Claire had gotten married two years earlier, had a baby, and was living in Hawaii with her naval husband. Craig was finishing up his undergrad degree at UNC-Asheville. Only Mike and I were consistently living in the house at that time, so the kids weren't around to be affected by this fallout.

As I lay there trying to find calm in my head, I brought myself back to two years earlier when Mike had laid another grenade at my feet. As usual, there was no warning or predictor for his abusive manipulation of my emotions.

Craig was home from college during the holidays and had joined me in the kitchen, where I was baking cookies and watching a fun holiday movie, The Out-of-Towners, with Steve Martin and Goldie Hawn. There was one scene near the end of the movie where Steve Martin's character found himself in an elevator with a random stranger on the way to an important interview. Steve Martin's character had a brief anxiety attack and almost refused to get off the elevator—until the stranger said, very creepily, "You don't understand us. We are one now."

That prompted Steve Martin's character to snap out of his anxiety and bolt out of the elevator—away from the creepy stranger.

Craig and I were laughing at the scene when Mike walked in and wanted to know what we were laughing about. I tried to explain the moment, and Craig and I both ended up saying, "We are one now," at the same time, which prompted us to laugh all over again.

Mike walked away but came back after the movie was over, once I was alone. When we were by ourselves in the kitchen, Mike lit into me with the most disgusting accusation.

He stood in the doorway between the kitchen and the living room, his whole body tense, his face tightened, and his eyes dark and menacing. I had seen this body language so many times—I knew he was on a mission to destroy my moment and my day. My body immediately went into survival mode as I put up my invisible shield to protect myself from the oncoming deluge of unhinged accusations.

He repeated the line from the movie—*We are one now*—and told me I was disgusting, that it *proved* I was having an incestuous relationship with our son.

Hold on now. What did he just say? Did he just accuse me of having an incestuous relationship with our son?

What the hell?

How disgusting. He was the disgusting one. How does anyone let their mind wander into such a repulsive idea? There is no way Mike could actually believe what he just said. No way. What an evil, sickening ploy to get attention, gain emotional control over me, and triangulate me with our son.

Mike had just effectively destroyed the holidays—again. And no doubt he walked away very pleased with himself, knowing that he had rocked me to my core. I hated him for making me question any loving feelings a mother would naturally have for her son. Because of what he said, I didn't dare hug my son for several years.

What a sick bastard.

That memory from a couple of years ago came flooding back as I lay there now, wondering what kind of evil possesses someone to make such bold, provocative, and revolting claims—knowingly causing emotional distress to the person they swore to love and protect. I could not comprehend how he could say something so despicable and then walk away as if nothing had happened, expecting me to just forget about it.

"You know I just blow hot air. *You* know I didn't mean it."

I tried to settle into my new surroundings with dear Xena by my side and eventually fell asleep.

My alarm woke me at 5:00 a.m., and I quickly put the blanket and pillow away in a closet in my classroom. I took Xena with me to the faculty bathroom, changed, fixed my hair and makeup, and was out of the school by 5:30, before any teachers arrived.

As I drove away with Xena by my side, I noticed the frost on the ground that had accumulated overnight—and the bare spot where my car had been parked. I worried someone would notice and figure out that my car had been there overnight and start asking questions. There was nothing I could do about it now, so I drove to get some coffee and waited for Mike to leave for work.

I realized I couldn't keep Xena with me at school, so I had to take her back home before the day started and take advantage of being there to grab some extra clothes. I hoped I could do all of that and still get back to school before the first bell—but I didn't want to run into Mike on his way out.

Eventually, I dared to drive back home. I kept a watchful eye in case Mike saw me and turned around to confront me at the house. Fortunately, I didn't see him, and he wasn't there when I arrived. I was able to put Xena in her kennel outside and grab a few more things for myself.

I didn't know how long I'd be staying at the high school. My mind was still whirling from the fallout of the night before. I wasn't capable of planning beyond one day at a time, and I had to get back to work. Thankfully, I made it back in plenty of time before classes started, and no one said anything about the only parking space without frost.

I made it through the day, held volleyball practice after school, then pretended to leave to go home. I picked up something to eat for dinner and made my way back to the school, now empty once again. This time, I parked my car in a different spot so no one would notice the telltale patch of frostless asphalt the next morning.

I went to my classroom, where I spent the evening watching a movie on the television and planning for the next day's class and volleyball practice. I worried about Xena. I hated that she was home alone with Mike. I didn't know what he might do to her—if anything—but I had to take care of myself.

Jillian was in the habit of calling and talking to me every night, and this night was no different. I didn't tell her that I was not sleeping at home. I tried to keep the kids away from the fray between their dad and me. We chatted like usual, and then I made plans to visit her in Wilmington for the weekend. I was going to leave right after school on Friday. It would be a place I could stay while I tried to figure out what my next move was with Mike.

I understand that it may seem to anyone reading this that, since the kids weren't at home, this would be a great time for me to leave him. I thought about that. But the kids were not yet ready to handle the truth about their dad. Craig was almost done with UNC-Asheville and was planning to enter the Marine Corps to fly jets like his father. I felt that any disruption at home could interfere with his finishing up his studies and might compromise his transition into the Marine Corps.

Jillian had completed her master's degree at UNC-Wilmington the previous spring and was frustrated that the recession of 2008 was stunting her ability to land a "big-girl" job. She was calling every day to vent and to tell me how little progress or hope there was for her. She was trying to navigate this economic climate with a master's degree but had only been able to find two part-time jobs—working as a cashier at Best Buy and as an archivist at a local historical foundation.

Claire was living in Hawaii and had just had a baby. I had flown out in August to spend a week with her right before school started. She was doing great in her marriage, and I felt she would be able to handle the truth—but the other two were still vulnerable. As much as I wanted to leave, I felt that Jillian and Craig would suffer from the fallout, so I put myself on hold.

I had spent Tuesday and Wednesday night at the high school. None of my colleagues suspected anything. But Thursday morning, John caught me sleeping in his office. I hadn't expected him to be at work so early, so I was surprised. He was kind enough not to ask about it, and I went about my day as usual.

When school was out, I dashed home quickly to grab a new set of clothes. I was planning to take enough for the weekend when I went to visit Jillian. As I was rushing through the house, I saw Mike pulling into the driveway.

He had noticed that I'd been coming and going the last couple of days, and he was trying to get home quickly to catch me before I left.

I wasn't ready to talk to him. He followed me around the house, trying to be sweet as I moved quickly toward the front door. I didn't say much, if anything. He wanted to get together for dinner and talk. I must have agreed, because later that evening we met at a local barbecue restaurant and had our first conversation since I left on Tuesday.

I basically told him that I was done with his B.S., and that over the course of our marriage I had changed—I had become a totally different person, someone I didn't even recognize or like. I told him I had tried my best to make him happy at the expense of my own happiness. He just sat there with contrite eyes, nodding yes to everything I said.

I told him I was going to spend the weekend with Jillian, and that if he ever threatened to leave me again, he'd better be sure—because I would not be coming back.

This was the first time I had the courage to give him any kind of ultimatum. He had already threatened to leave me numerous times and had put my body and soul through such a traumatic spin that I was no longer going to tolerate it. He was warned—and I intended to follow through.

He acted as though he believed me. He seemed contrite and didn't offer any defense for what he'd done the other night. But he also didn't apologize for it, either.

He had promised to change so many times in the past, and then he would alter his behavior for a little while—just long enough for me to believe he was changing. I wanted the original version of the person I married so badly that I allowed myself to believe it. Then I would let my emotional guard down and start believing he had really changed. I would live for a short while in that manufactured fantasy—until he started chipping away at me, little by little. Then, when he had me emotionally hooked again, he would spin around and turn into the most evil, vile being.

I had no real hope that he would change for good. I knew he wouldn't. I was just hoping to be able to stand it a little longer—until Craig got into the Marine Corps and Jillian was able to land a big-girl job. But if he ever threatened to leave me again, I was going to take him up on it, even if Jillian and Craig weren't fully on solid ground yet. At least I would be able to tell the kids that *he* was the one who ended the marriage, and they wouldn't have to hear the sordid details of what I'd been enduring all these years.

I spent that weekend with Jillian, and I believe I told her a little bit about her dad being a turd and that I didn't want him coming with me to Wilmington. Jillian quickly understood my vague explanations because she had seen a lot since Claire got married and Craig had gone off to school. Being just a couple of hours away, Jillian would often come home on weekends when she wasn't working. She had seen enough of her dad's selfishness and self-centeredness—clearer now through her adult eyes—so she understood what I was saying without me having to get into the ugly details.

It was a great weekend. I had access to a shower, and I didn't have to worry about a grenade exploding at my feet. Jillian and I window-shopped, went to antique stores, and watched movies. I was reluctant to go home and face Mike, but I knew I needed to confront this new phase of our marriage—and I wasn't sure what it would look like. I was also worried about my dear Xena, since I hadn't been home for a while. I knew she was missing me and likely living in her own fear of Mike.

We got Xena and her brother Ozzie as pups in the summer of 2001. It had been five and a half years since Briggs passed away before we decided to get another Boxer. Ozzie and Xena came from a puppy mill, and I felt sorry for them, so we got both instead of just one. They were pals and kept each other entertained when we were too busy to do so.

One night, when Mike was in the garage practicing welding and the dogs were outside watching him, I called Mike in to take a phone call. The call happened to be from his asshole friend who had sexually assaulted me back on the Fourth of July in 1990. I was hoping Mike would take the opportunity to finally tell him off—but no. Mike had a polite conversation with Ken and hung up without ever mentioning how disgusting it was for him to have grabbed my breasts.

The call lasted just a few minutes, and then Mike went back outside to continue welding. Xena showed up at the corner of the garage to watch, but not Ozzie. I walked all around the house and yard, calling for him, but he didn't show. We got concerned, so everyone came outside and started looking. Eventually, we found Ozzie on the other side of the highway from our house—dead. He must have been hit by a speeding car, since the distance from where we found his collar to where we found his body in the ditch was quite a stretch.

We had an invisible fence around the yard that gave off an electrical current, and both dogs were wearing their electronic collars. Lately, Ozzie had been busting through the electric field, enduring the shock just so he could explore beyond the yard. That night, he took advantage of us being distracted by the phone call to explore again. What a sorrowful evening that turned out to be.

Xena became the only dog in the house, and she showed signs of missing her brother's companionship. She was always looking for extra love and pats on the head—and I made sure she got them. I would sit on the floor so she could rest her head in my lap, and together we'd watch a movie and enjoy each other's company. Xena became very close to me and looked to me to protect her from Mike.

Whenever Mike got into an ugly mood and started shouting at me, Xena would start to shake and cower away. Mike hated it. Instead of recognizing that his tirades were causing the trauma in Xena, he would just yell at her even more, shouting things like, "Look at that cowardly dog. Look at her shake. She is such a wus." Or, "That goddamned dog is shaking again. I'll give her something to shake about." Then he would lunge toward her to intimidate her, and she would scurry back—her poor little nails slipping on the wood floor beneath her feet as she tried to get away.

I would step in and grab Xena by the collar, pulling her toward me where I knew she would feel safer.

My dear Xena was exhibiting outwardly what I had been enduring inwardly all these years. I understood where her tremors came from, even if Mike was too self-involved to see—or care. I hated leaving Xena behind at the house this past week while I was sleeping at the high school, but I had no way to properly care for her. I'd been concerned about her well-being all week and was hoping she would be okay when I got back home on Sunday evening.

On the two-hour drive back to the house, I thought about what I was going to do once I got there. I needed to do laundry and get ready for school the next day. Those were easy chores to keep me preoccupied. I had already decided that I wasn't going to sleep in the same bed as Mike. After all, he had said he didn't love me anymore, that he hadn't loved me for a long time, and that he didn't even want to touch me.

How do you climb back into bed with someone like that?

I had done it so many times before, always with concern for my own safety after the many times he intimidated me and made me feel less-than. The kids were home during those times, but now it was just me and him. I decided I was going to sleep in one of the other bedrooms.

I found Xena happy to see me, and I let her sleep with me in the extra bedroom. I slept the next few nights with Xena nearby and had very few words for him during the day. He had stripped me of any love or compassion I might have once had for him, and I was not ready to join him back in bed.

After the fourth night, I decided to find my way back to our bedroom. I really didn't want to be in the same bed with him, but I wanted to take away any story he could tell anyone—including himself—that he was now the victim. I had taken more of my power back from him, and I was just biding my time, waiting for the kids to be on solid ground before I left.

Things were very different between us after that episode. Mike knew he was on thin ground with me, and I had taken a big step forward by drawing a clear line in the sand for his behavior. I knew he would try to show me that he was changing—and I also knew I wouldn't allow myself to believe it. I was just playing the long game, waiting for Jillian and Craig to be on steady footing.

I was getting closer to my exit and regaining my freedom. I was determined to keep my energies focused on when that glorious day would come.

*   *   *   *   *   *   *   *   *   *   *

NARCISSISTS HATE: boundaries, being ignored, being wrong, criticism (constructive or not), people figuring out who they are behind the mask, being vulnerable, taking accountability, apologizing, being real, anyone who challenges their façade, not having power and control.

Maria Consiglia/@understandingthenarc

20. It's Not You, It's Me

*Loving myself is my greatest gift. I choose to love myself,
even on hard days.*

-GROWTH GEM

I was having dreams about our house falling down. It was about a year before Mike dropped his bombshell that led me to sleep at the high school. As I look back, I believe those dreams were symbolic of our marriage. It was the Universe's way of saying, "Get out"—out of both the house and the marriage. However, since I wasn't ready to leave the marriage at that time, the best I could do was just get out of the house.

We had kept up with the repairs, but it seemed like there was always something that needed to be done—something out of my skill set. That meant I had to rely more and more on Mike to get it done.

Mike was very handy and skilled with any kind of construction. I could trust that if he did something, it would be done correctly and we wouldn't have to revisit it. But he was getting increasingly annoyed with fixing problems around the house. I hated having to point out issues because it would set him off into a tantrum that was always directed at me. Somehow, he made all the problems my fault.

But I kept having those dreams of the house falling down—with us in it. It bothered me enough that I was able to convince Mike we needed to fix up the house and sell it.

In the beginning, Mike was all in. He was looking forward to having a house with a two-car garage or a workshop for his tools. With that motivation, it didn't take much to get him on board to renovate the house. One of the biggest updates we decided to tackle was removing the carpet in the living room. We replaced it, along with the entryway and stairs, with hardwood floors. It was a big transformation and much needed—but there were some issues along the way.

Mike had a hard time removing the old wood floors in the entryway because they were glued down. Unfortunately, he ended up having to remove the entire subfloor. It was a crazy sight to see Mike standing on the dirt in the crawl space under the house, trying to repair and replace it. He was not a happy guy, and he would lash out at me for the extra headache, as if I were the cause of it.

He'd put on his best-worst scrunched-up face of disgust and purse his lips tight as he glared straight through me. I kept a stone face and refused to engage with his baiting. I knew it was frustrating to discover the subfloor needed replacing before he could install the new floor. I tried to give him some slack for his outward attitude—but there was no justification for putting the angst on me.

I really did appreciate Mike's skill and talents, and I only wished I didn't have to ask him to do anything. He made me feel like he was doing me a huge favor—and that he expected repayment of some kind when it was over. It took a couple of days to replace the floors, but they eventually got done—and they looked great.

Even with the beautiful floors in place and that big task behind us, Mike started losing interest in getting the house ready to sell. Instead, he gave up his free time to help Laura, his work wife, with updates and repairs around her house.

Every weekend, for quite some time, he would head to Laura's house with his tools and supplies to fix whatever she wanted done. Laura had a husband, a brother, and a brother-in-law who could have helped her—but Mike, with his huge ego, felt like he was the only one who could do the job correctly.

Meanwhile, we had plenty of projects piling up around our house, but Mike didn't seem to have time for them because he was busy fulfilling his obligations to Laura.

He would come home and excitedly recap all that he had completed for her. He was feeling rather full of himself after a long weekend of showing off his handyman skills and flexing his testosterone in front of Laura. His weekly reports of accomplishments at her house were also peppered with opinions about her husband. Mike thought he was lazy and unskilled.

He used his opinion of her husband as justification for why he was spending so much time at her house: "He doesn't know what he's doing." And, "He just sits around and drinks beer."

It was obvious Mike thrived on getting attention from Laura and fixing things for her. Since I wasn't giving him the attention he craved, he needed new fuel for his fragile ego—and he found it in Laura.

Please understand—I always complimented Mike on the work he did. He was amazing at pretty much any project he tackled. But most of the time, he'd throw my compliments back at me: "No, I'm not talented," or, "I suck." He wouldn't accept the praise. He just wanted to be the "poor guy" who doesn't do anything right—just so I'd repeat the compliment.

But eventually, my compliments and my attention were no longer enough to fill his ego.

I can imagine he was getting his fill of praise from Laura by exhibiting his masculine skills for his fantasy wife to see. And I'm sure Laura was very appreciative of the attention he gave to her home. Any expression of gratitude from her made Mike feel powerful and superior—even above her own husband. That would have been important to Mike—to think he could fulfill a need for Laura that her husband couldn't.

He wanted Laura to think of *him* first if something needed fixing. He wanted to be her fantasy and savior.

You would think that maybe I would be jealous of the time he spent with Laura and the attention he gave her. I really didn't care. She could have him. I was just very disappointed that he was putting his energies into helping someone else fix up their house instead of ours. I was hoping to get the house on the market in the spring of 2011, and here we were, approaching fall and the start of my volleyball season. I was limited in what I could do, but I went ahead and started completing the minor updates without any assistance from Mike.

I painted all the bedrooms and installed crown molding in three of the four rooms. I cleaned out and painted all the closets. I took advantage of pulling everything out before I painted and made piles of stuff to get rid of or sell in a yard sale. Since volleyball was starting, I had to squeeze all these projects into whatever free time I had, so we'd be ready to put the house on the market in March. Eventually, I had to stop the updates when volleyball season picked up, and then the holidays arrived soon after.

This was about the same time Mike dropped his bombshell that led me to sleep at the high school. When I finally came back home after that damaging event, it was early November, and Mike was in a pouty and morose mood. He may have promised to change his behavior, but he had sunk into a self-pity state where he'd give a look of disgust, not say a word to me, and sequester himself in the family room to watch TV.

I wasn't going to go anywhere near him. I had school, the holidays, and plans for getting the house ready to sell. I was way too busy moving forward with life, while he was content sitting in and drowning in his own self-made misery.

It took me by surprise when he suddenly walked into the kitchen where I was working and told me he was going to get some counseling. I was surprised because it takes a strong sense of self-awareness to realize you need help—and Mike had never shown that before. Mike fully believed that he was always right, always justified in whatever he said or did to me. He never apologized. He never accepted accountability for his abusive behavior. Instead, he bullied, shamed, and guilted me into submission, and then got me to apologize for something I hadn't even done—just to end the torment.

It was his way of maintaining control. He never exhibited self-awareness. I was curious how he came to the decision to see a counselor, but I didn't dare ask. Partly because I feared he'd blow up, and partly because I just didn't care. Good, I thought. Maybe this will help him to heal his own traumas and stop taking his perceived shortcomings out on me.

Mike began going to counseling once or twice a week. He would come home, silently pull out a book, and sit in front of the fire reading for the evening. For me, it was peaceful. There was no yelling, no tirades, no intimidation—just quiet reflection. I found myself grabbing a book and sitting next to him, reading quietly as well. The peace was good for my body. I enjoyed the stillness and the lack of drama.

After a few sessions, Mike came home and said the counselor would like me to attend the next session with him. I was happy to help in any way I could. I was proud of him for taking this step, and I was willing to play my part to support his mental healing. I hoped, for his sake, he could find a way to change. I was still determined to leave him—because I had been cut too deeply, too many times, over more than twenty years of abuse. But I hoped the counseling would help him become a happier person.

We got to the session, and the counselor let Mike talk and set the topic for discussion.

Almost immediately, Mike started talking about how I won't wear high heels or put on a dress for him. I sat silently in shock. He continued for a few minutes about how I seemingly refused to fulfill this simple request. He was very clear that he interpreted my not dressing up for him as a sign that I didn't love him.

I sat and listened to his misogynistic drivel, laughing to myself internally. Does he really hear what he's saying? This? This is the reason for all the hate and abuse over the years? Because I didn't get dressed up for him when I came home from work? Really?

Are you kidding me?

All his angst toward me, all his mental instability, his untreated depression—it all boiled down to heels? Did he truly believe this somehow justified his behavior? Was he laying all blame on me, simply because I wouldn't dress up for him at home?

Did he not see how ridiculously submissive he wanted me to be? His insistence that I dress up for him was akin to wanting a concubine. A sex slave. Did he not see that he was exposing himself as someone who had little to no respect for his wife? That he saw me not as a partner, but as a tool—something to use for boosting his own power and ego?

He was painting himself perfectly as an abuser while trying to position me as the problem. As if I was the one resisting efforts to mend the marriage.

The counselor let Mike talk, and then she turned to me for my response. Even though I was totally disgusted with his view of me and our marriage—and even though I was laughing inside—I was very careful and respectful with my response. After all, I had years of practice at not adding fuel to his fire and being calculated with the words I spoke so that I wouldn't trigger him. I wanted to tell him how totally disgusting and demeaning his request was, but instead, I carefully pointed out several rational and logical reasons why I wouldn't comply.

First, my days were extremely long—being on my feet almost all day teaching and coaching. I pointed out that there were many nights in a workweek when I didn't get home until after eight o'clock or later, and the last thing I wanted to do was change into heels and a dress just so he could fulfill his own twisted fantasy.

Second, I had tried to find dresses for myself, but everything sucked. The dresses I saw were either poor quality, overpriced, ugly styles, or the wrong colors. I didn't have the time to make my own dress because of teaching and coaching. Plus—and I kept this last reason to myself—I felt like Mike's insistence that I dress up for him was his way of getting me to buy new clothes so he could wear them when I wasn't around. I already suspected that he was wearing my clothes, and it made me sick to think that he was parading around and fantasizing in them.

The counselor quietly listened to both of us and then offered this solution: "When was the last time you took your wife on a date? A real date, where the two of you dress up and make reservations? You could schedule the date for several weeks out. This would allow Pam enough time to look for a dress. There could be some excitement as the day gets closer and as you both prepare to dress up for each other."

What a great idea! He could take me out on a date! Up to that point, the best he ever did—besides dressing up for the Marine Corps Birthday Ball—was take me to a Chinese buffet for our anniversary. He always laughed about how lame our anniversary dinner was to his friends and family. He never planned out special times to be with me. He never planned anything special for Valentine's Day, my birthday, Mother's Day, or any other day. Doing something special for me was nowhere on his mind or in his heart. Because he had no empathy for anyone, he couldn't put himself in anyone else's position to see how they would feel. All he could see was what was in it for him. Why would he want to take me out and make me feel special when he's the one who wants to be the center of attention? I should be making him feel special.

I didn't care about going out with him. I didn't want to pretend that I enjoyed his company. He could never give me sincere compliments because he saw everything between us as a competition. I wasn't in love with him—I was only "in habit" with him. I came with him to the counseling appointment because I genuinely cared about him getting mentally healthy. I didn't come thinking we could save our marriage. But what I really wasn't prepared for was to find out that his main angst—the main reason for his brooding, sullen moods and his layers of abuse—was because I didn't wear heels for him.

Holy cow. You've got to be kidding.

Mike sat still, expressionless, with his eyes exhibiting a blank stare as he listened to the counselor suggest he take me out on a special date night. I could see the stone wall he was putting up to keep the counselor's insight from reaching him. It was apparent to me that Mike was not getting the support from the counselor he had hoped for. He pretty much shut down after that and didn't add much more to the topic. I don't remember if the counselor talked about anything else, and we left soon after.

On the way home from the session, it was mostly quiet. Eventually, Mike spoke up and said, "I now know it's not you. It's me."

Hell, yeah, it's you! How could you ever think that any of this madness was my fault? How could you even think that all these ugly issues would simply go away if I just wore heels? What an emotionally immature point of view from an emotionally immature person. If Mike was thinking I was going to chime in and contradict his statement, he was wrong. My silence at his revelation was my agreement that I wasn't the problem—he was.

It finally dawned on me: Mike didn't go to counseling because he believed he needed help. No. Mike went to counseling to get verification that I was the problem and not him. When the counselor didn't support his point of view but, in turn, suggested he take me out on a date, he felt deflated.

Did Mike ever make a date to take me out after that? No. Never. He never wanted the marriage to get better for the sake of the marriage—he just wanted me to be his servant and submit to him. He was hoping the counselor would support him in this so he'd have proof from a professional that I was the one falling short in the marriage. Him wanting me to put on a dress and heels after I got home from work is one of the most disgusting, misogynistic, and demeaning requests a man could ever make of a woman.

How did I ever get caught up with this monster?

Because Mike didn't get the support from the counselor he expected, he quit going. His ego couldn't handle the fact that he wasn't perfect and that he wasn't married to—in his words—"Donna Reed." Now we were heading into the holidays with a gloomy dark cloud hanging over us by the name of Mike.

Oh joy! Another holiday season walking on eggshells and trying not to trigger this giant man-child into exploding on me.

That December, our daughter, Claire, and her four-month-old baby girl came to visit from Hawaii. I really enjoyed having them with us, even though we still had to go to work. Claire was not staying through the holidays, so we made as good use of our time together as possible.

One cold morning, after I had already gone to work, I got a phone call from the front office saying that Claire had locked herself out of the house and needed me to come home and let her in. She had left the baby on the floor in the living room all alone and was afraid for her safety.

I dashed home as quickly as I could, all the while keeping my fingers crossed that Claire wouldn't break a window to get in. I finally got home and ran up to the door to unlock it, while Claire came running around from the back, hysterical and still in her pajamas. I gave her a big hug as she hurriedly pushed past me to get to her baby. She quickly picked up her daughter and held on tight as she tried to tell me what happened through her massive sobs.

Claire had been about to start getting ready for the day when she placed the baby on the living room floor and walked out to the back porch to take in the morning. She shut the door behind her to keep out the cold, not realizing she had forgotten to release the button on the door.

Just like that, she was locked out.

She tried all the other doors to the house, but none were open. She ran down the street and knocked on a neighbor's door to call me at school. She was worried the baby might spit up and aspirate, since she had left her on her back. Claire then ran back to the house, terrified I wouldn't get there in time, and tried to break the glass doors to the porch with a wooden stool. She did break the glass—but not enough to gain entry—so she was emotional about both locking herself out and damaging our doors. She kept sobbing and apologizing the whole time.

I felt so sorry for her. I understood the fear she had for her little girl, but now she was worried about her dad being upset. I told her not to worry about it; her dad would be OK. Privately, I knew Mike wasn't going to be OK, and I knew he was going to blow his top when he saw the broken glass. So, I decided to call him at work and tell him what happened. That would give him enough time to process the morning events and cool off before he came home later in the day.

I got Mike on the phone and told him what happened. In one ear, I had Mike blowing up and shouting obscenities, and in the other, I had Claire asking through her sobs, "Is Dad mad at me?"

I put on my Oscar award–winning performance once again and told Claire in a soothing tone, "No, sweetie. He's not upset." All the while, Mike was overreacting and popping a couple of veins on his forehead at the other end of the phone.

The priority for me was that the baby was OK, and that Claire didn't feel bad about trying to protect her daughter. That should have been the most important thing. But Mike isn't capable of being compassionate. He's only capable of creating drama.

Now, if Mike had been standing in front of Claire, he wouldn't have blown up. He only did it because he had me on the phone and no one else would hear him. Did Mike ever ask how Claire was? How was the baby? No. Because he has no empathy, he couldn't see that Claire was in real pain and had a real fear for her baby. She was genuinely sorry for breaking the glass and was really worried about disappointing her dad. No empathy from Mike. All he wanted was for the world (me) to know that he was cursed—the forever victim.

Mike came home from work that evening in a bad mood over the broken glass. He had all day to calm down, but he made the conscious decision that he was going to be mad when he got home. He just wanted to make a show and let me know that his life was miserable, that nothing went his way. Just the good ol' victim mentality he loved to hang onto. His mantra was, "God hates me. He really hates me." *Insert eye roll here!*

There happened to be a lot to be grateful for, but Mike chose to focus on the negative and stay ticked off. It ended up being very inexpensive and quick to have the windowpanes replaced. The guy came out the next day, and it was completed in no time. Mike was so reactive and toxic. He couldn't get out of his own way to enjoy life. I'm just glad that Claire never heard the obscenities he dished out to me on the phone. She didn't need that—she just needed someone to give her a hug and tell her she's doing a great job as a mom. Unfortunately, Mike was incapable of doing anything like that.

The holidays came and went, and now I had about two months to get the rest of the house ready to be put on the market. I say "I" because Mike was AWOL. He had purposely pulled back any of his motivation to make the needed repairs and left it all up to me. It was his way of punishing me. Mike may have felt like his indifference was sabotaging the renovation plans, but I wasn't going to give him any satisfaction. I thought, *Fine, I'll do it.* So, I got busy pulling up all the old tile from the kitchen and dining area, including the trim, to get it ready for the new tile to be put down.

Every day when I got home from work, and every weekend, I positioned myself on the floor in the kitchen, peeling off the old tile, scraping the glue from the subfloor, placing the new tile, and putting the trim back on. Then came the painting of the trim and the kitchen cabinets.

At some point, when I was about two-thirds of the way through the kitchen, Mike made his appearance in the doorway.

He stood there between the kitchen and the living room with his usual disgust on his face, hands on his hips, and said in a very nasty tone, "You wonder why I'm not helping." Then he walked away. It wasn't a question—it was a statement.

I didn't even respond. He wanted to be miserable, so I let him be miserable. He wanted to make a show of how disgusted he was with life, so I let him make a show of how disgusted he was with life. I was his audience of one, and I didn't give him any attention. As far as I was concerned, he could just blow away in the wind and never return.

Eventually, I got to the point where I was able to get a realtor to come out, set up a time for photos, and get the house listed. I worked the rest of the time packing boxes and putting stuff aside for a yard sale. We had lived in the house for eighteen years, and we had accumulated a lot of stuff. It took longer than I thought it would, but it felt good knowing that I was moving forward. Even if I wasn't leaving him just yet, I was still leaving this house and shedding "stuff" from my past that was weighing me down.

I was just moving on autopilot. I knew I needed to get out of this house. After that, I would see where I would land next. I knew whatever house we moved into after this would be a temporary stay for me. Mike had shown, over and over again, that he was incapable of being anything other than the small, selfish, self-centered, emotionally manipulating person that he was. I knew my time was coming soon to break free. I was pretty much just going with the flow.

Many times, I questioned myself as to why I was going through with the sale of the house and buying another one when I knew it wouldn't last. In many ways, it was like the events leading up to my wedding day, when I had that loud voice tell me not to marry Mike. Back then, I felt like too many tumblers were already in place and I just had to go through with it. I felt the same here. Jillian was no closer to landing a job in her degree field, and she was very much reliant on me for emotional support. I knew it was going to take longer for her to get on her feet, so I let the wheels roll with the sale of the house and figured I would see where I landed after that.

Interestingly, I found myself disconnecting from the experience. I felt like I wasn't really in my body anymore. It felt like I was just floating over the scene and watching a hollow version of myself move through each day. I had made the conscious decision that I was done—with him and with our marriage. I wasn't resisting much anymore. I just didn't care. I was getting good at grey rocking, and I was just existing as best I could. I was going through the motions of being a dedicated science teacher and volleyball/track coach. I had a lot of people who depended on me to help them make their dreams and personal goals come true. I didn't want to let anyone down. Teaching and coaching gave me a purpose for still being in North Carolina, and I was going to fulfill it the best I could until my time came to leave.

My personal life may have sucked, but I had enough great things going on in my professional life to allow me to focus on the positive impact I was making for others. I was making a significant transition in my personal and mental space. Selling the house was symbolic and imperative. I knew I still had a while before I could leave, but I also knew it was coming closer to the end. I knew I had enough strength and confidence to see this through.

After all, it was never about me. It was always about him.

*   *   *   *   *   *   *   *   *   *   *

To a narcissist, the relationship's only purpose is to serve them, not to be connected to you. They're willing to threaten you in order to keep you in line and under their control.

Kerry McAvoy, MD

21. The Fifth Wheeler and Shedding

One day you will look back and realize you did it. You were brave enough to want more, bold enough to chase it and resilient enough to create a life that feels like home. Keep going.
Your future self will be so proud.

-THE GLOW WAVE

We were getting so close to putting the house on the market. Mike finally started helping with the process, so we began looking for the next house to move to. He really wanted a bigger garage and a workshop for himself, so we were limited in what we found for sale. Somehow, the discussion turned to buying land and building a house. Mike could get exactly what he wanted, and he could start out with a new house requiring few repairs and updates. The next big question was: Where do we live in the meantime?

We decided on getting a fifth-wheel camper and placing it on a local campground site where we could live until the house was built. Since Mike loves to spend money, this excited him, and he got busy searching the internet for used campers. We eventually found one that needed a few repairs, and Mike said he was okay with fixing it up. We had it in our possession, sitting next to our driveway, when we had our big blowout yard sale in March.

There were a lot of people who showed up for our "moving sale," including friends who wanted to see our new camper. People were crawling all over the place, and Mike was in his element—able to show off his new camper while making "great deals" with the yard sale shoppers. I was surprised how much my energy soared just getting rid of the excess and cleaning out the house.

It wasn't long after the yard sale that we were able to put the house on the market. We got a lot of activity right away, followed by an offer to purchase. After negotiating the agreed price, next came the inspection. Mike was furious when he got a copy of the inspection and read all the needed repairs the inspector came up with. One of the most unsettling issues that was highlighted was the discovery that part of the foundation wasn't being supported by posts in the crawl space.

Mike took offense with all the findings since he considered himself to be perfect and on top of all the maintenance and repairs in the house. I tried to calm him down by pointing out that most of the issues were simple and could be easily fixed. Our biggest and most expensive issue was the foundation support. Unfortunately, due to that discovery, the buyer backed out of the offer, and we had to put the house back on the market.

It took a couple more weeks to get someone out to fix the foundation support and for us to complete the inspection list. Fortunately, we were able to keep the house listed while we made the repairs. That way, we didn't miss out on any offers that might come in.

The next offer that came in was at full price. They were so pleased with the interior that they asked us not to change or do anything else to the house. In addition, they wanted to buy any furniture we were willing to sell. I kicked up my heels at the news. I was happy to part with most of the furniture because our belongings were going to be sitting in storage for quite some time, and one of two things was most likely going to happen. One, we would get new stuff to fit the new house—or two, I would be leaving anyway, and I didn't plan on taking much with me. With the offer in hand, we loaded up our fifth-wheeler, put our stuff in storage, and moved to a campground nearby.

I was so happy. I had shed a big part of the dark energy from the last eighteen years we had spent in that house. Now I was moving closer to my time to leave and not look back. I know it may seem crazy to be building a house I may never live in, but life was still happening. I had to move forward somehow until I could leave him and North Carolina. It might as well be in a fifth-wheeler while we went through the motions of building our "dream house."

Mike was also in a good mood. We had just made some good money on the sale of the house, and we were moving toward buying property to build his dream workshop. This charade of building a new future together was worth it to me. It seemed to keep him preoccupied with reaching his personal goal of having a grand place to work with his tools. It also kept him happy enough that he wasn't dumping too much of his dark energy on me. I called that a "win-win."

We settled into our transitional life in the fifth-wheeler in a campground outside a nearby town. Our entourage included four cats and Xena. Plus, Craig stayed with us during the summer between semesters at college. It was a tight fit. But it was also very enlightening to discover that we really didn't need much to be comfortable and survive.

The camper had many unique storage nooks, so we had plenty of room to put things away. The appliances worked decently enough, and the layout of the camper was very comfortable. Our site was directly across from the public showers and bathrooms, so we decided to put the cats' litter box in our shower. We could simply walk across the driveway to use the campground's shower.

Living in the camper felt like I was on vacation. Since I didn't have a yard to take care of and it was quick to clean, I had more time to dedicate to myself and get healthy. I would get up early that summer and go for walks, runs, and lift weights. The meals were simpler, so I was freed from spending extra time in the kitchen. We grilled more and even put up a movie screen to watch films outside. There were others in the campground who were in a similar situation to us, so we were able to get to know our neighbors quickly.

The extra time I gained from not having to do yard and house maintenance allowed me to get busy looking for house plans and move forward with purchasing property and starting the build.

The summer of 2011 seemed to be moving along well without too much drama from Mike. We had purchased property not too far down the highway from where we sold our house, and we had hired a builder. We agreed on a house plan and were meeting with the architect to finalize the blueprints before breaking ground. I was busy with summer volleyball camps and teacher workshops. Summer was almost over, and the volleyball season and new school year were about to start. There was plenty to keep us busy, and Mike was doing a good job regulating his emotions—at least for now.

I thought everything was moving along just fine. Mike hadn't given any indication that he was unhappy, so I was caught off guard when I got back to the trailer from one of my summer volleyball practices to find him in a dark mood. Who knows what it was about this time. He just gave me the silent treatment and dirty looks when I asked what was wrong. I knew not to go anywhere near him, so I just walked past him to our bedroom at the back of the camper and stayed there for a while.

It was hard to find space to get away from him, so I buried myself in planning volleyball practices at the small dining table in the camper. I figured if I didn't make eye contact with him, I'd have a better chance of escaping whatever it was he wanted to unleash on me. Eventually, he got up—apparently disgusted that I didn't inquire hard enough into his dark mood—and left the camper, letting the door slam behind him.

OK. Noted. You're not happy.

Mike came back a little later and said, "You wonder why I'm mad? The cost of building this house is more than I thought. You have to scale back the plans for the house, or I won't be able to afford my workshop."

Fair enough. The house isn't for me anyway.

I spent several days looking at the plans and redrawing room sizes, but the cuts I made were only going to shave maybe $5K off the cost of the house. Five thousand dollars wasn't going to get him any closer to his dream workshop. I told him that maybe he needed to cut back on the size of his workshop.

Oh, holy hell! What did I just suggest? Did I just suggest that he cut back on his dream?

Mike flipped out in that tiny space of our camper, and poor Xena ran to our bedroom in the back. He said there was no way he was going to compromise on his workshop and that I had to find the savings. There was literally no way I was going to meet his demands, so I just sat quietly, letting him rage on.

I had to remind myself that I wasn't planning on staying in North Carolina, so if he wanted to have a giant workshop, then he could have it. I suggested he take money out of our investments to make that happen. I even said something like, "After all, why did we invest our money all these years if we can't use it for our future?"

He calmed down after that and got happy again. I was giving him permission to take money out of our investments to build his dream workshop—even though that never stopped him in the past, and he always loved spending money. He was in heaven. At least for now.

School and volleyball season started again, and I was entrenched in long days away from the camper. Mike's work schedule was very accommodating, and he was able to get away early every day, which meant he had more time on his hands. I would have loved to have his schedule, but he seemed to find a reason not to be happy no matter how good he had it. He complained that he didn't have anything to do and was getting stir-crazy. I suggested that he take advantage of the extra time he had and join a gym or start a fun little hobby.

Oh, no. Those suggestions were not what he wanted. He wanted me to believe that his life was miserable. How dare I solve his problem that fast. He wanted to wallow a little longer so he could squeeze more sympathy out of me. I, coming up with options so quickly, would strip him of the opportunity to stretch out this ploy for attention.

I thought about his pouting and how resistant he was to any suggestions about what to do with his extra time. It reminded me of a child who wanted his mommy to find something for him to do because he was just too little to be creative on his own. In any case, I had little time in my day to fall prey to his emotional manipulations. I gave him one last encouraging suggestion and then had to turn my attention to grading papers.

The volleyball season of 2011 was looking to be a repeat of the previous year when I coached our team to the state playoffs. We were the 8th seed and ended up beating the #1 seed in the first round. We were eliminated in the second round, but the girls had accomplished a great feat—getting our volleyball team back into the playoffs after several years of missing it.

Here we were a year later, back in the playoffs—this time as a #5 seed—with several seniors I had coached their entire high school careers.

It was a special time, and I was so proud of the girls. I was also very fortunate to have been given an assistant coach. The year before, I did not have an assistant and had to coach both the varsity and JV squads. That was beyond exhausting. So, I was really enjoying this season—watching the girls reach their personal best while having an assistant to help carry the extra load.

2011 was shaping up to be another great season as we headed south of Wilmington, NC, for the first round of the state playoffs. We were playing the number 4 seed, New Hanover High School, at their place. The teams were perfectly matched, and the scoring went back and forth for quite a while. Eventually, our squad lost in the first round of the playoffs, and it was now time to walk the slow walk to the bus and head home.

New Hanover High School is over three hours from our school, and it was dinnertime when we started heading back. It was customary to stop somewhere for the athletes to get something to eat, and this time we had special permission to stop at the mall on the way home. It was great to see the girls with smiles back on their faces as they ate and took some time to shop. I had given the team their rendezvous time to be back on the bus and sent them off to get food and unwind from the season.

A few parents were following the bus and joined me in the food court to visit while the girls enjoyed the release from their loss. Even though we lost in the first round, everyone seemed to be letting the loss go and just enjoying the moment. It was turning out to be a nice way to finish the season. Soon, it was time to get back on the bus and head home. As usual, all the girls were present at their assigned time, and off we went.

The ride back was mellow. As I was driving the bus, I was discussing with my assistant coach the plans for the team's season-ending awards ceremony. All was well until we smelled something funny coming from the back of the bus. My assistant knew right away that it was marijuana and shouted back at the girls to put it out as she moved to the back to get the evidence.

Apparently, the seniors on the team were all sitting in the back with the windows rolled down, smoking a joint.

I pulled over and called our principal, who planned to meet us—along with the police—at a small town approximately thirty minutes from our school. I pulled in and got off the bus to briefly chat with the principal and the police. Phone calls were made to parents, and the principal spoke with the seniors who had been smoking. This was not how anyone wanted our season to end. It was such a shock and a huge disappointment. The rest of the ride home was quiet, as everyone was trying to anticipate what would happen next.

The principal had no other option but to suspend the girls. In addition, those who were smoking were automatically kicked off the team with no athletic awards or recognition given to them for the year. We had four girls on our team who had been nominated by the press for the First All-County Team, and two players nominated for Second All-County Team. I had to call the reporter and tell him that the girls were no longer on the team and, therefore, could not be awarded that title by the newspaper.

The reporter, who I had worked with many times, tried to find out what happened, but all I could say was that it was a policy decision. There was a long silence on the other end before he thanked me and hung up.

The fallout from the event kept rolling. Teachers were giving me an earful about what I should or shouldn't do. The remaining girls were upset with me because they felt their teammates were being treated unfairly. I found out that other teachers were pulling my athletes aside and shaming them for not backing me. Players were going home and complaining to their parents, and the parents were then calling the principal to complain about me.

Before I knew it, I was being called in by the principal to find out what was going on. I had no idea that other teachers were chastising my players, and I assured the principal they had done so on their own. Then The teachers who were part of the problem got mad at me because they thought I threw them under the bus.

It was a hot-holy-hell mess, and I was emotionally spent. I found myself visibly shaking and unable to focus on delivering any lessons, so I called the front office and told them I had a personal emergency and had to go home immediately. One of my science colleagues came directly to my room and took over for the rest of the day. I left, emotionally crumpled and sobbing uncontrollably as I drove home.

So many emotions poured out of me. I could barely see the road through my tears, and it was hard to breathe. Unfortunately, there was a roadblock up ahead with police checking driver's licenses and registrations. I was so emotional that I couldn't think straight when the officer asked for my ID and what was wrong. He had a shocked look on his face when he saw just how broken I was. He was kind enough to recognize that I just needed to go home. He let me go without asking for any documents and gently encouraged me to get home safely.

Somehow, I made it back to our camper, and I crawled into bed, sobbing.

Mike got home from work soon after I arrived and found me curled up in bed. He asked what was wrong, and I tried to tell him. I could barely speak with all the sobs coming out of me. Instead of offering comfort, he just started yelling at me. He told me he was tired of my crying and didn't want to hear it. He said he was going to leave, and I had better not still be crying when he got back.

I was stunned through my sobs—but not surprised. I couldn't remember the last time I had cried so deeply. Mike had never seen me that upset, and you would think he'd be so disturbed and affected by my emotional collapse that he'd try to soothe and comfort me. But no. He yelled at me—for my emotions. Emotions that had nothing to do with him. Not one smidge of empathy or compassion. Not one. I should have been even more devastated by his dismissal of my pain, but I was already too far removed from his abuse.

I hadn't cried in front of him in over twenty years. The last time I did, he verbally abused me for crying—because he had just verbally abused me. Stupid, right? But that's what narcissists do. They get upset at you because you dare to get upset with how they treat you. Then they blame you when you try to hold them accountable for something they did.

I had given so much of my energy and soul to coaching, and now it seemed I was being censured by the very ones I had poured that energy into. It was a ridiculous series of events that were out of my control, yet I became the target of their resentment and outrage. It was a very emotionally low time for me—and yet, no loving husband to offer compassion.

I knew my life wasn't in Havelock, North Carolina. I knew I would eventually have to quit coaching and leave. I took this as a sign that the Universe was helping me start breaking away from my familiar life to prepare me for the next one. So, I made the decision that 2011 would be my last year coaching, and I called the team together to let them know.

It was a heavy conversation, but it also felt liberating— to shed one more thing from this current life while I got ready for the next one.

*   *   *   *   *   *   *   *   *   *   *

Emotional abuse warning signs... They make you feel bad about yourself. They try to control you. They constantly ignore your boundaries. They enjoy making you feel powerless and scared. They are constantly dismissive of your feelings. They use threats to guilt or manipulate you. They continually criticize you. They like to humiliate and belittle you. They call you names or put you down. They gaslight and isolate you.

@mentalhealth.with.emma

Part Four: Awakening and Renewal

22. The Loaded Gun

No matter how hard things get, I know I'll never again let anyone convince me I'm crazy, unhealthy, or insecure for having a normal reaction to their hurtful behavior.

-Brandi Clark/Stardust Poetry

It was now November 2011, and we were heading into the holidays in our camper. Mike always found a way to sabotage the holidays, so I was intent on keeping things simple. Jillian was living in a condo in Wilmington while working at Best Buy, and she wasn't going to be able to get away for Christmas, so we made plans for all of us to join her in her little place. Craig was also home, so there were four of us—plus Xena—spending the night together in a 250-square-foot space.

We didn't exchange gifts since we didn't have any extra room in the camper, so we just gave the kids money. I enjoyed keeping it simple. We drove around, looked at Christmas lights, and found some fun places to dine. I value quality time over material gifts, while Mike is the opposite. He would much rather spend money than find time to spend with me or the kids. Surprisingly, Mike didn't blow this Christmas up, so it was a relaxing time together.

Winter in North Carolina can be gray and dreary. When you put that together with longer nights and fewer hours of sunshine, you can struggle with seasonal depression. The post-holiday blues can be very real. When you're cooped up in a small camper with someone who doesn't need an excuse to be gloomy, then the small space seems even smaller. The nights and mornings were colder, which also made that walk across the driveway to the campground showers more dreadful.

Mike was sulky, and every conversation was laced with negative energy. I was pulling up my emotional wall to protect myself from swirling into the dark void he wanted to go to. I purposely avoided any conversations that might trigger him. I allowed him to set the topic and then just let him vent. He liked to hear himself talk, and he liked to think that his opinion was the only opinion, so he would dominate all conversation by talking over me. I wasn't allowed an opposing view, because he would interpret that as me thinking he was wrong—that he wasn't perfect. He always needed to control the conversation, so I let him. It was more important to me to have peace in our small space than to offer my differing opinion.

It was getting closer to the spring of 2012, and the builder still hadn't broken ground on the property. We were getting anxious to get started—it had now been almost a year since we sold our house. I could understand Mike's frustrations, but he couldn't moderate his emotions. The old familiar "blame it on Pam" outbursts started to resume. Somehow, it was my fault that the new house construction was moving slowly.

One of the worst places I could ever be alone with Mike was in the car. There was nowhere to escape, and he would use the car as a tool to torment and traumatize me. We had to make many trips sourcing materials for the new house: lighting, flooring, appliances, sink fixtures—you name it. He loved to use those opportunities to remind me he still had power over me by accelerating and braking abruptly, or taking sharp turns so my body would fly all over the car. I hated him for that. But I didn't fight back—because I knew it only gave me greater resolve to leave him when the opportunity came. I was making lists in my mind of his never-ending abuse so I wouldn't get caught in a weak moment—fooled by one of his manufactured kindnesses—into thinking he had changed.

He needed a distraction other than the camper and the new build, so I suggested we visit our old neighbors and friends, the Bowmans. Doug and Barb Bowman had been friends for over twenty years—practically the entire time we had lived in North Carolina. Mike enjoyed visiting with Doug, and I enjoyed catching up with Barb. I knew that if he could spend some time with friends, it might lift his energy out of the dark abyss.

The Bowmans still lived in the same housing development where we had just sold our house, down the highway from where our new house was going to be. I had known them since Claire was in preschool with their son, Matt, and Barb was a regular substitute teacher at the high school. That was over twenty years ago, and I considered them truly great friends.

Here's an interesting side note. It was Mother's Day, a year later in 2013, that Barb and I found out we were cousins! Jillian and Barb's oldest daughter, Kim, had been tracing family genealogy—independent of each other. We found out that Barb's son, Matt, and his wife, Amy, were expecting their first baby, a boy. Barb shared that they were going to name the baby *Corbin*, after family ancestors from the 1700s.

Jillian heard the name and said, "Huh. That's funny. We have family with the last name of Corbin."

Barb replied, "So do we."

Jillian came back with, "Ours was from Culpepper County, Virginia."

Barb excitedly answered, "So is ours!!"

Barb promptly got Kim on the phone, and Jillian—who had been carrying her genealogy book with her wherever she went—ran out to the car to retrieve it. Together, she and Kim were able to verify that we both shared the same family of Corbin brothers from the Revolutionary War! Barb's ancestor had stayed in Virginia, while our ancestor moved west to Missouri.

How cool is that? All this time we were friends, and we never knew we were also related! We now get to call each other "cuz."

Anyway, back to the story.

Doug and Barb's daughter, Mary Beth, was getting back on her feet after a divorce. She had obtained a great IT position at the hospital and had just purchased her first home in Havelock. We had already been to her new house several times for visits and celebrations. We found out from Doug and Barb that Mary Beth needed help with some downed trees at the back of her property. They were planning on going over to her house Saturday, March 10, to celebrate her birthday and help clean up the debris. Mike volunteered our services to help that weekend, so when we left Doug and Barb's, Mike was in a better mood.

Mike liked to feel important. Don't we all? Everyone has a need to feel that they make a difference—a positive impact on the lives around them. But Mike used this feeling of being important to define himself. He needed that outward affirmation from others. If he didn't get it, he viewed himself as unworthy. His ego was reliant on praise and compliments from others to get the validation he didn't know how to give himself.

I felt sorry for him. He relied on others to give him that confirmation through their praise of his talents. Subsequently, he was always chasing the compliments—putting himself down to play the victim so others would repeat the words he needed to hear. It was so exhausting, but I knew helping Mary Beth would make him feel better, and I hoped it would lift the dark energy he was putting out.

It was a gray Saturday, a bit chilly. Doug and Mary Beth's fiancé, Rudy, were already there when Mike and I showed up. The guys got busy playing lumberjack in the back while the rest of us watched safely from afar. I don't remember all that they did, but the three of them seemed to enjoy each other and the task at hand. We ended the day with a birthday celebration for Mary Beth and visited for a while before heading back to the camper. The cleanup wasn't completed, so we planned to return to Mary Beth's house the next day to finish up.

The ride back to the camper seemed uneventful. I got no indication that Mike's mood had turned dark. I was completely caught off guard when I found him in the bedroom of our camper—with a loaded gun in his hand.

Oh my God.
Not again.

The gun he had loaded was a black powder pistol. The bullet was a round ball. I remembered when he got it and how excited he was to show me how it worked. He loved that there was a slight delay from the hammer going down to the ball being discharged by the ignited black powder. I remembered him telling me that kind of ammunition would do a lot of damage as it passed clumsily through muscle and bone.

And now, here he was—with the hammer pulled back, his shoulders slumped, and a pitiful look of despair on his face.

My first instinct was to turn around and leave—just like the last time he pulled out a gun on himself. I had too much to live for, and I did not want to be around while he did himself in. I almost did turn around to leave, and then I thought: If I did, Mike could view my retreat as the ultimate insult. Narcissists fear rejection. He could shoot me in the back as punishment for leaving. Then, once he realized what he'd done, he would kill himself. A murder-suicide.

These thoughts flashed through my mind in an instant, and then I thought about the kids. They may be adults, but they would be devastated beyond measure if their dad followed through with such a selfish and evil act. So, instead of getting the hell out of there, I moved forward and placed both my hands on the pistol along with his.

I had no idea what had made his mind go down this dark route. I saw him earlier at Mary Beth's, enjoying Doug and Rudy's company. There was nothing there that gave me pause—no dark clouds to look for. There's usually a "tell" with him. I'm usually sensitive to his mood changes, especially if he's about to go deep down a dark hole, but I missed this one.

We were standing there—on his side of the bed—both with our hands on this loaded pistol. I was very aware of his fragile state, and I believed that any wrong word out of my mouth could send him over the edge. I was very careful with the words I chose, trying to coax him back from the cliff. My heart was racing, my mind was cloudy. I kept my gaze on him, searching for any hint that he was about to escalate this into tragedy.

I don't remember what I said to him. But I do remember that we stood there—both with our hands on this loaded pistol—for over an hour. I was so exhausted. My legs were getting weak from standing. I hesitated to adjust my stance because I didn't want any slight movement to break him out of his trance and cause him to pull the trigger. So I stood still and firm in place. My hands, arms, neck, and head were aching from holding the same tight position for so long. My lower back started to throb from being frozen in place, and I could feel my legs going numb.

All the while, he never said a word. He just held his head down with an intense look of deep shame.

My body was about to give out on me, so I started to plot my hurried exit. I visualized where I had left my purse—so that when I turned to run, I wouldn't have to take time to look for it. I visualized where the keys were inside my purse, so I wouldn't have to dig. I visualized the angle where the car was parked so I wouldn't waste any steps once I got outside the camper.

I knew I couldn't take Xena with me. She would just slow me down. I couldn't take the time to look for her leash. I couldn't take the time to put the leash on her. I couldn't take the time to round her up and put her in the car if I let her out of the camper with me. I hated to leave her behind, but I couldn't take the chance that

Mike would use those extra moments to follow and turn the pistol on me.

I was about to turn and run—while I still had strength in my legs—when he finally put the pistol down. I watched him place it in a cubby next to the head of his side of the bed. I watched him let out a series of deep breaths that allowed his shoulders to relax. I watched him turn and exit the bedroom and collapse on the sofa in the camper.

I usually have a good memory, but I can't remember what was said—if anything—after that. I don't remember my emotions. I don't remember how I went to bed that night next to him, knowing that the pistol was still loaded and near his pillow. Maybe it was the shock of the event that didn't allow me to remember. I don't know. But I do know this:

He was poisonous.
He was deeply flawed and troubled.

Somehow, we both got up on that Sunday, March 11, 2012, and went back over to Mary Beth's house to finish the clean-up. It was another gray, cold day, and I set up a lawn chair in the backyard where I could keep an eye on Mike. I was still in shock. My body was still humming from all the adrenaline running through me. I could feel my elevated heart rate by how fast my chest was pounding. Barb and Mary Beth were in the house with Mary Beth's daughter, but I chose to stay outside in the cold gray air so I could monitor Mike.

Yes. A person with a clear mind would have reached out for help. Maybe they would have called the police. I didn't have a clear mind. My mind, my body, and my soul were deeply traumatized. My brain was in "fight or flight" mode. That doesn't mean you literally fight the abuser or take flight from the abuser. It means you're in a heightened state of survival. The survival mode each person chooses will vary. Someone may choose to run. Someone else may stay and fight. My body and mind chose to freeze. All I could do was be in the moment— monitoring each second, watching for clues to see how he was doing.

That Sunday seemed to go on forever. The seconds ticked by so slowly as I sat and watched him. I remembered thinking what a good actor he was—showing no residual effects from the traumatizing event of the day before. He chatted and laughed easily with Doug and Rudy. He didn't even let his mask slip when we were alone in the car, safely away from everyone. There was no mention of what happened the day before, and I didn't dare bring it up. After all, he still had a loaded gun next to his bed.

For the next few days, I got home from work before Mike. Each day I quickly made my way to the pistol, trying to figure out how to unload it. I had no idea how to handle a gun, let alone load or unload one. I hoped it would be easy. I didn't want to fumble and risk it going off on me.

I thought about calling the police to come unload it for me, but they would ask questions, and most likely confiscate the weapon. That would lead to Mike being questioned—or worse. It would be disastrous for him. He could lose his job. He would lose the respect of his peers. And he would never have the personal strength to recover from the public shame. I imagined that would be the final push he needed to kill me and then himself. I couldn't do anything that might set him off while I didn't yet have a full exit plan.

Eventually, by Thursday of that week, I found that Mike had unloaded the gun. I allowed myself a moment of peace.

Listen, when you're outside looking in, you can see everything so clearly. It's easy for armchair analysts to judge and assume what they believe would have been the smartest course of action. But they have the advantage of a mind that's not clouded by trauma. Try hitting your head a couple dozen times against a brick wall and then try to think logically through the pain. Now imagine that trauma bypassing your skull entirely and being directed straight at your unprotected brain. That's what prolonged mental, emotional, and psychological abuse does to you. Your brain gets beaten up repeatedly over such a long period that you struggle to make even simple connections in logic.

I knew he hated himself. I knew he hated me because I knew his secret about cross-dressing. I knew he was struggling with depression. All of that—I knew. And I still gave him some allowance for it.

But I also knew how calculating his cruelty toward me was.

He knew that the way he treated me wouldn't be tolerated by anyone who saw it. He knew it was wrong. That's why he made the conscious choice to wait until we were alone to unleash his demons on me. To everyone else, he was the great guy who'd do anything for anyone. I was the lucky woman to have him as a husband.

Little did anyone know just how calculating, cruel, and demeaning he truly was.

This last episode—his suicide attempt—threw me back under the train where my emotional and mental health was crushed. The past several years of me putting up walls to protect my mental health from his abuse didn't serve me this time. No. This time, it all came back with a fierce flood of emotional confusion and physical pain.

It took me a long time to mentally recover from it. Somehow, I was able to shift my consciousness to perform the mundane tasks needed to get through a day. Somehow, I was able to push it aside so I could function as a teacher. No one knew my pain. No one. Mike knew that he hurt me, but even he couldn't fathom how deep his cuts went.

I was walking this path very much alone. I was becoming hollower and hollower inside. There wasn't much left of me. You can't even imagine the amount of strength it takes to gather yourself up and put on a happy mask for the world to see. Jillian wasn't any closer to getting her feet on the ground, and I knew she still needed me. I couldn't leave and have her take on the extra emotional burden of the fallout. I was praying and praying.

I was looking for some strength from somewhere, and I decided to cling to a quote from Lucy Maud Montgomery in one of her Anne of Green Gables books. It said, "You know what tomorrow is? Another day, fresh, with no mistakes in it."

I hung onto that promise. Somehow, I would make it through this day—and then have another chance to get it right tomorrow.

*   *   *   *   *   *   *   *   *   *   *

The personality and very character of a narcissist is a smoke screen. They are all pretty lights that lack substance and depth. Beneath the grandiose façade is an extremely fragile ego which, when starved of attention and acknowledgement, struggles to cope.

@myexisanarcissistandimadeitout W. Hardy

23. Breaking Ground Upside Down

THE WIN IS COMING. DON'T LET THE WHEN WORRY YOU.
-lawofattraction

It was somewhere around the spring of 2012, and we were finally breaking ground for the new home. It was in a new development—just a single street—that backed up to the Croatan National Forest. We bought the largest lot at the end of the cul-de-sac, and ours was the only custom home among all the other spec homes. We started planning the landscaping and slowly accumulated trees and shrubs that we tucked around our camper. Even though I knew I wasn't going to be there long, I still allowed myself to get distracted by the planning and building of the house.

I was moving forward, but I felt like a shell of myself. I was always on guard, watching for any sign he might blow. I continuously monitored his pistol to see if he had loaded it again. I wanted to be ahead of any drastic change in his demeanor or mood swings. I had already decided that if I ever found the pistol loaded again, I would leave with Xena and go to Jillian's condo in Wilmington. I knew I couldn't handle another episode like the one I had just gone through, and I figured I probably wouldn't be so lucky a third time to get away alive. Eventually, Mike moved the pistol to its case and stored it under the bed. I was able to relax a bit more—but I never completely let my guard down.

Mike's mood was always a crapshoot from day to day. He had been on edge, growling about the lack of progress on the house. He was better once the foundation and walls went up. It helped to see the house taking shape, and then he was able to regulate his emotions a bit better. Mike created a positive distraction for himself by buying a small motorboat and trailer so he could take advantage of his free time. He would take it out to the Neuse River or the Intracoastal Waterway in Morehead City and boat around. Sometimes, I would go with him. I admit, the water was very therapeutic. The soft bump of the boat over the waves was soothing and helped to keep my nerves in check.

Craig was finishing his degree at UNC–Asheville and would be joining us full-time in the camper at the start of summer. He had an internship at a local furniture upholstery business that he needed to complete. Once finished, he would have met all his graduation requirements for his B.S. in Engineering. He was planning to go into the Marine Corps, like his dad, and had already been awarded a flight slot for flight school. He just needed his diploma before the rest of the tumblers could fall into place.

It was good having him around. He was an extra buffer between me and Mike. Mike only came after me when we were alone, and with Craig living with us in the camper, there was basically no opportunity for him to get me alone. Craig took his internship seriously and put in a full day's work every day with the upholsterer. He would come home with amusing stories of how this old guy he was learning from could put a handful of upholstery nails in his mouth and somehow not swallow any of them.

Summer continued to roll on. Mike and Craig would take the little boat out, and Craig would toss his net into the water, trying to catch fish. There was a small pier off the campground where we were staying, and I would often go down there with Xena to watch Craig practice tossing his nets. The summer was fairly quiet. It was easy living. I wasn't coaching volleyball anymore, so I didn't have summer camps to prepare for or run. It was my first summer free of coaching obligations in over seven years.

By the end of summer, Craig had completed his internship, received his diploma, and was sworn in as a second lieutenant in the Marine Corps. His start date for TBS—The Basic School—was delayed until the spring of 2013. I knew he was anxious to get started with his chosen career, but he still had several months to go before his class date. In the meantime, he lived with us in our tight little camper with four cats and Xena.

I could see that Craig was about to launch his personal and professional life, and I was counting down the days until Jillian would follow. Here she was—three and a half years older than Craig—with both an undergraduate and graduate degree, but still no job opportunities. She was trying so hard to stay positive, but there were very few openings in her desired archivist profession, and since she didn't have experience, she was constantly being passed over for consideration.

I made sure that Jillian didn't feel any pressure from me. I only offered words of support and encouragement. But this delay in the personal launching of her career was taking a huge toll on her. We had taken a day trip to Wilmington to visit her and stopped by her place of work at Best Buy, where she was a cashier. We got in her line, and I watched her interact with the customers. She looked tired, beaten down, and could hardly muster a smile. I knew she was slowly dying inside every day she showed up to work—feeling less-than because she had a master's degree but was working as a cashier.

Jillian was a high achiever. She loved academia, she loved history and research, and she buried herself in any task put before her. She enrolled in all the honors courses in high school and was accepted into the Honors College at UNC–Pembroke. She had received a lot of scholarship money to help pay for college. The university also rewarded her academic excellence by selecting her for several trips abroad as an ambassador for the school. She spent three weeks in China, a week in London, and five months studying at Macquarie University in Sydney, Australia.

In high school, she worked at the local movie theater and saved so much money that by the time she graduated college, she had no student loan debt and about $15,000 in savings. Then, when she finished her master's program in only two years, not only did she pay for it herself, but she also had over $20,000 in savings. Who does that? Who finishes two degrees in six years, with no debt and a huge amount of money put away?

Jillian does, that's who.

She had every right to be proud of what she had accomplished. She had big plans for herself and such optimism. But unfortunately, she got caught up in the big financial collapse of 2008, and it was taking a long time for the economy to recover. Now here she was—with a master's degree—stuck as a cashier at Best Buy.

As we waited in her line, I could see how beaten down she was, how emotionally exhausted she had become with her situation. When we got up to her register, I told her, "Jillian, you don't have to do this. You have plenty of money saved up, so you can afford to quit. You can take care of yourself and have more time to look for a better job."

That was all it took. She just needed someone to give her permission to quit and take care of herself.

Jillian walked into her manager's office at the end of her shift and quit that day. She found another job working for a mediation lawyer, joined a gym, hired a trainer, and eventually cut ties with the historical foundation she had been working with. Her personal energy level skyrocketed, and she began developing a more positive outlook on her situation. She was my last holdout. I needed her to get her sails set—moving in a healthy direction—before I could do the same.

Summer was ending, and there was significant progress on the house. Mike was looking into getting a hydraulic lift for the monstrous workshop he was planning. He had spent many days and evenings driving around eastern North Carolina, buying used tools and equipment for his new shop. Even though he was in his element and happily distracted, it came at a price.

I was born with a calculator in my head—mostly because I had been responsible for my own finances since third grade. It was easy for me to keep a tally of all the money he was spending. Mike only saw the price tag of individual items. He never totaled them up. He would say, "I got a great deal. It was only two hundred and fifty dollars."

Well, when you get ten items at a "great deal" of $250, the total comes to $2,500. I could hear the cash register in my head going cha-ching with every purchase.

Where were we getting the money from? He didn't care. He was giddy and on a spending spree. To him, it was only "$250."

It didn't take long for Mike to blow past several thousands of dollars. He never considered how much money he was spending—or that I would have to be the one to sacrifice to cover the bills. I would try to carefully point out the excess spending, but any comment from me, no matter how delicately I framed it, triggered a defiant and nasty response from him. I reminded myself that we were living in tight quarters and there was nowhere to get away from him when he erupted in anger. So, I had to swallow my comments and remind myself that I was getting closer to the end.

I decided to withdraw into myself and find ways to avoid the tension. Since I didn't have volleyball to preoccupy me, I had extra time, so I joined a gym and began rediscovering parts of myself again. I couldn't let myself get too happy. I knew what kind of person I was married to, and I knew the floor could be pulled out from under me at any time. I took advantage of the time I got back from not coaching volleyball and allowed my personal schedule to slow down. I took long walks after work and read books for leisure. It was interesting to observe how different my life felt when my mental load lessened.

We had a short time left before the new house would finally be turned over to us. The estimate was the end of October. Unfortunately, the campground we were staying at would not extend our monthly lease, and—even though we pleaded for just one more month—they wouldn't budge. We were forced to find another spot for our camper.

This was stressful for all of us. The problem was that Mike wasn't good at regulating his emotions. Any challenge, any change in the status quo would rock him. He was not good at adapting, and the dark energy started emerging once again. We were fortunate to secure a spot at a campground on the Marine base, so we moved our camper there. It was just for a month. I told myself, I can do this for a month.

The dynamics were different at this campground. More eyes were on our dear Xena. I kept her on a leash when I took her out, but there were still plenty of campers who didn't want her there. I would walk Xena away from the campsite, and when I saw open land, I'd let her off her leash to run. She didn't seem to notice any of the side-eyes from others—and she loved our outings together.

We didn't have the luxury of having a bathhouse across from us like at the last campground. We still had four cats, and their litter box still lived in the camper's shower stall. So if we wanted to take a shower, we had to drive to the base gym. It wasn't convenient, but you do what you have to do. That last month was trying for all of us—and it didn't help when Hurricane Sandy began heading our way.

The hurricane came near the end of October. We were so close to moving into the house, but there were still parts of the construction that were vulnerable to the storm. So we headed out to the property in the intense rain to try to protect what we could.

There was no grass yet, so the ground was pure mud all around the house. The gutters hadn't been installed yet, so water was pouring off every edge of the roof, causing massive erosion to the soil we had brought in.

I don't remember everything we did, but we worked for a couple of hours and were soaked and muddy by the time we finished.

We were all exhausted and disappointed with the storm—but I didn't take it personally. Who would? Mike would, that's who. He continued with his familiar mantra: "God hates me. God really hates me." I would just sit quietly, letting him exhaust himself with his rants. It amazed me how much energy he put into being negative.

I secretly called it "Eyoreing," after the *Winnie the Pooh* character who was always brooding and gloomy. I'd turn my head toward the passenger-side window—away from his dark monologue—and give myself a very satisfying eye roll.

It's just dirt. We can get more. Get over it. Life will move on. And we will still be able to move into the house.

The storm passed, and the day finally came for us to move into our new home. Yay! Our energy lifted knowing we were at the end. There was much celebration as we carried our stuff out of the camper and into the new house. We had the rest of our belongings in storage, and over the course of the next few days, we got everything moved in.

When you first move into a house or apartment, there's so much to do. There are countless trips to the store for the organizational stuff you didn't know you needed. There are trips to the dump and to Goodwill because you realize some of what you had in storage didn't survive the wait. Normal chaos. I was used to chaos, thanks to Mike. I was bending like willow branches in the wind. Mike was snapping like dried twigs under your feet. I just kept myself occupied with getting organized. After all, Thanksgiving and the rest of the holidays were coming, and I didn't have time to get swallowed up in his madness.

The days flew by because there was so much to be done. Mike was completely in love with his new workshop. He spent all his time out there, setting everything up just the way he wanted it. It was a very huge workshop— complete with a hydraulic lift, an automotive side, and a woodworking side. He had a roll-up door at both the front and back, a concrete pad for the riding lawn mower, and even a huge attic space for extra storage. He spent a lot of time and money finishing out his dream space. I was happy for him. It cost us a lot of extra money, but I figured if he was going to stay in North Carolina after I left, he might as well get what he wanted.

Craig was still with us since he wouldn't start TBS until the spring. He was working at an Advance Auto in Morehead City to fill his time before he left. The four cats were slowly adjusting to their new surroundings, but Xena loved it. After spending a year and a half in a tiny camper, she finally had the space to run and be free. We had almost two acres set back against the national forest with no one ever building behind us. She had the room and the freedom to explore as much as she wanted. She was in her own heaven.

Thanksgiving came and went, and now Christmas was coming. The days were getting shorter, the darkness was getting longer, and the chill was setting in. I hated being out after dark in the wintertime. The roads seemed harder to navigate, and at Christmastime, everyone was in a hurry. I always gripped the steering wheel tighter and kept an eye out for crazy drivers—and for the random deer that might jump out in front of the car.

It was the Thursday before Christmas, and there was an electric current running through the air as everyone rushed to get somewhere. I had a hair appointment right after school, then had to go to the commissary on base to get the Christmas groceries. Jillian was coming up from Wilmington for the holidays, so I was trying to be efficient with my errands. I was heading home, hands tight on the steering wheel in the December dark, when my life was almost taken from me.

North Carolina is notorious for having no shoulders on the highways. All you get is a white line on your right and, if you're lucky, maybe four inches of asphalt. Anything after that is pure vegetation and soil. On top of that, eastern North Carolina has a thick layer of red clay beneath the soil. It acts like a barrier and limits the amount of rain the ground can hold. When there's heavy rain, the surface water can flood neighborhoods and roads. Our part of the state has miles and miles of ditches dug to collect the excess water and direct it to rivers or holding ponds. The day before, we'd had a massive rainstorm—so the soil was soft. Fortunately for me, the ditches were empty.

I was heading home, ten miles outside of town. I was nearing Havelock's city limits and accelerating to reach the 55-mph speed limit on Hwy 101. There's a slight curve to the right as you pass the city limit sign, and the road itself slants rightward. That slant is designed to help surface water flow more quickly off the road and into the nearby ditch.

I accelerated the car to 55 mph. As I approached the slanted turn, the car drifted too far to the right. Unexpectedly, the right front wheel went off the edge of the road and caught the mushy soil of the shoulder. The soft soil caused the car to jerk toward the ditch. I took my foot off the accelerator, hoping to slow down. Then I turned the wheel, trying to urge the car back onto the road.

The car jolted up over the ledge of the asphalt, hurling me into the opposite lane, the headlights of oncoming cars blinding me.

I quickly turned the wheel the other way to get out of the path of the car. The vehicle jerked again, this time to the right, and I felt something break underneath. Now I was headed straight toward the ditch. I remember thinking, *Airbag,* as the car hurled into the ditch.

I had my foot off the brake, but the car's momentum was strong enough to carry it up the other side of the ditch at an angle. There was a brief hesitation—no airbag. I thought I might escape okay.

Then the car started rolling over onto the driver's side.

Don't let this be my end. I'm so close.

   *   *   *   *   *   *   *   *   *   *

An abusive person is not a "nice" person who's being "occasionally" abusive. They're an abusive person who can sometimes fake "nice" qualities.

untamedhero

24. More Shedding

Your boundaries are not making you lose friends or family members. Your boundaries are making you lose gaslighters, emotional abusers, needy and greedy manipulators, self-centered narcissists and energy draining vampires. Keep standing up for yourself. You're doing great. Keep going. -elite.mindsets

It was a weird feeling being upside down. My body had started to fall out of the seat, but then the seatbelt and shoulder harness tightened and kept me in place. My cell phone had been on the seat next to me, but now it was right in front of me—on the headliner of the car, fully lit in the dark. It seemed my angels had placed it right where I could find it.

I calmly picked up the phone and dialed 911 to report the accident. The 911 operator was shocked to hear I was upside down in a ditch, and she verified that I wasn't in danger of any water. I was so disoriented. I had a hard time visualizing where I was in relation to the ground. Since I was upside down, I was now on the right side of the accident scene—even though my body's right side was on the left side. It's hard to put into words or paint the picture of how I was positioned in relation to my surroundings. I was momentarily confused.

I fumbled for the electric window controls and, fortunately, there was still power. I was able to get both front windows rolled down. Immediately, a man was there, and I heard him say, "She's alright." I carefully released my seatbelt. My body slipped a bit, and I climbed out. My right foot was caught under the brake pedal, so when I climbed out, my shoe came off. I ended up hopping and standing on one foot in the cold, mucky soil.

I was so lucky. I could have been hit head-on by cars going at least 60 mph. I could have caused someone else to swerve and get into an accident. There could have been gushing water in the ditch like there had been the day before. I had lost a shoe, and my car and groceries were upside down, but other than that, I was okay.

Since I had just passed the city limit sign, the local police weren't called. I had to wait for the state patrol. Fortunately, I didn't have to wait long. I knew Jillian was on her way to the house and was due to pass by at any time. I had to call her and let her know what happened so she wouldn't be shocked when she came upon the accident. I then called Mike at home. Soon, Jillian and Mike joined me on the side of the road as the state patrol officer took down the information.

The officer recognized the inherent danger at that point in the road—where it slanted away and where there was no real shoulder—so he didn't give me a citation. The tow truck arrived shortly after and righted the car. The body looked amazingly intact. I didn't see any damage. But the tow truck driver assured me the car was totaled. I was so bummed. I really liked my Ford Focus wagon.

It had been paid off for a while, and I was counting on taking that car with me when I left. I was already trying to manage the debt Mike kept piling on us, and I didn't want the added expense of another car payment.

I had to remind myself that I was lucky to be alive, and I tried to let the other worries pass me by.

The tow driver hauled the car back toward town and pulled over at the Havelock Parks and Recreation Department so I could retrieve my personal items. Mike helped me clean out the car. I found my other shoe, and we emptied the glove box and center console. I was taken aback when I saw the groceries.

I had at least ten dozen eggs, eight gallons of milk, and ten loaves of bread. Remember, I started buying in bulk years earlier because Mike would lose his temper if we were ever out. Many of the eggs had fallen out of their cartons and were lying on the car floor. Surprisingly, not one egg was cracked. Even the bread wasn't squished by the eight tumbling gallons of milk. I was so, so fortunate. The only casualty was the car.

I was worried about what Mike was going to say. I imagined he would go off on me for the accident. He surprised me by acting concerned for my safety. Could he really care about me? It was always so confusing trying to figure out his emotions toward me. He would be sweet and caring for a moment—just enough to make you think he was softening, maybe even changing—then he'd go right back to being an asshole.

I was relieved he didn't blow up, but I had been conditioned not to expect the calmness to last. I figured, give it time.

There's never a good time to have a car accident. It can be fun to look for a new car, but all I could think about was having another bill to pay. And I really liked my wagon. Having this happen at Christmas—when I wasn't expecting to spend that kind of money—made it even more stressful. One blessing was that Mike's dad was retired from Ford, so we were able to get an employee discount.

I don't enjoy shopping for a car with Mike. He gets so giddy about purchasing that he doesn't think about the practicality of it. He allows himself to get emotional about the purchase. I don't. I think about how the car will be used, its fuel efficiency, and its price. Craig came along with us to the dealership, and the two of them paired up and left me to myself.

They were all over the sales lot, jumping in and out of cars. It was like two kids in a toy store. They were having a great time together, imagining themselves behind the wheel of each car. I kept my wants in check. I knew this car would come with me when I left, and I wanted to make sure I could afford the payments when I did. I hated that I had to get a car right away. I didn't want to have to settle. But you can only do what you can do in a given situation, so I settled on a silver C-Max Hybrid. It was the only one on the lot, and the dealership wasn't sure when they would get another.

It was nice enough. A small four-door sedan with a gas mileage of 46 mpg. I loved that. And I loved that it was relatively inexpensive once we used the employee discount offered by Mike's dad. I hated to spend the money. Debt and no ready cash had kept me a prisoner in this marriage for way too long. I had been trying so hard for so long to get out from under debt. But this time I didn't have a choice. At least I chose a car that I felt I could afford.

Christmas was here. Craig and Jillian were home, and I got busy doing the usual baking. There were always the cookies I liked to make, but I would always ask everyone if they had a special request for a Christmas dessert. Everyone had a favorite: Jillian wanted an apple pie, Mike wanted a cherry pie, and Craig wanted a pumpkin pie. I had been disappointed in past holidays—baking their favorites only to have no one eat them. They would just go to waste. On top of that, Mike wanted me to make cinnamon rolls.

Cinnamon rolls are not easy to make. I've tried countless times and adjusted the recipe many times to get it right. Sometimes they rise too high and turn out dry. Sometimes I have a hard time getting the dough to rise due to drafts. Maybe once every four tries the cinnamon rolls turn out great. Half the time they're just okay. And other times, they're terrible. I try. I try. I try. It gets very frustrating, and the last thing I want is extra criticism from Mike.

He never hesitated to brag about his mom's cinnamon rolls. "She lets them rise six times!" "You need to get my mom's recipe." I reached out to his mom, and she told me that she hated making them and that it was always hard to get them to come out the way she wanted. She'd quit making them years ago and didn't even have the recipe anymore. So much for her "fabulous" cinnamon rolls.

It takes a long time to make cinnamon rolls, and I have to commit to several hours in the kitchen. I tried so hard to make this batch turn out great. Unfortunately, I didn't have any area warm enough for the dough to rise. Everywhere I turned there was a draft. I tried to manufacture the right air temperature, but nothing worked. The results were not good. Mike started in, making fun of the cinnamon rolls and comparing me to his mom's once again.

I explained the issue—not having a warm enough place for the dough to rise—but he just kept making jokes at my expense. I wasn't taking the criticism well. I was tired of his "holiday takedown" of me and the cinnamon rolls. It was every holiday. He never once acknowledged the effort I put in.

When I told him I didn't appreciate his condescending words, he got upset and said I was too sensitive—that I couldn't take a joke. I told him, "I'm not laughing. I don't get the joke."

Instead of recognizing that he'd hurt my feelings, he just doubled down and said, in an irritated tone, "It was just a joke. I guess you can't take jokes, and I'm just an asshole." And then he walked away.

I was done making cinnamon rolls. No more. They were too hard to make, and I rarely got any recognition for the effort or the difficulty in trying to meet his standards. It was bad enough that I made everyone's personal dessert request and then they didn't even eat it. I was taking back some of my power by refusing to make the cinnamon rolls again.

The holidays ended, and 2013 began. I was trying to figure out the point of making this house a home. I didn't have any idea when I was leaving, but somehow, deep inside, I could feel it was near. Jillian certainly couldn't go much longer without a big-girl job. I was floating above myself most of the time—just going through the motions of someone who cared about their marriage.

With Mike spending endless hours in his workshop, I decided to get some baby chicks and start raising chickens. It was so much fun. I was so grateful to have such a joyful distraction while I could. Mike was okay with it, and he helped me get a chicken coop and create a secure compound for them.

I called them my "babies." I eventually had fifteen chickens. Each one was a different variety. It made it easier to tell them apart, and they were so colorful as they wandered around the property. I named them after dead relatives so no one would be insulted. There was Lavinia, Hazel, Jolly, Georgia, and Lizzy, to name a few.

They would roam our almost two acres and eat all kinds of insects, baby lizards, snakes, and even mice.

My babies loved scraps from the kitchen and could eat an entire watermelon rind—except for the green skin. They would come running when I brought out popcorn because they knew they were going to get some. All I had to do was call out, "Hey babies, hey babies," and they would come running from all directions. It was so much fun to have them.

I was getting up to a dozen eggs a day from my babies. I had so many that I encouraged my coworkers to give me empty egg cartons, and I'd fill them. I was so grateful for the distraction my chickens provided. They gave me something that would put a smile on my face—and I needed a reason to smile.

That spring of 2013 was going to be our 30th wedding anniversary. Mike had never done anything special for me. My wedding ring had lost several stones years earlier, and I'd stopped wearing it. I had asked him repeatedly for a new ring, but he never made it a priority. There was always something more important to him—something he wanted for himself.

This time, it was the big thirty years, and I was determined to make sure we did something meaningful.

I know—why should I care? I didn't love him, and I was planning on leaving him. But I gave him one more shot to show me that I was a priority to him, that our marriage was a priority—even if just for one evening.

After thirty years, I felt I deserved at least one nice dinner somewhere, and I was determined it was going to happen.

I brought it to Mike's attention that it would be thirty years in April, and that we should do something nice. It was on a Tuesday, and the plan was that when we got home from work, we would dress up and go somewhere nice. I even told my colleagues in the science department about the plans.

I surprised myself by actually getting excited about dressing up and going out. It had been many, many years since we'd done that. I wanted to feel special and be treated special. Our thirtieth anniversary was a good excuse to finally do it. I had planned what dress to wear and had the shoes and jewelry picked out. Now I just had to wait for Mike to get home.

It was around four o'clock when Mike came home from work. He barely said a word and went straight out to his shop. I had no idea what he was doing. I figured I would give him twenty minutes to take care of whatever he was working on before I went out to check on him. I had my clothes laid out on the bed and was touching up my makeup when I decided enough time had passed.

So, I went out to the shop and found him absorbed in some project—one that clearly showed he had no intention of taking me out.

I was very disappointed. He had one more chance to prove that I was a priority—that our marriage was a priority. And once again, he proved that neither I nor the marriage ever was. I just stood there, watching him, waiting for him to take a break and notice I was there. When he finally did, I reminded him that it was our anniversary and that we were supposed to be going out.

I think I said something like, "I guess we're not going out for our anniversary."

He stopped what he was doing, looked at me with disgust, and said angrily, "So I forgot. So what? I guess you're mad at me now? Just one more thing I can't do right."

Instead of backing down and avoiding "poking the bear," I said in a very disappointed tone, "It's our thirtieth, and we made plans just last week. How can you forget our anniversary?"

I knew it would make him mad instead of contrite. I didn't care. He never, ever owned up to any of his shortcomings. He would only get defensive and try to turn everything around until somehow, I ended up apologizing for his bad behavior. How twisted and sick narcissists are.

I just turned around and walked back into the house and put my clothes away. I didn't have anything planned for dinner since we were supposed to be going out, so I don't remember what I ate. I'm sure it was something very simple. He eventually came back inside—along with his defensive attitude for forgetting our anniversary.

No apology. Nothing. We didn't talk, and I just kept to myself for the rest of the evening.

I read somewhere that if you really want to know how important you are to someone, watch how they treat you—especially during the times that matter most to you: your birthday, your anniversary, Christmas. Don't listen to hollow words. Watch how they put their true feelings into action. That will tell you exactly where you stand in their heart and in their life.

I knew I wasn't anywhere near the front of the line for anything. He had one more opportunity to put my feelings first, and he just let it evaporate—right out of his selfish, self-centered head—because I was NEVER important to him. My feelings were NEVER important enough to be validated.

At work the next day, my colleagues asked how dinner was. I got the pleasure of telling everyone that he forgot. I got the pleasure of seeing eight pairs of eyes looking at me with pity. They may not have known how bad my marriage really was—how emotionally discarded I had been for so long—but they had an idea that things weren't great. Mike had done me a favor. If I had subconsciously given him any credit that he might change after thirty years, this just solidified the truth for me: he never would.

Maybe I should have been more wounded by it, but I was already so hollow inside. It was just another example of him discarding me—one more in a long, long list of discards.

I kept busy and happily distracted with my babies. The summer came and went, and here we were again—back in the holiday season. Craig had graduated from TBS in Quantico and was waiting for flight school to start. I made my usual request for Thanksgiving dessert preferences and got busy preparing the traditional meal for everyone.

It's a lot of work, and it takes a lot of planning to make Thanksgiving dinner. I usually had little help from anyone, and I was getting tired of working for several days leading up to it, only to have everyone eat quickly, then get up from the table and leave me to clean up. I was hoping this year would be different—but I was wrong.

Mike was in his shop; Craig may have been with him, and I don't recall what Jillian was doing. Claire was with her family in Oklahoma City, following their move from Hawaii the year before. It was just me, getting everything ready. The least I had hoped for was that everyone would linger at the table with good conversation. But dinner came and went. In fifteen minutes, Mike and Craig were up from the table and had gone back out to the workshop.

Jillian helped me clear the table and put the food away. No one ate dessert.

Evening came, and Mike and Craig eventually came back into the house to watch TV. I offered them dessert, but neither of them wanted any. I really didn't want any either, but I was determined that someone would eat it—so I had a slice of something. Jillian may have had some too. But by Saturday evening, the pies were still there. I just picked them up and threw them away. I was done.

You know you're near the end of a situation when you start to shed old habits and beliefs that no longer serve you. I was done with not feeling appreciated or valued. I was done with Mike taking me for granted. I was done giving him consideration when it was rarely reciprocated. I was tired of being an afterthought—if even that.

Who says you have to have turkey and pumpkin pie for Thanksgiving? I was done.

I remember telling everyone, "That's it. I'm not making Thanksgiving dinner anymore." Mike and Craig laughed at me, thinking I was just being dramatic.

I wasn't. I was serious. And to this day, I still have not made another Thanksgiving dinner.

I was done. I had spent a lot of money and put in a lot of time to fix a meal no one seemed to be grateful for. So I made the decision that I wasn't going to waste any more of my time.

Ta-da!

It felt good to shed one more thing that I felt shackled to.

I did not want to be home for Christmas. I didn't want to cook for people who didn't appreciate it. I wanted to change my surroundings and do something for me. I declared that we were going to go to Durham and stay at a nice hotel next to Duke University. I had found it online and thought it would be a great way for me to escape the drudgery of the holidays. Craig was going to be at his girlfriend's house, but Jillian would come with us.

The only bummer in the whole plan was that Mike was going to be there. He always found a way to make the holidays a drag—but what could I do?

I was making these plans out of pure selfishness. I rarely ever put my desires or needs above everyone else's, but I was reaching the end of tolerating the crap I had put up with for so long. I had been a hollow person for a while. I needed something to fill my emotional bucket. I needed to treat myself to a trip—away from the sadness.

It was just unfortunate that the source of my sadness was coming along.

Sometime around Thanksgiving, Mike made a huge purchase without my knowledge. He bought himself a recumbent bicycle. These bikes are not cheap. I know he spent close to a thousand dollars—if not more. I was so disgusted. He tried to rationalize the value of having the bike. All I knew was that we couldn't afford it, and I knew he wouldn't use it.

He wanted to take the bikes with us to Durham. So we put three bikes on the bike carrier and, along with our luggage, headed to Durham. The hotel was very nice.

The rooms were expensive, but I got a great deal for those two days. I wanted to treat myself to something nice. Mike and Jillian thought it would be fun to go to Denny's for Christmas Eve dinner—just like in the movie The Santa Clause. I didn't care. I just wanted low-stress, quality time together. The next morning, we planned to ride bikes around Duke University.

It was a chilly day, and there was a slight breeze that made it feel cooler than the temperature suggested. It didn't matter. I wanted to go for a delicious bike ride where I could feel the speed and get my heart pumping. It was going to be cold, but I buttoned up and prepared for the adventure.

Mike was the hesitant one. He hadn't ridden the recumbent bike yet and was hoping this trip would allow him to learn. It was an unusual-looking bike—low to the ground and reclined back, with a single tire in the back and two up front. The controls for steering and braking were by the seat. It required a different kind of balance, and it was tricky taking turns. Mike had a hard time sustaining any forward movement. He kept tipping over and then getting pissed. He would cuss and flash me dirty looks. I just ignored it. *This was your wonderful idea to buy this bicycle. You can just rot with it for all I care.*

He tried repeatedly to get going, but he couldn't find his balance. Every time Jillian and I started riding, we had to stop and wait for him to regain control. I should have been patient—but I wasn't. I was counting on having a great bike ride, feeling the speed and the wind. Instead, I was barely going anywhere. I thought, *How do you like your thousand-dollar bike now?*

We went back home with a sulky Mike in the car. He kept trying to justify why he couldn't ride it. He made excuses about the conditions not being right, saying he needed a long, straight road. So, he decided that when we got back to Craven County, he wanted to stop and try riding his new bike on the side roads next to Highway 70.

We stopped, and he got his bike out and tried again. He still couldn't find his balance and kept stopping to get it back on track.

He was furious but didn't say a word when he got back into the car. He knew he had made a colossal mistake buying that bike—and he couldn't return it. He also knew I was unhappy with him, even though I didn't say a word. I didn't have to. He was angry that he couldn't ride it, and he was angry because he knew I was right about wasting the money.

I just kept silent.

It was another Christmas that was a bust. Even though I had tried to make the holidays different—tried to create something we could actually enjoy—Mike still brought his rain cloud.

He tried several other times—when the weather got better—to master the bicycle, but he never did. It just hung in the garage, out of the way. Every time I went into the garage, it was hanging there—a constant reminder of his selfishness and his obsession with spending and wasting money.

You might think he would have been humbled by the lesson. No. Not him. Spend, spend, spend.

I was getting fed up. Over thirty years of marriage, and I was getting depressed at the thought of spending another year fighting to stay out of debt, fighting to keep my head above water.

I had shed my coaching positions. I had shed the traditional Thanksgiving dinner. I was cutting back on my emotional investment in him. I grew quieter and quieter every week, pulling further and further into myself. This year had to be different. I couldn't keep going at the destructive pace he was setting. Mike was suffocating me in so many ways.

There was an entirely different *me* waiting for the opportunity to expand and breathe.

I was determined that 2014 would be the year I prioritized myself and got emotionally stronger. I just needed Jillian to move forward in her life. If she was the holdout, then I needed to get her going.

This was the year. It had to be.

*   *   *   *   *   *   *   *   *   *   *

Narcissists will go out of their way to charm others, so when you try to speak up about their abuse, it's you who appears unreasonable. By maintaining a perfect image in public, they make it difficult for others to see the reality behind closed doors.

JENNALEA_COACHING

25. The Dream

You do not have to prove or justify why what you went through was hard. -selfcare.recipe

It was a new year—and hopefully, a time for new beginnings. I had made New Year's resolutions before but never kept them. It's easy to get sidetracked by life. It's easy to allow distractions to pull you off course if you don't have the deep resolve to stay true. Most likely, my failed resolutions were because it was more comfortable to stay in the same mode I was in than to go through the discomfort of change. Even if where you are is not healthy or safe, deep down you accept it because it is your "normal." It's what you're used to.

It may seem cumbersome to dig deep within yourself and get rid of what's been keeping you from your goals. It can be scary to acknowledge the part you played in your own discomfort. And it can be gut-wrenching. But it's a necessary step so that your new path forward will stick—so that once you're on your new path, you know you have the tools and strength to stay on it.

I believe that in the past, I wasn't ready to put in the necessary work. I may have wanted parts of my life to change, but I could never really move forward if I was still carrying the wrong energy with me. I had to transform from within and let that transformation show itself to the rest of the world.

It was 2014. I had been married almost thirty-one years. I had been putting my energies into the belief that Mike was capable of change—and that I was the only one who could help him. It was this belief that kept me anchored to him and his abuse. I also believed that I deserved it.

I kept going back to that Memorial Day in 1981 when I broke up with Jack just to "explore" my sexuality, not realizing I was using Mike in the process. There was so much shame I carried for what I did to Jack—and what I did to Mike. I believed I could pay back my karma by helping Mike become happier with himself and more whole. Now I was starting to see more clearly. A bit of the veil I had placed over my eyes was beginning to lift. Just a bit. My poisoned brain was still functioning in a fog, but it was starting to clear. I could see part of the path in front of me.

The first thing I wanted to do was start feeling better about myself. I had gained twenty pounds in the last two years due to stress and menopause. So I got busy clearing out all the obstacles I had allowed to stand in my way—obstacles that had kept my health from being a priority.

I started simplifying my life. I cut back on volunteering and extracurricular activities at work. I prioritized simple meals that didn't take long to prepare or clean up. I rearranged the furniture in the living room so I would have space to work out, and I sought out some workout DVDs that were simple and focused on the whole body. I also declared that I would create quiet time for myself every night by taking a bath—without interruptions.

Once I had everything in place and had cleared the perceived restrictions from my new goal, I started taking care of me. I made sure I left work by 3:30 p.m. every day. No more staying late to get extra stuff done. Then I would come home, change, and work out. The cats and the dog always ended up on the floor with me, so I had to allow for their love and distraction.

There were many times Mike would come in from his workshop while I was working out and make comments— or make fun of what I was doing. I just ignored him and tried to stay in a positive state during this "me" time. He was busy doing his thing in the shop, and I got busy doing my thing—my physical and mental health. We really didn't have anything in common. I liked simple things. I liked quality time. He needed stuff to validate himself, and quality time was not important to him. It was what it was. I took care of me, and he took care of himself.

I realized that no one was going to make me a priority— so I had to do it for myself. I started telling Mike "no" more often. "No, I will not go to the store with you." "No, I will not watch a movie with you." "No, I don't want to go out to the shop and see what you've done." Instead, I was telling myself "yes" more often. "Yes, I deserve peace and quiet." "Yes, I can go for a walk by myself."

"Yes, I can spend the money on fresh blueberries and hide them from Mike." "Yes, I can have a glass of wine if I want." I was getting some power back by putting myself first—and I liked the results.

Unfortunately, I had to take a brief interruption from my wellness overhaul and tend to my dear Xena.

Xena was failing fast. It was just a week before, when I let her out of the house, that I witnessed her doing her last zoomies. She took off like the younger version of herself, skirting this way and that all over the backyard. I was so surprised by the burst of joy she was exuding— she was almost thirteen years old and getting very gray.

Wow—thirteen years! Could it really have been that much time? I remembered when we got her and Ozzie as pups. I remembered how she was always eager and ready to go for long walks when I got home from work. Now, she was shaking uncontrollably and couldn't muster the energy to stand up and go outside.

Knowing Xena's limitations, I would climb down off the sofa and sit by her, stroking her head. She would gaze up at me with what little strength she had, as if to say, "Thanks—I love you too." I realized her days were coming to an end, and I wanted to spend as much time with her as possible.

When it came time to take her to the vet for her last trip, I went alone. I don't recall if I even told Mike I was going. It didn't matter. It had always been me and Xena anyway. I drove carefully so she wouldn't feel the bumps and turns of the road too much. I walked her slowly into Dr. Jeff's clinic. I had called ahead, so the ladies took me immediately into one of the exam rooms, where they had placed a comfortable blanket on the floor for her.

My tears had started flowing before I even left the house, so I kept my sunglasses on. I made myself comfortable next to Xena on the floor, and soon Dr. Jeff came in to evaluate my beautiful little girl. He agreed that she was failing fast. He was so empathetic. He kindly gave me some alone time with her before returning with the barbiturate that would put her to sleep for good.

I loved on that little girl as much as I could in the short time I had to say goodbye. I thanked her for the love she gave me and her selfless attempts to protect me from Mike's assaults. I thanked her for going with me to sleep at the high school that night, and I apologized for ever leaving her alone with him—especially when I wasn't sure if Mike would keep his promise and shoot her. I told Xena I'd be looking for her when it was my time. All the while, she just kept her head on my lap, listening and looking up at me.

Dr. Jeff came back in, and I gave him permission to give Xena her last injection. I held her as I watched her breathing slow and her eyes gloss over. I could feel her life energy fading. The office staff was so kind—they left me with my dearest Xena for a while longer. I left with my sunglasses still on and my heart very heavy. What was I going to do without my dear one?

The days and weeks following Xena's death were an adjustment. Every time I came home and walked into the house, I expected to hear her toenails clicking on the floor as she ran to greet me. When I went for a walk, I would absently reach for her leash—and then remember she wasn't there anymore.

I lost Briggs after Jillian returned from the hospital in January 1996. I lost Ozzie the night he busted through the electric fence and got hit by a car in 2006. But losing my Xena really hit me hard. It seemed like parts of my old life were continuing to shed, making room for the new one ahead. I knew she wouldn't live forever, and I knew this day would eventually come—but I was still deeply affected by her passing.

Mike's workshop became a blessing for me. He spent most of his free time there, which meant I didn't have much contact with him. I was okay with that. I felt nauseous being around him. He was still spending money like we had an endless supply. He was always finding another tool he just had to have. Even though he spent, on average, at least $500 per tool he bought for the workshop, it was never enough for him. I was trying so hard to clear the negative energy from my body, but I couldn't escape the reality of the monthly bills.

I developed a great method for paying down our debt. But as soon as I got close to being debt-free, Mike found a way to set us back. The crazy thing was, together we made good money. I was the one making the least with my teaching position, but Mike made over $100K with his government contractor job. Together, we were bringing in close to $140K a year. Once you took out the taxes, we were averaging close to $10K a month. If we were making that much money, then how were we always close to being broke?

It was a disgusting amount of money that he would spend. If it wasn't in cash, then he charged the credit cards. He would buy something, then turn around and sell it for less. What a great financial strategy—especially if you want to stay in debt. It made me sick to my stomach. All the kids were now out of college and pretty much on their own, so where was the money going? I wasn't spending it. I was still trying to justify spending $20 on a new bra.

I got tired of him bullying me about money and acting like we didn't have enough. I finally asked him how much money he thought we made every year. He said, "I don't know, close to $80K." Wrong. He was shocked when I told him how much we actually made. He demanded proof, so I showed him our income tax forms. How do you not even know how much money you make? He was always disengaged from our finances. He never cared to know how much money was coming in or going out. He just wanted to spend however much he wanted, whenever he wanted.

When we built our new house, we had wanted to extend the driveway around to the back where his shop was. But the cost of laying down a driveway was too much at the time, so we had it stop at the front of the house.

Here we were, starting our second year in the house, and Mike wanted to have the driveway extended—but this time with the cheaper material, marl.

He hired a guy to come out and lay the marl. It was a big job, and it came with a big price tag. Mike never really consulted me about it. He just said he was going to do it. I questioned how we were going to pay for it. Mike said the guy would take payments. Whoopie. That doesn't make the cost any cheaper. It's still an X amount of money that has to be paid back. I was pushing money everywhere, trying to plug Mike's holes. He had no clue—and he didn't want to know. I felt the weight of his reckless spending starting to crush me again.

I can't keep doing this. I can't keep living like this. We make too good of money to be living like we have none. I was constantly sacrificing my own wants because of the debt. Mike didn't get it, and he didn't care to get it. Just stay out of his way—or suffer. I chose to stay out of his way and try to find a way out.

I remember feeling this deep sense of sadness. I had been working hard on myself to climb out of this mental darkness, and here I was—still fighting the same battle I had tried to win over thirty years ago when we were first married. I was losing the battle. I had given and given so much of my energy over the years, trying to guide him toward being a supportive and loving partner and more responsible with money. I realized I had lost. If I stayed another year, it would crush me.

The last piece of my puzzle was Jillian. I realized that getting her on her feet was going to be critical to my wellness journey. We talked every night, and she was always so bleak about her prospects. I would listen to her as she recounted her daily job searches and the few interviews she was able to line up. There were a couple of times she felt good about her prospects, but then she would get ghosted by the interviewer.

I got busy on my end looking at job market trends and where most new job hires were coming from. It seemed that technology and medical were the two fields hiring like crazy. It would require that she go back to school and get a second master's degree. I knew she wouldn't like it, but the economy wasn't favoring her degree in public history and archival work.

When I proposed to Jillian that she would need to go back to school for another degree, she freaked out. She hated that she couldn't get a job in her desired profession. She hated the idea that she would have to go back and get another master's degree when she hadn't even been able to fully capitalize on the one she already had.

I totally understood her frustration. She—and many more in her peer group—had been stunted professionally by this long, drawn-out recession. I was doing my best to help her see other options. She had to move on from where she was, and she knew that. It was a hard pill to swallow, realizing she might have to go back to school before she'd even had a chance to fully explore the career path she had originally chosen.

I looked up the most prevalent job opportunities and their pay scales. Most of them were in the medical field. Jillian was a hard no to anything medical, ever since her traumatic experience of nearly dying when she was in the fifth grade. It didn't matter if the position was a technical one—her anxiety about hospitals and doctors' offices kept her from pursuing anything in that field. That left her with a path in technology.

I looked through UNC Wilmington's catalog to see what master's programs they offered in technology. I figured if she was already living in Wilmington, it would be less disruptive for her to stay there and pursue another degree locally. I found one program that was so popular with employers that students were being hired before even finishing their degrees. This sounded promising, so I forwarded the information to Jillian. It didn't take long for her to reach out so we could discuss it.

She knew she had to do something different. She knew it was inevitable that she would have to go back and get a second master's degree. But she didn't like it, and I didn't blame her. I finally asked her a hard question: "What is it you really want to do with your life? And I don't mean professionally. What is it that you really want to do?"

She replied, "I want to travel."

Okay. Then I asked her, "How much money does an archivist make in a year?"

She gave me a number—something modest. Then I asked, "How much traveling are you going to be able to do on that salary? Remember, work is not your life. Work is there so that you can afford to do the things you really want to do. You can do so many different things with your skill sets. It doesn't have to be as an archivist. So, how much traveling are you going to be able to do on that salary?"

Now I got her to really think. She paused for a moment and said something like, "Man, I wish someone would have told me that before. I wouldn't have wasted so much time."

I just happened to have a pay scale for people with this technical degree, and it was triple what she'd be making as an archivist. I also pointed out that the technology degree would be more recession-proof if we had to go through another economic downturn. Jillian finally saw the benefit of going back to school. She didn't like it, but she understood. She went ahead and applied for the master's program at UNC Wilmington, and then waited to hear if she got in.

This was early March, and I felt a little victory just getting Jillian to inch forward a bit. It was out of my hands now, so I continued to focus on putting my positive energies back into me again. I had now been working out six days a week, eating cleaner, and taking a calming bath at night—for two months. I started seeing the change. I was physically stronger, and I found some mental calmness. I was creating a little pocket of comfort and self-healing in my hollow world, and I was very careful about what energies I allowed into my life. I was still sleeping next to Mike every night, and I was sitting down with him for dinner—but I was not allowing him into my sacred mental circle.

I realized that if Jillian went back to school, it would be at least another two years before she would be ready to stand firmly on her own. I felt my mood and energy drop significantly. I had been waiting a long time for the kids to become fully self-sufficient so I could leave Mike without it harming them. I never would have thought that my oldest would be the last to get her life going. The idea that I would have to wait another two years made it hard to stay positive.

How do I go through two more years?

I needed more than just my daily workout routine. I needed to feel grounded in who I really was. I needed to go back to when my life was the happiest. I needed to go back to Yakima.

I stayed strong in my resolve to prioritize myself. I wasn't going to let two more years with Mike keep me from loving myself. But I needed to go back home for a visit—to recharge. I wanted to go alone, and I wanted to go to Yakima. I needed to reconnect with the happiest time of my life, and I didn't want anyone else's mental baggage tagging along.

I spoke to Mike and told him I wanted to go to Yakima— only Yakima. I wasn't going to visit his family or my family. It was just going to be me, going back to fill my spiritual soul. I immediately booked a flight for the Monday after Father's Day.

The prospect of going back to Yakima in June was so exciting. It gave me the energy I needed to lift me above the daily sadness that threatened to take over my soul. I started looking up old friends' information online and reached out to let them know about my planned visit.

I had missed several high school reunions due to living on the East Coast, and it had been twenty years since I had seen any of them. I was getting so excited. I looked up Lisa, who had been a bridesmaid at my wedding, and found she was still living in the area. She was so shocked and delighted when I called her. It was almost like the past twenty-plus years had blown away as we quickly reconnected with each other's energy.

Lisa offered to let me stay with her while I was in Yakima, and she said she would organize a reunion so I could see everyone. I was flying high. I needed that. When I got off the phone, the doomsday veil that had been trying to cover me again lifted a bit. I shared my excitement and plans with my colleagues at work, and they were so happy for me. They mirrored my excitement back to me, which only amplified the energy I was already feeling.

I started looking up all things Yakima again. What was the weather like? What was going on in the news? What was the real estate market looking like? I imagined buying one of the houses and moving back to stay. I got onto Google Maps and walked around all my old neighborhoods, tracing the familiar paths I used to take. I was flying so high with the plans I had made, and I ended up with so much energy running through me because of it.

With all this energy blasting out of me, I had to burn it off somehow—or I was going to blow! I never drank regular coffee because I couldn't handle the effects of caffeine: the jitters, the shaking, my blood running fast through my brain. But this was how I was feeling with the idea of going back home. I had so much energy that I would come home from work and grab my bicycle for high-intensity rides. I needed to release the electricity shaking from my body, but I also needed to allow myself space to reflect on the healing that was happening inside me.

The good vibes kept happening. Jillian called and told me she had been accepted into the grad program for the technology degree. I was so happy for her. I knew she wasn't excited about going back to school, but she realized this was an important redirection that would allow her to start moving forward. We talked for a while about what this would mean for her. Luckily, she didn't have to adjust much—she lived literally two blocks from the university. I was so happy for her, even though I knew it meant two more years for me in hell.

Life was still happening around me. I couldn't help but be pulled back down to the reality of my day-to-day obligations—and the reminder that Mike's dark energy still loomed large over me. We completed our taxes for

2013 and received a refund of about $5,000. Instead of using that money to pay off the guy who laid down the marl, Mike wanted to use it for something else. I was left to stare at the bills and try to create some magic.

I got quietly ticked off that I was once again put in the position of making all our bills just go away. And then I realized—my lack of self-confidence and my lack of self-love had allowed me to take on that extra burden. It was a startling discovery.

Yes, Mike was selfish and self-centered. Yes, he was a bully and cruel to me. Yes, I had been afraid to push back because I had seen the physical destruction he was capable of. And yes, he had traumatized me many times with threats of self-harm. But I was also starting to realize that, because I was more concerned about pleasing him than pleasing myself, I had put myself in those horrible situations—and let him walk all over me.

I consciously decided not to participate in this anymore. I paid the bills, as usual. But I did not pay the gentleman who laid down the marl. I was not going to sacrifice my needs anymore by financially supporting Mike's selfish habits. So, I let the bill sit unpaid. I felt bad for the guy who did the work on the promise of money, but that was between Mike and him. I wasn't going to allow Mike to think he could continue to spend recklessly without any consequences. This was my passive-aggressive way of taking back some of my own power—and it felt great.

I was working out regularly. I was isolating myself from as much negative energy as I could. I was looking forward to my trip to Yakima, and I was enjoying the distraction my babies gave me. All of that was great. But I still had this deep feeling of sadness creeping up through my brain. It was the knowing that I had to push through two more years. I would sit back in my own quiet presence and just observe Mike.

He was repulsive to me. All I could see was a man who had deliberately been cruel to me—someone who had consciously decided he would treat me as less than. I remembered all the opportunities he had to publicly thank me for the sacrifices I made for his career, and how he chose not to, because "it wasn't important." I remembered all the bombshells he dropped on me. I remembered how he accused me of having an incestuous relationship with Craig. I remembered when he said that he didn't love or like our kids. I remembered how he chased me through the house and grabbed my legs as I was running up the stairs, causing me to fall on my face.

It seemed that no matter how much I was trying to heal and move forward, I couldn't—because I was still with him. And now I had two more years until Jillian completed her next master's degree and could start a self-supporting career. I kept trying to push those thoughts away. I kept trying to hang on to all the good things surrounding me. But the mental sadness was starting to win, and I was slipping into a depression.

Then Jillian called with the greatest news. She had received a job offer from the North Carolina State

Archives—and they wanted her to start in May! This was a big-girl job with big-girl benefits. I was stunned. I had resigned myself to the fact that it would be two more years. And now here she was, calling to tell me that her dream job had finally come true.

I was so happy for her. She had been in limbo for so many years, fighting her way out of her current state and trying to get her adult life going. She couldn't contain her happiness as she related every detail of the job offer and what it would mean for her. She declared that she was going to continue with her second master's degree, since she wanted to ensure she had a recession-proof option. She was going to talk to the department chair at the university and see about switching her acceptance to an online format. We set a date to go to Raleigh to start looking at apartments and exploring the area. She was flying high—and I was flying high.

It was incredible, the feeling I got when I received the news of her job offer. I could feel the weight fall off my shoulders. It caught me by surprise—how noticeable and real the weight shift felt to me. I knew then that Jillian was going to be all right. And almost immediately, I saw this imagined curtain pull back. The light blazed through and surrounded me. I could feel the sun shining on me, and I could see the promise ahead.

Then I had the dream.

Out of nowhere, Jack came to me. He was smiling his most beautiful smile. He reached out to me and took my hand, and I immediately felt home. I could feel his love for me surrounding my entire being. And then he said to me, "You don't have to live like this anymore."

I woke up immediately and started sobbing into my pillow. I was afraid Mike would wake up and ruin it for me, so I just held the pillow close to my face as I allowed the deep sobs and tears to come over me. It felt like a lifetime of emotions I had held back was pouring out of me. I was giving myself permission to be happy. I was finally giving myself permission to leave.

*   *   *   *   *   *   *   *   *   *   *

The effects of narcissistic abuse: After the...criticizing, manipulation, name calling, intimidation, belittling, financial control, pathological lying, blaming, guilt tripping, shaming, threats, jealousy, rage, isolating, disrespect, and gaslighting, you are left feeling...lonely, confused, exhausted, helpless, anxious, hopeless, intimidated, depressed, ashamed, full of self-doubt, trapped and scared. The long-term impact of narcissistic abuse may include...chronic stress, depression, c-ptsd, addiction, self-harming, emotional shutdown, physical health issues, severe isolation, severe mental health struggles, an inability to function in daily life. This is abuse.

LOVE.leaxo

26. Making Plans

It feels so good knowing that little me would run to a woman like me for help.

-AlphaFemal.inc

Having Jack come to me in my dreams was so prophetic. He had always been there for me—even though he didn't know it. My breakup with him was supposed to be temporary. In my mind, we were always meant to be together. Even though we never did reunite, I never lost that deep connection I felt toward him. He was always in the back of my mind, and many times, he would push himself to the front just to remind me that I was worthy and deserving of all good things. Of course it would be his voice that came to me and told me, "You don't have to live like this anymore."

Instead of feeling euphoric now that I knew I could leave, I was surprised by how quickly and deeply my sad emotions started to flow. I couldn't understand what was happening. I knew I had been living in trauma for many years, and I knew that I would somehow—some way—break free. I thought that when the time finally came, I would be deliriously happy. So where did all this sadness come from?

I found myself becoming totally detached from my surroundings. I was numb everywhere. I don't know how I functioned from day to day because my senses seemed to stop working. My eyes were open, but I couldn't remember seeing anything. My ears were working, but I couldn't detect any sound. I had never been as numb as I was then.

I went to work, and I came home. I know I interacted with people, and I know I got through my lesson plans for the day, but I didn't remember any of it. I could barely recall what I had done the moment before. What was going on with me? Then, after a few days of this, I realized—I was in mourning.

My poor brain should have been focused on my escape. Instead, I was feeling a deep sense of sadness for all that I had lost over the past thirty-three years: the loss of not having a loving and committed partner by my side, the loss of opportunities for real happiness, the loss of my own self as I became smaller so Mike's ego could stand taller, and the loss of what life could have been with Jack. So many years of my life were lived in fear, torment, and darkness. So many years of my life were gone.

I tried looking back to find a glimpse of the happy times, but the only ones I found were with me and the kids. I couldn't find any with Mike. It was all dark. I might have thought I was happy early in the marriage, but now—with time passed and the privilege of hindsight—I realized any perceived happiness was built on lies.

He pretended to be this wonderful person, but he wasn't. He showered me with gifts and attention early on just to get me emotionally hooked. Then he methodically stripped me of my self-worth and self-confidence and caused me to believe that I was the one responsible for his misery.

All the gaslighting, the angry self-projection, the mental and emotional turmoil that came out of nowhere, and the criticism disguised as love. Then there was the huge betrayal of finding out he was a cross-dresser—after we were married and had a family.

He destroyed almost every holiday or special event. He filled celebratory moments with tantrums, explosions, and selfish redirection of everyone's attention. Mother's Day plans he hijacked, anniversaries he let slip by or dismissed, and that trip to Seattle in the summer of 1990 when I was a single married parent on a family vacation.

I had actively sought his company so we could be more emotionally connected, but he rejected it. I would go out to the garage to try to spend time with him, only to be told I was weird. I asked him multiple times to go on a cruise with me, or to take a weekend trip somewhere. My suggestions were always rejected.

Eventually, it became easy for me to associate those rejections as personal rejections—of me. I wasn't important enough to him. If I had been, he would have recognized that I needed quality time with him. But he was never in tune with my emotional needs, and he walked over them like they were just shadows on the ground.

The mourning extended to my own accountability. How did I not see who he really was? Why did I ever put up with so much of his abuse for as long as I did? Why didn't I leave when I found out he was a cross-dresser? Why didn't I leave when he dragged me down the stairs? Why didn't I leave when he tormented Craig and busted open his bedroom door? Why didn't I leave each time he pulled out a gun to use on himself—or me?

All of these moments felt like lost opportunities. And I started heaping the blame on myself for the abuse.

It would take me many more years to understand that blaming myself was just another symptom of the deep psychological wounds I had accumulated over the thirty-plus years we were together. Logically, I could tell myself I wasn't to blame. I could tell myself that the real and prolonged trauma had caused brain damage and cognitive dissonance. This neuro damage was what kept me tied to him.

I could logically tell myself all of that—but my brain wouldn't let me believe it. I took on a large amount of self-blame as I slid into that deep, dark well of mourning.

I tried to hide it. I thought I was doing a pretty good job functioning day to day. I was still meeting the needs of my colleagues, my students, and my family. But Jillian noticed. She was visiting for a weekend, and I didn't realize she would be able to detect my sadness while we were watching TV.

"Are you okay, Mom?"

It took me by surprise. I didn't realize I was giving off low vibrations. I assured her I was okay. I thought how nice it was that someone was in tune with me and knew something was off. For many years, I felt invisible because no one knew about the pain I was going through. Now, here was my daughter picking up on the fact that something wasn't right. I really appreciated her thoughtful detection. It made me feel valued.

I kept trying to move through the darkness that was engulfing me, and I kept willing my body to pretend that everything was okay. The earth was still spinning, the sun was still rising and setting, and I still had things to get done. The first of many tasks was finding an apartment for Jillian in Raleigh. We took a weekend trip to look at apartments. I was doing a great job hiding my sorrow. I didn't want to ruin this joyous occasion by allowing my sadness to spill over.

Fortunately, it didn't take long for Jillian to find a great place just north of the Capitol building where she would be working. Now we just needed to get her packed up from our condo in Wilmington and moved into her new space by the first of May.

At the same time, I was pushing myself to move beyond the mourning and start planning my exit. When would be a good time for me to leave? I was scheduled to fly to Yakima after school let out for the summer. I could come back from that trip and start packing things up and leave by the end of July. But what about Mike? I couldn't tell him I was leaving. He would take that as the ultimate insult—and he could lose his mind and come after me with a gun. When could I pack up without him seeing and asking questions? It would have to be done in secret. But when?

Mike's mom was doing poorly, and she wasn't expected to last past fall. I thought about how hard her passing would be on Mike, and with me leaving, it would only make things harder. Should I wait until after she passed before I left? But when would that be? How much longer? If she didn't pass until fall, I would have already started another school year. That would mean waiting until after Christmas, when the semester ended, before I could leave.

But that would be nine more months.

I couldn't stand the thought of waiting another nine months. Once I had made the decision to leave, I had to leave as soon as I could. I couldn't wait any longer. I had already emotionally detached from Mike, and the longer I was with him, the more I detested him—and the closer I was moving toward a mental breakdown. I couldn't wait another nine months. Not with this deep sense of sadness blanketing me every moment.

Then I realized—no time would ever be a good time. Here I was in this deep, dark mental state, and instead of putting my own health and happiness first, I was still concerned about everyone else but me.

Enough.

I've done enough. It's time for me.

I made the decision that instead of going home for a visit in June, I would be going home to stay.

It was only six weeks before my deadline. Six weeks. I had a whirlwind of things to do in just six weeks. I had to move Jillian out of her condo and into her new apartment in Raleigh. I was still teaching, and I had to get my students ready for their state exams. I was in charge of the high school graduation ceremonies, and it was time to start getting those plans into action. I had to contact a lawyer, look for and apply to a teaching position in Yakima, look for a place to live, organize all my legal documents and investment information, carefully set aside and pack up essentials—and more. All of this had to be done in just six weeks. And all of it, without anyone knowing.

I couldn't trust anyone with what I was going to do. Not because my friends would purposely betray me, but because I knew this information would be so traumatic for them to bear alone. Remember, no one saw the abuse. Friends would be so shocked by the contrasting image I would present to them. It would be hard for them to wrap their minds around the stark difference between the Mike they knew—and the Mike that I knew.

I imagined that the weight of knowing I was leaving Mike would be too heavy and traumatic for any of my friends to carry alone. I imagined it would be so burdensome that they might feel the need to share it with someone they trusted—just to ease their own pain. I could understand the impulse. But I couldn't take the chance that Mike would find out and snap. I was sincerely afraid for my safety.

We had lived in this small town for over twenty-five years, and I knew a lot of people: the chief of police, the fire chief, the mayor, generals, business owners, my colleagues, and parents of students and athletes—past and present. News of me leaving Mike would be huge. It would travel like wildfire. It had to be done in secret. I had to protect myself. But I also had to protect my friends from the guilt they might feel if their loyalties between the two of us were tested.

I had to get started immediately—putting all the pieces together for my safe exit. I began searching through my phone for lawyers and making calls to find out what I needed to do to get the divorce started. I began researching the credentials I would need to teach in Washington state. I looked for apartments in Yakima and started trying to figure out where I would live. I needed to get a credit card in my own name, and I looked into how to cash out the vacation time I had acquired at work.

I had so much to do—and I had to keep it to myself. I did most of my searches on my phone or on my computer at work because I was afraid Mike might see what I was doing on the home computer. I realized I needed my own laptop. That way, I could keep my documents and folders secure from his knowledge, and I'd need one for myself when I left anyway.

There was so much that had to be done—so much planning racing through my mind all at once—that I didn't have time to entertain sadness anymore. I started thinking more and more about Jack and how timely his message had been for me. Then I decided to try to get in contact with him. It had been a long time—over thirty years—but I had always felt a deep connection with him. Deep in my soul, I knew he would still feel the same for me. I had to try.

I was able to find his mom's phone number online, and I placed a call on an afternoon when Mike was out. Barbara answered the phone, and I immediately recognized her voice. She was so delighted and surprised to hear from me. We talked for quite some time, and I filled her in on my abusive marriage and my plans to leave.

She was so sympathetic and supportive. When I asked her about Jack—if he was married—she said, "No, but he does have a girlfriend." She told me he had been married twice and had two girls and a boy, just like me. I told her how I had tortured myself all these years over the way I broke up with Jack. That it was supposed to be temporary. I told Barbara that I felt like there was so much unfinished business—and I owed Jack a complete and honest explanation for what happened.

She agreed to give Jack the letter I was going to write. So I got busy putting my thoughts together, sealed the envelope, and mailed it to Barbara to pass on to him. I was moving back to Yakima, and Jack was a big part of my past there. It was one of the many wrongs I felt I needed to make right so I could move forward with peace in my new life. I just had to wait to see if he was interested in reconnecting with me.

Meanwhile, I had reached out to a lawyer in New Bern and found out how much it would cost to retain them. It was more money than I had on hand, and I didn't feel safe taking it out of our investments for fear Mike would find out. So I had to reach out to my dad and my stepmother, Norma, for help.

Me, my lawyer, my dad, and my Norma—that was all who knew about my plans to leave. Dad and Norma were super supportive. They sent me the money I needed for the lawyer almost immediately, with instructions to reach out again if I needed anything else. There had been a few times in the past when I had let a few things slip to my dad that hinted my marriage was not healthy. Dad was always very compassionate and simply said, "If you decide to leave him, I'll support you. If you decide to stay, I'll support you." He was unconditional with his love and support, and it meant a lot to know I had someone in my corner if I needed them.

Before my first meeting with my lawyer, I grabbed all our investment documents and took them to the school to make copies. I made sure the originals were placed back in our file cabinet so Mike wouldn't have any suspicions. Over the thirty years we were together, we had systematically made monthly investments. Mike had taken a lot out for one thing or another, but there was still a substantial amount of money in the accounts. I wanted to make sure all the money was accounted for when it came time to split the assets.

It was emotional recounting some of the highlights to my lawyer as to why I was seeking a divorce. I asked if I had the right to take the car with me. After all the years we were married, I never had a car in my name. I was worried I could be accused of stealing it. The lawyer assured me that since it was the primary car I drove, it would be considered mine and I would have no problem taking it with me. That gave me some relief—I couldn't afford to get another car, and I knew I wouldn't have the money to buy one.

So many layers of life were continuing to move through me and around me. I could check the box on securing a lawyer, but I still had so much more to do. It was near the end of April, and Jillian was packing up her condo in Wilmington, getting ready for her move to Raleigh. So Mike and I took a Saturday to help her. As usual, Mike hijacked the purpose of the trip to scout out more tools for his garage, and then we made a side trip to Dick's Sporting Goods for him to look at guns. It was here that I received a phone call—from Jack.

I was so excited and nervous to hear from him for the first time in over thirty years. I walked outside the store to the car so I could talk freely. It was amazing to hear his voice. I could hear his smile through the phone as we chatted excitedly. He seemed genuinely happy to reconnect. I know that on my end of the line, I couldn't stop smiling. He sounded just the same—he sounded so good. I had just turned fifty-three, and Jack would be fifty-six in July, but his voice sounded just like it did the last time I saw him when he was twenty-five.

I quickly told him I was moving back to Yakima to start over. I wanted to get together with him once I got there so I could go over what had happened between us. He was so sweet to me, and he promised that we would make it happen. While I was on the phone with Jack, Mike and Jillian came out of the store, and I worried Mike would ask who I was talking to. I didn't have a good response. Fortunately, Mike didn't say a word. Then again, he rarely ever took notice of what I did.

I got off the phone with Jack, and we both promised to keep in touch. I was flying high. I was so grateful that Jack wanted to reconnect as much as I did. Just hearing his voice lifted my energy and gave me more resolve to continue carefully extracting myself from Mike.

We got Jillian packed up out of the condo and moved into her apartment in Raleigh. It was a nice apartment— with a deck, fireplace, and room for a washer and dryer. It felt good to see her finally moving forward with her adult life. She was almost twenty-nine years old. It had been seven years since she earned her undergraduate degree, five years since she finished her first master's.

She had been waiting five years for the economy to tilt her way. And it had been five years that I had been waiting for her to get her feet solidly on the ground.

Now I was finally tucking her into her new apartment and her new life—while I was making my own plans to move forward with mine.

I had just gotten started on my long list of "to-dos." Getting Jillian moved into her apartment was huge. Now I had to move on to the other pieces—I was running short on time. I discovered I would need to take a couple of competency exams in my teaching specialties so I could get my science credentials in Washington State. The nearest exam center was in Wilmington, and I quickly scheduled to take them the next week while Mike was going to be gone.

Mike had made plans to fly back to Seattle to be with his mom and help with repairs around her house. He was going to be gone for a whole week. I decided to take advantage of his absence to do some aggressive packing and get things into storage. Every day when I got home from work, I packed up essentials I needed and wanted to take with me. I was careful not to pack anything that Mike might notice as missing.

I wasn't taking a lot with me, but it still felt like it took a while to pack what I did. I realized that if I was going to keep Mike from finding out about my exit, I'd have to do a lot of last-minute packing. I couldn't take the pots and pans just yet. I had to wait on the coffee maker and all the pictures on the walls. I was taking very little furniture with me, but even that would have to be loaded onto the moving truck at the very last minute.

I didn't write anything down. I didn't make any lists. I didn't want him to find any evidence at all. There was too much at risk. Everything was in my head. I made mental lists every day and would visualize myself taking down the pictures, packing the last-minute items, and loading the furniture in a very methodical order. I didn't want to forget anything that was important to me, and I didn't want to waste time when it came time to load the U-Haul.

I took a day off work during the week Mike was away visiting his mom, and I went to Wilmington to take my competency exams. I was flying high when I finished, knowing I could now officially apply for open teaching positions in Yakima. I needed someone to share my excitement with. I called my dad and my Norma. They cheered for me and celebrated the progress I had made. Then I tried calling Jack. After all, he was one of only four people in the entire world who knew I was leaving Mike. I left an excited message, and the next day, Jack got back to me.

Once again, it was so nice to hear his voice—and to hear him be excited for me. I told Jack all the progress I had made so far, and he was genuinely surprised. He gave me more encouragement to keep going and wished me well. Everything was moving in the right direction for me. I just had to be careful not to tip my hand.

When Mike returned from Seattle, he never noticed that anything was missing. The linen closet was less cluttered since I had packed up towels, blankets, and sheets. If Mike asked, I'd just tell him I was donating things to Goodwill. To further support my story, I cleverly placed extra open boxes in the spare bedroom in plain sight. I wanted Mike to see them. That way, if he asked about them, I could say I was using the boxes to pack things up for donation. I wanted him to get used to seeing a few boxes out. It would give me the opportunity to continue packing right under his nose if needed—and I needed those boxes ready to go when it was time to leave.

As it turned out, Mike never noticed that the linen closet was nearly bare, nor did he ask about the extra open boxes in the spare bedroom. He was perpetually caught up in his own world and rarely noticed anything I did. This was the perfect time for me to be invisible to him. I was able to continue putting all the moving pieces in place so that I could blast off when the time was right— and he had no clue.

But when would the time be right?

My flight reservations to Yakima were for the Monday after Father's Day. I wasn't going to cancel them, even though I knew I wouldn't use them. I didn't want Mike to find out the flight was canceled and start asking questions. I still needed to pack the rest of my things and leave while he was at work. That meant I had to leave during the workweek.

The high school graduation was scheduled for Saturday, June 7, and since I was in charge of the ceremony, I would have to wait until the following week to leave. School would be out by then, and only the teachers would remain—cleaning up classrooms and turning in equipment.

I figured I had a short window of opportunity. I was shooting for the earliest—Wednesday, June 11—but no later than that Friday the 13th. It would all depend on Mike's work schedule for the day. Mike was working at the AV-8B simulator building on base as a civilian instructor. His hours changed daily, and he never knew what his schedule was going to be until the night before. Plus, Mike might be scheduled to work anywhere from three to five hours. He never put in a full eight-hour day, even though he was paid for eight hours. I needed him out of the house for at least four hours. That part was totally out of my hands, so I just hoped that at least one of those three days in June would work in my favor.

Next up, I had to get a credit card in my own name. I needed to get one soon so I could reserve the U-Haul truck and the car trailer I'd need. I was able to get the credit card immediately, and fortunately, it came with a large credit limit. That was important. I wanted to be sure I had the money I needed to get home. There was hardly any money in our savings account, and I still couldn't take any out of our investments for fear he would find out. The credit card would be my lifeline.

I called around and found that the only U-Haul business that had a car trailer was in Morehead City, about twenty-five minutes away. I went ahead and reserved it. I was able to reserve a modest U-Haul truck at the dealer in Havelock. I would have to pick up the truck first, load it up, drive to Morehead City to get the trailer attached, then return to Havelock to load my car onto the hauler. So many details—and they were all tucked safely in my head.

It was obvious I couldn't pull all this off on my own when the day came to leave. I needed someone to help me. It had to be someone I could trust, but someone I wasn't socially close to. I had a lot of friends, but because of their relationship with both me and Mike, I just couldn't ask them. It wasn't fair to get them emotionally caught up in something that would tear them apart. Friends would be torn between their loyalties to me and to Mike. It would be unfair to put anyone in that situation.

But a casual colleague wouldn't have emotional ties to either of us—they could help me pack without getting caught up in the emotion of it.

There was an English teacher I really clicked with professionally, but whom I wasn't socially active with. I approached Dawn and told her my story. She was so, so supportive. She was one of those people who was like a pit bull if you needed her to be. I knew she could keep my secret and be there for me when the time came.

I told Dawn my plans and my fears. I explained the small window I was working with and how I wouldn't know which day would be the day until the night before. She was all in. The plan was that I would call her the night before, as soon as I found out Mike's schedule. What a big relief it was to know I had someone who would help me in those final hours.

It didn't take long after I submitted my applications for teaching positions to start receiving phone calls. Math, Science, and Special Ed teachers are highly sought after, so when the three schools I applied to received my application, they reached out immediately. Washington State is three hours behind North Carolina, so when the administrators called to talk to me, it was after 6:00 p.m. our time. Mike was home, and I had to scurry into the bedroom to chat.

One by one, the schools contacted me. I set up phone interviews for the following week and made plans to be out of the house when they called. I needed to be able to talk freely without Mike walking in on the conversation.

The next step was to line up job references. Unfortunately, that meant I would have to confide in more people about my plan to leave. I was worried—but I had no choice. The time had finally come when I had to tell John, my department chair, and my principal, Dr. Murphy, that I was leaving. I would need both of their recommendations for my job applications. I knew it would be very emotional, but it had to be done.

I first reached out to John. He was the one who had the sofa in his office that I slept on when I left Mike several years ago. He was also the one who had caught me sleeping at the high school—but kindly never brought it up. Now I had to tell him I was leaving, trusting that he would keep it private.

I met John after school in his classroom. He was always an empathetic and compassionate person. He was skilled at just listening and making you feel like you were the most important person in the world in that moment. I shocked him when I told him I was leaving—and that Mike didn't know. The tears started flowing as I implored John not to say anything to anyone.

"If it gets back to Mike," I said, "then I'm out of here just like that." I snapped my fingers. "I'll leave with nothing."

John gave me a big hug. He told me how much I was going to be missed, and he assured me that he would keep everything private.

Next, I met with Dr. Murphy. It was pretty much a re-run of my meeting with John. I got emotional and told him I would leave in a heartbeat if Mike got word of it. He promised it would stay confidential. Then we talked about who my successor would be as graduation chair, and how to turn in my keys at the end. Two band-aids ripped off, one after the other. It was painful to say it all out loud. I had no choice but to include both John and Dr. Murphy in my plans. Now, there were seven people who knew I was leaving.

Immediately after talking with Dr. Murphy, I contacted the central office for the school district and got the paperwork for my resignation and for cashing out my vacation time. I rarely took any time off work, so I had a ton of vacation and sick leave that I never used. I was able to get close to $5,000 for my unused vacation days, and I was reminded that I would still receive a paycheck for the month of July. Super. I could use every penny to help me relocate to Yakima.

What I needed now was a place to live when I moved back. Jack had been reaching out to me from time to time during my workweeks in May. We chatted about how my plans were going, and I asked him for recommendations on apartments. He suggested the Lake Aspen apartments off River Road and said that if I had the option, I should choose one with a lake view. I thanked him and reached out to the office manager right away to get my application started.

They quickly accepted my application and told me I could expect to move in by the first of July. Sweet! I was crossing more tasks off my mental list.

It was now the end of May. I had less than two weeks left before leaving. I had kept up with my six-day-a-week workout routine and was looking and feeling stronger. I had lost almost twenty pounds and my clothes weren't fitting anymore. It was time to shop for some new summer clothes.

I headed down to Morehead City and stopped at the local Marshall's. I could afford their discounted clothes, and I quickly found some items that worked well for the season. While I was there, I ran into a friend, who started chatting with me about who knows what. I wasn't really listening. I was just marveling at the fact that this was probably the last time I would see her—and she had no clue.

I had to interrupt our conversation because I received a phone call from Davis High School in Yakima. I stepped away to talk in private and was thrilled to hear that they were offering me the science position for the next school year. They had already checked my references and didn't want to wait through the weekend to get back to me—they were afraid the other schools would beat them to it.

Holy cats! I was ecstatic, but I couldn't show it. My friend was still nearby, and I didn't want her to ask what was going on. I had an apartment, and now I had a job offer. Everything else was just whipped cream with a cherry on top. I knew then that it was really going to happen. I was going to be free.

It was Memorial Day weekend, and Craig came home. He was stationed in Pensacola, Florida, for flight school and drove home in his new blue Ford Ranger pickup for the long weekend. I was still running around, taking care of the little details and getting ready for my departure. Early one morning that weekend, I backed into his truck while heading out to run an errand. I put a big dent in both his truck and my car.

Holy crap! This is not what I needed right now. I was going to be leaving in less than two weeks, and I didn't have the luxury of waiting around to get my car fixed. What if I took it in and they didn't finish in time for my deadline? I knew Mike would want to take the car to the body shop right away, and I was afraid I wouldn't get it back within the nine days I had left. Plus, I still had so much to do—I couldn't be without my car at that time.

Just as I expected, Mike wanted to take the car in immediately. Somehow, I convinced him to wait. I insisted I couldn't be without it until after graduation this coming Saturday. He backed off and said he'd take it in when I flew out to Yakima in two weeks. *Yes, good plan. Just keep believing that I'm flying out to Yakima.*

I was so driven to get all the details tucked in my mind taken care of. So far, I was doing great. Step by step, task by task, I kept moving forward. My mind was spinning constantly, trying to keep tabs on what I had done and what remained. I would come home from work with so much adrenaline running through me. I'd grab my bike and take off on a long, hard ride. I used that time to quietly reflect on everything left to do—and to find peace within my soul.

Mike was usually content to be by himself in his workshop. He rarely showed interest in anything I was doing. So I was surprised when, as I got ready to go for a bike ride, he asked if he could come with me. Fine. *I don't care. Just don't ruin it for me.*

We rode all around the housing development with Mike leading the way. At one point, he stopped to wait for me. When I caught up, I could tell he wanted to talk. In a very somber tone, he said, "Don't leave me."

What the heck? Where did that come from? Why would he say that? I knew he had no idea I had actively made plans to leave, but somehow, he must have detected me pulling away. Even though he paid little attention to me—and even though I was playing it cool—he must have noticed how I had emotionally detached, and he was worried.

I didn't say a word. I just looked at him with no expression on my face. After a moment, we got back on our bikes and headed toward home.

It was June 4, less than a week before I was leaving, and it was hot and humid in North Carolina. Sweat rolled down my back as we arrived home. I was counting on a quick dinner, a bath, and bed. I had no intention of discussing the comment he made during our bike ride. I just wanted to get through another day so the next one would bring me closer to leaving.

I got busy making dinner while Mike went out to the workshop. I mentally ticked through my last-minute packing list while I cooked. I was still taken aback that he sensed my detachment. *Good. I'm glad he's feeling a bit unstable.* He kept me off balance for all of the thirty-plus years we were married. He could stand to experience a little of what he put me through.

I got dinner on the table and called him in to eat. We sat down, side by side, each of us quietly eating. The TV may have been on, but for me, it was just silence. Halfway through dinner, Mike tried to reel me back in from my emotional distance by playing the poor victim.

He lowered his voice and said sadly, "I know I'm not a good person. You should have married Jack."

Yes, I should have. But I didn't say anything. I just sat quietly, eating my dinner. I had no response.

In the past, I might have felt compelled to say something to counter his statement. I might have said, "Oh no, Mike. Don't say that. You know I love you." I would've said it just to pull him back from that dark ledge and prevent an emotional or physical explosion. But I wasn't going to relieve him of his worries this time. This time, I sat in silence. I'm sure my silence frightened him.

I didn't care.

I had one more week. Just one more week.

It was the final week for students. Final exams were underway, and graduation was scheduled for Saturday. I still had a lot to do before I could walk away and leave. I had to administer and proctor exams. Final test scores needed to be recorded and posted to report cards. I still had to pack up my classroom supplies and put them in the storage unit I'd rented in town. I also had to run graduation practice on Friday and finalize edits to the graduation program before they were printed for the ceremony. And, of course, there was still graduation on Saturday.

One of my colleagues walked into my classroom after I had packed everything up and questioned why I had taken everything down off the walls. I couldn't tell her the truth, so I casually said something about how school maintenance was going to paint my room over the summer. She just smiled and walked away. I didn't like the lies. But no one, except me, knew the real risk of Mike finding out. I had to lie—but it made my heart heavy.

Graduation practice came and went on Friday, June 6. It was an early rise the next day to get ready for the morning graduation ceremonies. It would be my last big responsibility for school, and I was feeling the bittersweetness of it all. My soul, my spirit, had to leave everything behind so I could find my own peace.

I had been blessed with a great group of teachers, many of whom were kind enough to volunteer with me for graduation. I loved every one of them. I wanted to pull them aside and give each a goodbye hug or tell them how much they had meant to me over the years. But I couldn't. So, I just quietly observed each one of them at graduation and offered a silent blessing for their friendship.

The weekend passed, and now it was Monday, June 9—two days before my earliest departure on Wednesday. I reached out to my friend Lisa, who was going to let me stay with her when I got to Yakima. I told her that I was now coming for good. She was so supportive. She had also gone through a divorce and knew how hard the transition could be. She gladly extended my stay until I could move into my apartment in July. She was person number eight who now knew.

In my head, it was check, check, check as I kept rattling off all the tasks that needed to get done. There wasn't much left. I still needed to pack up the clothes in my closet and dresser, and all the last-minute items I wanted to take with me. You'd think my mental load would have gotten lighter—but it just kept shifting to the next phase of my exit.

I had pulled out my laptop to do some personal work and was surprised to see it had linked up with the home computer. I started seeing online searches and prompts that I hadn't made—searches for power tools and movies. Then, I saw something that made my stomach turn. Right there in front of me were online feeds for cross-dressing.

Mike had been uploading videos of men dressing as women. I was disgusted. If I had ever felt any remorse for what I was doing to Mike, it ended there. I had suspected that he was still dressing up in women's clothes—and now I had confirmation. Ultimately, I didn't care what he did. I just didn't want to know about it. It had been so difficult all these years to push the thought of him wearing women's clothes—my clothes— out of my mind. If I didn't know about it, I could pretend it wasn't happening anymore. But this realization made me physically ill.

I am so out of here.

Another realization hit me: if I could see what Mike was doing on the home computer, then he might be able to see what I had been doing on my laptop. I panicked. From that point forward, I decided I would only use my phone for anything online. I only had two more nights in this house with him—if I was able to leave on Wednesday. I had come too far to risk him finding out now.

On Tuesday, I went to work and finished turning in all my assigned equipment and closing up my classroom. We had a retirement lunch for one of our science teachers, and some of our previously retired teachers had come to celebrate. It was nice to see everyone together one more time. Even though the party wasn't for me, I pretended it was. I pretended I was able to give a fond farewell to my partners in the trenches. I took pictures and gave hugs.

John, the department chair, had created a sweet goodbye gift for our retiring colleague. When everyone left, he quietly slipped one of those gifts into my tote bag. It had a heartfelt message from him about how I would be missed and how he wished he could have given me a going-away party.

I was very mindful of the loss I would feel when I left. But I was also very mindful that I didn't have a choice anymore. Go away and survive and thrive—or stay and die.

Heading home, I called Dawn to make sure she was still up for tomorrow morning if Mike's work schedule accommodated it.

She said a very strong, "Hell yeah."

I hung up and managed a small smile at her comment. I realized I was conserving my emotions. There was still too much to do, and I remained cautious of Mike finding out.

My stomach was in knots, knowing that tomorrow could be it. I had to go for a bike ride to work off the stress and calm my nerves. One more ride around the neighborhood. Would I miss it? No. I had mostly experienced pain and darkness during the twenty-eight years I had lived in North Carolina. I would miss my friends—but not North Carolina.

I returned home and put my bike in the garage, right next to his disgusting recumbent bicycle that he never rode and wasted money on. Just another confirmation that I was doing the right thing.

Mike was in his workshop. He was due to get his work schedule within the hour. I busied myself writing my farewell letter to him and gathering all the house and condo keys to put in the envelope. I went outside and spent a little time with the chickens, then made sure they were secured in their coop for the night.

Mike came in shortly after. I was hoping he had the information I wanted to hear—that he would be working for several hours the next day. I hesitated to ask, unsure whether it would come across as too suspicious. With so much at stake, I was getting paranoid. I wasn't sure if Mike would be able to pick up on my true intentions.

I was busy making dinner for us when he offered the magical words I had been waiting for: "I'm working tomorrow from 9 to 1."

Glory, glory, hallelujah.

I called Dawn and said, "Tomorrow is it."

*   *   *   *   *   *   *   *   *   *   *

You don't need to have that last conversation with the toxic person. You have told them how you felt thousands of times before. They will not give you closure, nor will they have any real remorse. They will just try to manipulate you like they always have and then they will twist everything around to make it your fault.

Maria Consiglio @understandingthenarc

27. Breaking Away

You don't owe them closure. The only closure you need is accepting that they were never going to change. Walking away is the closure. -evolvewith_sophie

The time had finally come. Tomorrow was the day. Thank goodness. I had no Time for celebrations—even if only internal. I wasn't gone yet. I wouldn't allow myself to really feel or believe the end was here until I was safely on the road and gone. In the meantime, I needed to mentally go over everything I had left to do before tomorrow morning, as well as how I was going to extract the last of the things I still needed to pack.

While Mike was busy entertaining himself in front of the TV, I got busy packing my clothes out of the closet and dresser, and my personal things from the bathroom. I used one of the open boxes I had left in the spare bedroom for the past two weeks and quickly made good use of it. I stayed vigilant in case Mike started my way. Fortunately, he was so caught up in his show that I didn't have to worry. I was taking a chance that he might notice my empty closet and drawers, but I was betting on his indifference to me continuing.

I walked around the house, making a final visual plan of everything I was going to take. The extra boxes were ready in the spare bedroom. I just needed to act quickly tomorrow morning in case Mike came home sooner than expected.

I put my beautiful chickens to bed in their coop for the last time and blew them all a silent kiss goodbye. I picked up our two black cats, Jack and Lilly, and gave them each a long hug and kiss. I had wanted to take them with me, but I knew having pets would make finding an apartment difficult. I just hoped Mike wouldn't take out his anger on them after I was gone. They were such sweet souls.

It was finally time to go to bed, and it didn't take long for Mike to join me. The lights were already off, and I was trying to calm my spinning mind so I could sleep. Not long after he came to bed, we heard what sounded like a series of high-pitched squeals. Mike scared the shit out of me when he jumped up, reached under the bed, grabbed his rifle, and had it loaded and cocked in less than twenty seconds. He ran to the sliding glass door in our bedroom, opened it, and went outside to find the animal making the noise.

I lay there, shaking. If he could get to that gun and have it loaded so quickly, then I wouldn't get very far if he found out what I was doing. It was another reminder of why I was leaving—and not looking back. I didn't trust him, his ever-shifting emotions, or his self-control. I certainly didn't trust that he wouldn't use the gun on me in a fit of rage.

I was so, so glad this was my last night with him. I just had to get through tomorrow without discovery.

The morning finally came, and I went about getting ready for work like I always did. Mike was up too, even though he had a later start than me. My last image of him was bending over to pick up one of the cats as I said goodbye and walked out the door.

I headed to work, staying calm and carefully going over the plan I'd made with Dawn. She would come into the science department around 8:30 a.m. and pretend she needed me to help her with something. That was the cue. I'd greet my colleagues, get busy doing something, and wait for her to come get me.

I was cleaning glass beakers when she walked in. I left without any goodbyes. Just silent farewells in my head. I hated doing that. I could only imagine how shocked and devastated my colleagues would be when they realized what I'd done. I felt bad for John, one of the few people who knew I was leaving. I knew he'd have to field all the questions once the word spread through the school and the town. I would've liked to protect him, but I needed his reference for my job applications.

Thank you, John. I'm sorry for any pain you had to go through after I left.

Dawn and I went straight to the parking lot and got into our cars. She followed me to the nearby elementary school where I parked my car far out in the lot, then got into her car. We drove to the U-Haul in Havelock to pick up the truck I had reserved.

After we got the truck, we stopped at the McDonald's at the far end of town. Dawn suggested we wait a few more minutes to be sure Mike had left for work and we wouldn't run into him on the road. She even recommended that she drive the truck, just in case we passed him—so he wouldn't see me driving.

Smart lady.

Sure enough, as we took off toward the house, we passed him. I ducked slightly to my right to avoid being seen. I looked at my watch—it was 9:00 a.m. Mike was late for work. What did that mean? Did his schedule change since the night before? Sometimes that happened. It didn't matter. It was now or never. We just needed to move fast.

As we pulled onto our street, I hoped no neighbors would see and question what was going on. Just another reason to hurry. Dawn backed the U-Haul up to the garage, and I opened it using the remote I'd taken from my car—one of the many details I'd made sure to handle.

I told Dawn which pictures I wanted from the walls, and she got busy. I grabbed the open boxes from the spare bedroom and packed up the last of my kitchen items—my pots and pans from college, the coffee maker, silverware, and a few small appliances. We loaded the boxes into the truck and then took apart one of the beds in the spare bedroom.

I wasn't taking much, and we were moving quickly, but it still took nearly two hours to pack everything. The humid June morning left us hot and sweaty, but we didn't stop to drink water. Adrenaline kept us going. Eventually, everything I wanted was packed and secured.

Dawn suggested I go back in and say goodbye. She sat on the front steps, lighting a cigarette, thinking I would take my time.

Nope. Not me.

I had already said my goodbyes. I placed the farewell letter on his pillow, took one last look around to make sure I hadn't forgotten anything, and walked out.

Dawn was surprised when I returned so quickly and said, "Let's go."

I closed the garage door and drove off down the street without looking back. I had no emotions left to give. I kept myself neutral and focused all my energy on the next phase: getting my things out of storage.

I felt a bit calmer. At least if Mike had come home early, I wouldn't have been there. But I still wasn't ready to release all my emotions. Not until I was officially out of town.

About that time, I started getting texts from some of my colleagues—probably asking if I wanted to go to lunch. I hated ignoring them, but I had no choice.

We pulled into the storage unit and quickly rearranged the truck to make space for the boxes I had already packed. We loaded everything quickly. Then I stopped at the front office, turned in my key, and we took off to Morehead City, where the car trailer was waiting.

It was about a twenty-five-minute drive to Morehead City, which gave me some time to talk with Dawn about everything it had taken to get to this point. She had been such a great friend. I chose well when I picked someone to help me escape. She wasn't close to Mike or to me, which protected her from the emotional weight that my other friends would have carried. She was a bulldog when needed—and here she was, sitting next to me, offering encouragement and congratulations for taking back my life.

We got the trailer hooked up to the U-Haul truck, and then we took off back to Havelock to get my car and put it on the back. Another twenty-five minutes on the road, chatting with this beautiful, compassionate soul. We both knew she would be pulled and tugged by many people after I was gone, trying to explain my shocking departure. She knew more about why I was leaving than anyone at the school. John and Dr. Murphy could only guess, since I had only intimated the seriousness of my secret departure.

I had asked Dawn to keep what she could to herself. Mike still had to live and work there. No one knew what I had gone through—Dawn only knew a small part. I wanted Mike to be able to go about his life and not have to worry about who knew that I was leaving. I wanted him to be able to walk into any business, anyone's home, and not have to wonder, Did they know? Did Pam tell them about my cross-dressing? Did Pam tell them about the abuse? I wanted him to be able to tell whatever story he wanted to. That was my final gift to him.

We got to the elementary school, and together, Dawn and I got my car up on the car hauler and secured it. I was very proud of what we did in such a short time. I had never put a car on a trailer, and I had never towed a trailer before. These were all firsts for me as I was working feverishly to get out of town. It was now just a short drive to the other U-Haul business where Dawn had left her car.

Dawn recognized that having me pull into the U-Haul parking lot with the truck and trailer would be too difficult to get out of, so she insisted I just let her out at the intersection in front of the business. The light had turned red; we stopped. I gave her a hug and took one last picture of her sweaty, smiling soul—and off she went. The light turned green, and I put my foot down on the accelerator, trying to get out of town before anyone recognized me behind the wheel.

That was it. She was gone that quickly. A hug, a picture—and then she was gone. And now I was gone.

I still couldn't relax. I was still in town where someone could recognize me. I kept my two hands tight on the wheel, my head lowered, and my foot pressed on the accelerator. It was now about 1:30 p.m. I knew Mike would be getting home soon, and I still hadn't told the kids. I wanted to be the one to tell them before their dad did. I was getting "pings" on my cell phone as more and more people tried to reach me, so I turned the sound off to ease my already overloaded, stressed-out body from any more mental torture.

When I got to Kinston, an hour west of Havelock, I stopped at a gas station, used the bathroom, got some water, and then called Jillian. She was in Raleigh, and I'd be driving right through. The news of me leaving would rock her. She had relied on my presence to help her through the tough times while waiting for the economy to shift in her favor. Now I was leaving her and moving back to Yakima. I also realized that my leaving meant she would bear the brunt of her dad's emotional fallout. There was no getting around the collateral damage that was yet to unfold.

Up to this point, I had remained very neutral in my emotions. I was so tense while driving. My hands stayed tight on the wheel and my shoulders were braced as I leaned forward in the truck, making my way down the highway. I hadn't afforded myself the release of any emotions. But when I got Jillian on the phone, I lost it. I simply told her that I was leaving her dad, that I was already packed up in a U-Haul, and heading her way. I wanted to see her and say goodbye.

Jillian didn't seem shocked. Her voice was soft and comforting. We planned to meet at the Crabtree Mall parking lot in Raleigh. It was going to be another hour and a half before I got there. She hadn't heard anything from her dad yet, and I was glad I got to her first.

I pulled out of the gas station and headed west again. I didn't feel safe until I was several hours away. I was still too close to Havelock, and who knew if he was in his truck, heading this way to look for me. I called Claire and Craig next. They were shocked into near silence. Their words were minimal, trying to take in what I had just told them. Craig was in Pensacola going through flight school for the Marine Corps, and Claire and her family were stationed outside of Oklahoma City. It was Wednesday, June 11. I made arrangements with Claire that I would stop by Friday on my way through.

My heart was heavy for my kids. This was huge. They had no suspicion that anything was wrong between their dad and me. That was because Mike always chose to hurt me in private. He waited until no one was around to emotionally torture and abuse me. They never saw it. Here they were—28, 26, and 25 years old—and they were shocked to their core. I couldn't even imagine the emotional damage it would have done to them if I had left when they were younger and had fewer emotional tools to work through it.

I got to the Crabtree Mall, and there was Jillian waiting for me. I climbed out of the truck and gave her the biggest hug through my sobbing tears. Finally—after holding back the emotions of the last thirty-plus years—I had permission to let it all out. And it came out in torrents.

Jillian had stopped at the grocery store and gotten me some supplies for the road. I had been going since I first woke up that morning, and other than the water I got at the gas station, I hadn't had anything to eat. Here she was, with water and food for my trip.

I looked at my phone and saw that I had over fifty texts and more than twenty missed calls. There were a couple of voicemails from Mike, and I made the mistake of listening to one of them. I heard the most pitiful wail and sobs coming from him. They were so intense that I had to delete every one of them. I knew it would be hard on him when I left, but I had no idea the depth of his suffering that he would experience.

Jillian told me she had been receiving calls from friends wanting to know what was going on. She had called some of her dad's friends to go over and be with him. While she was talking to me, one of those friends called, and I could hear only her side of the conversation: "Yes, my mom left my dad. Yes, she left him. I don't know, I just found out myself. Could you go over and check on him? Thanks."

It was now around 4:30 p.m. I didn't know where I was stopping for the night. I had no idea how far I'd get down the road, so I never made reservations. I had to get going, and I hated leaving Jillian with the fallout—but I had to go. I promised I would call her and let her know where I was staying for the night.

And then, off I went. Sobbing the entire way. Holding the steering wheel tight, shoulders pinched in stress, and my foot pressing down as hard as I could, just trying to get further away. North Carolina is a very wide state, and it can take seven hours to drive through. I made it somewhere around Winston-Salem or Hickory before I stopped for the night.

I don't remember eating anything other than what Jillian had given me. I was driving a big truck with a trailer, so I had to be careful wherever I stopped, making sure I could position myself to get out easily. I remember being worried someone would break into the back of my U-Haul while I was sleeping, but there wasn't much I could do about it. I had to trust that the lock I got from U-Haul would be enough to deter anyone.

I checked into my room and saw that I had another forty-some texts and dozens of missed phone calls. My heart was so heavy for every one of those people who were so worried about me that they kept trying to reach me. I couldn't read the texts. I couldn't talk to anyone. I could barely stop sobbing just to breathe, let alone recount to everyone what was going on. Plus, I also needed to protect my friends.

You might think it's crazy for me to want to protect my friends since I was already gone, but the truth about why I had to leave would traumatize them even more. They had no clue the enormous emotional load that would fall on them if I purged the details. They were friends with Mike, and they had to live in the same town with him. I knew the truth would devastate them and further traumatize them.

It was already bad enough that I had ripped myself from their lives without any explanation. My explanation would have only added to their trauma. It would've been selfish of me to cleanse myself by adding more unbelievable pain to their lives. I chose to bear the pain of losing my friends—and having them lose me—rather than have them also lose the image they had of Mike as a friend.

I was finally able to check in with my dad and Norma. They were heading to Lake Roosevelt to go fishing and would be out of cell phone range for a while. The plan was for them to reach out to me when they had coverage.

Then I called Jillian. I told her about all the texts I had gotten. I told her to tell her dad that I was not coming back, and that I was not going to be answering any of his calls or texts. He needed to know there was no hope of me ever returning to him again. Never, ever. I told Jillian to let all my friends know how much I loved them and that I was sorry I had to leave the way I did.

I got off the phone and collapsed. I needed to get some sleep. It had been a draining day, and I still had a long way to go. I found it hard to fall asleep. I kept reliving the whole day, and I couldn't believe I was on my way to a new life. Somehow, my body found the sleep I needed. It wouldn't be long before the sun came up and I'd be on the road again.

Morning came, and I was quick to get behind the wheel. I don't remember eating anything. I must have, but I just remember getting up and going, going, going—as fast as I could.

As I approached the North Carolina–Tennessee border, it occurred to me to take a picture of the "Welcome to Tennessee" sign. I was going to try to take a picture of each state's sign along the way. Tennessee is another very long state, east to west. I was determined to make it to Arkansas for the night, so I just kept pushing forward.

The last time I'd driven through Tennessee was in September of 1986, when we were moving from Yuma, Arizona, to Havelock, North Carolina. A totally different experience this time. Instead of looking forward to our life together, I was now looking forward to my life without him. Tennessee has a lot of rolling hills, and in the fall the trees are beautiful. But now I was paying more attention to my gas gauge than the scenery, making sure I started looking for a gas station when I got close to a quarter tank.

Every time I stopped for gas, I went to the bathroom, got something to eat and drink, and checked to make sure the car was still secure on the trailer. It was a good thing I checked at every stop, because the strap was working itself loose with each leg of the drive. I was still so high on adrenaline. I had this urgency to get to Yakima. Anywhere else in between still felt like a danger zone. I logically knew Mike wouldn't catch up to

435

me now. But I was still in fight-or-flight mode. My heart and blood were pumping out the word: Go, go, go, go.

Somewhere on the interstate through Tennessee, I got a phone call from Jack. He knew I was hoping to be on the road by now, but he wasn't sure. It meant a lot to me that he cared enough to check on my well-being. It was hard to hear him. The truck was loud and the road noise didn't help. I had to keep two hands on the wheel, so I put him on speaker. It was still hard to hear, but I told him my plan was to be in Yakima by Monday afternoon. We made plans to connect once I got there.

It was good to hear from Jack. That call filled my emotional bucket that seemed to be leaking continuously. I decided to make another call—to my friend Lisa, who I was going to be staying with. I told her I was on the road and would be in Yakima on Monday afternoon to unload my U-Haul truck into the storage unit I'd rented. She volunteered to find some male friends of ours to meet me there and help unload. I was so grateful for her friendship. What a blessing to know I had someone in Yakima advocating for me.

I made it through Tennessee and snapped a picture of the "Welcome to Arkansas" sign that was attached to the bridge over the Mississippi River. I could tell I was in a completely different state—the roads were terrible. Big potholes were everywhere. Driving the truck at sixty-plus miles per hour and then hitting one of those potholes caused it to drastically shimmy and shear. I didn't want an accident before I got home, so I kept a vigilant watch on the road ahead of me, trying to avoid the holes when I could. It was getting dark, and I was determined to stop somewhere in Little Rock for the night.

I found a motel close to the interstate, and it was across from a fast-food restaurant. Fortunately, there weren't a lot of cars in the parking lot, so it was easy for me to pull in and pull around, making sure the truck and trailer were pointed headfirst out of the lot.

I got a room and then went straight over to the restaurant to get something quick to eat. I didn't realize how hungry I was until I sat down with the food in my hands. I ate quickly, but it still felt like my stomach was empty. *That's OK*, I told myself. I figured I'd feel differently in a bit once the food settled and my nerves eased up.

I reached out to Jillian again and told her I was in Little Rock. She said her dad told her that I must have been planning this for months. That was a laugh. I had been dreaming about it for years, but the actual plan didn't take place until six weeks before. I recognized that what I did—the surgical nature of it, the secrecy—was incredible. Don't ever underestimate your own personal resolve once you've made up your mind to do something. My resolve came with thirty-plus years of darkness. Of course I was able to extract myself so quickly. I was like a spring in a box, tightly coiled. Now the lid was off, and nothing was going to stop me from getting away.

Next, I reached out to Claire. I told her to expect me in the afternoon. Oklahoma City would be my halfway point. I was looking forward to seeing her and her little family. I was grateful that my path took me right through OKC—it would make it easier to get on and off the interstate with the big load I was towing.

This was now the second night since I'd left. My nerves were still burning, but I was calm enough to start planning the next leg of my trip. Up to now, I had just gotten in the truck and driven until I was tired. I didn't have any plans other than to keep heading west. But now, I felt a little more relaxed searching through my phone and mapping out the next two legs of the trip. Interesting how just that simple act of planning my route helped me sleep more peacefully.

I got up Friday morning and was able to grab a quick breakfast before heading out. My next stop was Oklahoma City to see Claire and her family. Claire had been married and gone from the house for five years. She and her husband, who was a chief in the Navy, had lived in Virginia, then Hawaii, before moving to OKC. She hadn't lived close enough to visit often, so she didn't see the nuanced selfishness and self-centeredness of her dad the way Jillian had. I knew Claire would have a hard time understanding what happened. My visit with her was important to help her manage some of her own conflicting emotions.

It was a sunny day when I pulled up in front of her cute house. My three-year-old cutie granddaughter, Amelia, was waiting out front, and I snapped a picture of her as she came running down the driveway to greet me. It was such a sweet reunion. She gave me the biggest hugs, and then I put her down to hug my dear Claire.

I was only staying the night. I had to get up Saturday and hit the road again. Claire told me she was flying out to North Carolina the next day to be with her dad for Father's Day. Jillian and Craig were going to triangulate there as well. They wanted to be together to support him.

I was proud of my kids. They were rallying around their dad when he needed them the most, and they didn't hesitate to put their personal lives aside to make that happen. I had worked hard over the years to keep the abuse away from them. I wanted them to have whatever relationship they wanted with their dad, without my influence. They were grown adults now with their own lives and careers. It warmed me to know they were collectively coming together to be there for him.

Claire and I talked for a while about why I left. I kept most of the details from her. I assured her that my leaving had been coming for many years. I told her I knew that leaving when they were younger would've done more harm, so I stayed until I knew they'd be OK. There was absolutely no benefit in revealing the truth now, not after hiding it all these years.

Saturday morning, I was up and gone after breakfast. Little Amelia and Claire gave me a big hug outside by the truck. We waved our goodbyes, and I blew kisses to the two of them. My next stop: Wyoming.

I had to head north through Kansas before I could turn west again toward Denver. I found myself a little more at ease on the drive. This time, instead of just driving until I was tired, I had a destination in mind. I figured if I made it to Cheyenne, Wyoming, for the night, I'd be closer to Boise on Sunday and then reach Yakima by Monday.

Driving I-35 north through Kansas was an eye-opener. It was the first part of the trip where there were no hills—just long, straight roads with wide-open fields. I remember thinking, *No wonder tornadoes move through here so fast. There's nothing to slow them down.* Then I remembered it was tornado season. I hadn't paid attention to the weather, so I had no idea if I should be watching for them. Another mental load to tuck into my brain as I drove toward Salina, where I'd head west on I-70 to Denver.

The long, straight interstate was making it hard to stay alert. I didn't realize how the monotony of an unchanging road could lull me to sleep. I was grateful for the simple shift in direction when I finally turned west toward Denver.

The sun was getting lower in the sky, reminding me that I had to make good time to reach Cheyenne before dark. I stopped at a gas station just southeast of Denver to refuel and use the bathroom. I was a bit taken aback when the people who had arrived just after me said a tornado had been on their tail for the past couple of miles. Yikes! No thank you. I didn't need that experience—especially not now, while I was fleeing with my few precious belongings to start over.

I was about two and a half hours from Cheyenne, and it was after 6:00 p.m. I had hoped to get there before nine. I eventually made it through Denver and got on I-25 north to Cheyenne. So far, no real issues—except for the tornado behind me that I luckily missed. I started to feel good once the mileage signs for Cheyenne began to appear. I was pleasantly surprised to see it would only be another hour and a half drive. That was good, because I was ready to call it quits for the day.

I had noticed my feet were starting to hurt. I looked down and saw my ankles and feet swollen from sitting so long. My bent legs had been restricting the return of blood to my heart and lungs. I tried shifting my position a bit to relieve the pressure from the seat, but that wasn't easy in the kind of vehicle I was driving. It didn't have cruise control, so I couldn't just set it to 65 and take my foot off the gas. I did the best I could—leaning my body a bit to the right, then to the left.

It was dark when I arrived in Cheyenne and pulled into my hotel. I chose this one because it was near a restaurant and the interstate. It would be easy to eat and get back on the road. This time, I made myself walk around a bit, and I made sure to elevate my legs with extra pillows when I slept.

I couldn't check my phone while driving, so every stop was an opportunity to see if there were any messages from my dad, Norma, or the kids. There weren't any that day, and I was relieved not to see texts from concerned friends. I'm sure they gave up after I didn't respond. I could only imagine how they must be feeling—knowing I was gone for good.

I didn't call Jillian or any of the kids, but I did text to let them know where I was. By now, they were all at the house with their dad, and I didn't want to interject any of my energy into the energy they were supplying for him.

I still had one more night before I made it to Yakima, and I was feeling the effects of my adrenaline, the stress, and the long drives. I still wasn't letting myself get too excited about going home. It had been a traumatizing exodus, and my kids were now part of the collateral damage, trying to work through what it all meant for them. I remained mindful of the heavy hearts they were carrying—and how my actions had put them in this situation. Celebrating my escape didn't feel appropriate.

I woke up that Father's Day morning knowing I had another eleven hours of driving ahead. I needed a decent breakfast, so I took advantage of the restaurant next to the hotel and ordered an omelet and coffee. It was incredible how the simple act of having someone else wait on me eased some of my stress. I had been scorching the roads since Wednesday with little time in between. It was finally time to relax, if even for a moment, knowing I was going to be OK.

It was still so surreal. Just a week ago, I was in North Carolina, nervously waiting to see which day would be the day I could leave. Now, here I was in Cheyenne—just a day and a half from home. It was still hard to believe that I was finally on my way to start over. You'd think I would've been smiling from ear to ear—but I wasn't. I still had two more legs of this trip, and the experience had left me emotionally and physically drained.

There was no opportunity to truly relax. The truck was difficult to drive. I had to keep both hands on the wheel, constantly monitor the gas gauge, and shift my position regularly to relieve the pressure on my legs. I tried to let myself take in the changing scenery as I moved from state to state, but it wasn't easy—not in that truck.

However, Wyoming proved to be a beautiful state—at least from what I saw from the interstate. I was grateful that my route took me through part of the Rockies, and I got to witness the stunning rock formations. You definitely knew you weren't in Kansas anymore.

Somewhere in Wyoming, I got a call from Craig. He was on his way back to Pensacola after spending time with his dad for Father's Day. We didn't talk long, but I hung up the phone with mixed emotions. He said, "Mom, when you first told me you left Dad, I was so mad at you. But Dad told us the truth, and now I understand. But I want you to know that I still love my dad."

I was grateful that my son wasn't mad at me, but I worried about what his dad had actually told him. I didn't fully find out until Jillian called to recount how the visit went.

"Mom, I am so mad at Dad. He didn't have to tell us what he did. We didn't have to know. He said the only reason he was telling us was because it was 'cathartic' for him."

I asked her to clarify, and she said their dad had told them about his cross-dressing.

I was so deflated. I could only imagine the trauma the kids felt learning that after all the years I had protected them. But the truth was, I didn't leave him because of the cross-dressing. I left him because of the years of abuse I endured. He didn't tell them any of that—only the cross-dressing.

I never wanted the kids to know any of it. I had kept it to myself all these years to protect them. And now he goes and dumps the cross-dressing on them in one swoop. I was furious. How dare he be so selfish? He thought only of himself and didn't consider the emotional toll it would take on the kids.

Now I understood what Craig meant when he said he understood why I left. Unfortunately, he never got the real story—only the version that would elicit sympathy and pity for his dad. And that was exactly the kind of attention Mike thrived on. He was proficient at playing the victim. Now he had a big one he could pull out and use for the rest of his life. He'd use it to get an endless supply of sympathy from the kids and anyone else he chose to tell. About how he suffered because he couldn't fully express himself in drag. *Poor dear. Poor, poor dear.*

Would he ever come clean about the endless abuse I suffered at his hands? No. Because that would cast him in a negative light. He wouldn't get sympathy—only condemnation and the realization from others that they had never truly known who Mike was. He wouldn't be able to hide behind the mask of being this wonderful guy anymore.

Those two conversations—from Craig and Jillian—weighed heavily on me and preoccupied my mind. It was just another example of his selfishness and another confirmation that I couldn't get far enough away from him.

Eventually, I made my way into Utah. I shoved the disheartening conversation aside and focused on the road. I had to turn north outside of Salt Lake City toward Boise, and the roads were a little confusing. Driving the truck and towing the car didn't give me the luxury of quick lane changes if I missed an exit or took the wrong one.

During the trip, I always made a point of stopping for gas when the gauge got to a quarter of a tank. I didn't want to ever be caught without gas. But now I was on a stretch of road where the towns were spaced farther apart, and the roads were an up-and-down ribbon that sucked the gas quicker than I expected.

The gauge was getting low, and I had been scouting for gas stations. I started coasting wherever I could and took advantage of going down the hills without any accelerator assistance. I was getting nervous with every hill I had to climb, and I paid close attention to how quickly I was accelerating when I got to the top and had to regain speed again. I eventually coasted into a gas station with very little fuel. What a relief to have the gauge show full again as I took off toward Boise.

It was dark, once again, by the time I reached Boise. I had taken advantage of my stop in Little Rock and made reservations ahead of time for a nice hotel. It was going to be my last stop before I drove into Yakima, and I wanted to treat myself. Everywhere else I had stayed was just somewhere cheap and quick so I could get back on the road. This hotel had an indoor swimming pool, and I intended to take advantage of it to relax before bedtime.

The last leg to Yakima was going to be my shortest—only five and a half hours. I didn't have to get up as early, so I allowed myself to sleep in. I took advantage of the comfortable bed and the fluffy towels. The hotel had a decent breakfast for a Monday morning, so I didn't have to go looking for food.

Sometime that morning, after I had gotten back on the road, my dad and my Norma called me. They were heading back from Lake Roosevelt and now had phone coverage. We planned to meet up at the U-Haul in Yakima around two p.m. Now I was getting excited.

My phone was automatically adjusting for each time zone as I passed through, and it had been a fun distraction to see the progression from Eastern Daylight Time to Mountain Daylight Time. It wouldn't be long before I crossed into Pacific Daylight Time. With every hour, I was getting more and more excited.

I had never driven through the Blue Mountains of Oregon before, and I was surprised at the elevation the truck had to attain before hitting the summit and starting back down the other side. I had to really focus on the road since it seemed to wind as much as it climbed. But then I started seeing signs for Pendleton, which is close to Washington's border. My excitement grew. I knew it wouldn't be long before I would see signs for the Tri-Cities and Washington State.

I realized that I hadn't told my mom I was moving back. So, I gave her a call.

"Hi, hon. What are you up to?"

I told her I had left Mike and that I was going to be driving into Yakima this afternoon. Her voice didn't register any surprise, and she simply asked if I was OK. It was great to hear her voice and to know that she would be close by. I had truly told no one who didn't need to know. I thought about the ripple that went through Havelock when I left, and now I was contemplating the ripple I would make in my return to Yakima.

I made a stop in Pendleton for gas. This was a monumental one—it would be my last before I got to Yakima. The next time I climbed out of the truck, my feet would be firmly planted on the ground in my dear city. I fueled up, checked my car on the trailer, went to the bathroom, grabbed some water and some fruit.

Then I climbed back into the cab of the truck for the last two hours of my trip.

Holy smokes, it was hard to contain my excitement. I started seeing signs for the Tri-Cities. I knew I'd be crossing over into Washington State real soon. I had been taking pictures of every welcome sign for every state I went through, and now I was quickly coming up on the one for Washington!

Even though I was super excited to be crossing the border into Washington, I was disappointed with the size of the sign that greeted me. It was a relatively small sign—green, with a simple white profile of the state. Very understated. Nothing flashy. It didn't matter. I still let out a big whoop when I crossed over from Oregon.

I was now on very familiar ground. I didn't need the map on my phone anymore. I knew where I was going, and I couldn't keep the tears from filling up my eyes. I was now on I-82 heading west toward my beautiful city of Yakima.

Every little town from here on had some great memories for me. Flashes of my past and the times I had spent there were flooding back. There was Prosser, where my oldest brother was born. I could see Mt. Adams looming large in front of me as I flew down I-82. Then came Sunnyside, where we had gone to church at Holy Trinity Episcopal Church for several years.

Now the little towns were flying past me too quickly for me to properly pay them respect. Outlook, where I used to live for a short time when I was in the fourth grade. Granger, where my dad was a teacher and football coach—we lived there until I finished seventh grade. I made a promise to myself to come back and wander around once I got settled in.

Then came Zillah, my mom's hometown. So many memories of attending the Community Days pancake breakfast and marching in the parade. Then came Toppenish, where we would go grocery shopping and visit with my Uncle RC and Aunt Betty. Then there was Wapato and all the wineries. I was seeing signs for Yakima over and over again, and my body was electric with so much anticipation.

I had tried to keep my emotions tamped down since I left on Wednesday. Except for the outpouring of sobs when I spoke to the kids, I had held back. But now, I was giving myself permission to just let go. I was speeding past all the familiar orchards that dotted the interstate, and I remembered picking the fruit when I was little. The rolling brown landscape of Rattlesnake Hills and the beautiful easterly reveal of Mt. Adams were both giving me a welcome-home kiss.

I would catch myself momentarily forgetting that I was in the heart of Washington. Every time I saw a Washington State license plate, I got excited. *Oh look. There's one, there's one. Oh, wait. That's right. I'm in Washington!* The U-Haul place was in Union Gap, a little municipality directly annexed to Yakima. The two cities are basically one, so I was flying high, high, high when I finally took my exit to Union Gap and was on First Street heading toward my final destination.

I called my dad and my Norma to tell them I was heading down the street and would be there very soon. I was so excited that I was shaking. My entire insides were vibrating, and I could feel this invisible string pulling me toward my journey's end.

I had spent thirty-three years of my life with a monster. He hid his true self from me in the beginning and showered me with attention and gifts. Then, little by little, he started pulling back the attention and started dishing out the little slights, the subtle digs. I got caught up early in an emotional back-and-forth of getting love and attention from him, then criticism and control. I was left reeling every time he pulled his love away from me, not knowing what I did to deserve his disapproval.

Now here I was, thirty-three years later, returning to the city that held my happiest days. I was getting emotional. Tears were falling faster from my eyes. I had finally made it. Now it's my time—time for me to rediscover who I really am by remembering who I used to be before Mike.

The truck rolled up to the turn lane across from the U-Haul lot, and I looked to my left. There were my dad and my Norma, with big smiles, waving to me. There were my old high school friends, Ray and Matt, who lovingly gave up some of their personal time to help me unload.

My tears and my whoops for joy seemed at odds with each other, but they were perfectly matched. All the emotions of the last thirty years were condensed into one week with my epic escape.

I turned into the lot and pulled up beside my dad. My beautiful dad, who loved me unconditionally and gave me money when I needed it. I knew I had to be breathing but there were so many emotions swelling up and through me that I couldn't seem to catch my breath. All I could do was to jump out of my truck and throw my arms around him. It was now my time. After thirty-three years, I knew that I was finally going to be ok.

*   *   *   *   *   *   *   *   *   *   *

You are healing and that terrifies them. They've never met a woman who shatters and does not stay broken. They expected you to beg, to break, to need them. Instead, you looked into your own reflection and found everything you sought. A woman who heals herself, owes no one her scars, her softness, or her survival. That is why they fear you. Because they have seen what you survived, and they know...nothing can stop you now.

@femmefatalism

28. My Plea

Don't negotiate your value with anyone.

You're worth it.

Been worth it.

Forever be worth it.

-unknown

It takes a massive amount of bravery to leave an abusive relationship. You have to navigate a poisoned brain and the fog just to formulate a foolproof plan. You have to figure out who you can trust while simultaneously trying to keep others from being caught up in the collateral damage. You realize that there are friends and a community you have to let go.

It won't be the start of a new chapter in your life—it will be a whole new book.

Your new life won't resemble anything you had before, and it won't be long until you wonder who that person was that went through all that hell. It did happen, but there will be enough time and space between the two lives that you'll begin to disconnect from it.

A big part of me writing my experience was to help others identify the toxic relationship they are in—and for others to recognize toxic relationships that a friend or loved one may be in—so they can offer support and assistance to get away. That is an honorable intention, but I want to go one step further and try to help break the cycle of narcissistic abuse altogether.

So where does it start? It starts with the subconscious programming of how we raise our children and the environment they grow up in. Our brains grow rapidly in our early years, acting like sponges, picking up all the cues around us—stowing away information that guides how we think about ourselves, our place in the world, and the roles we assume in romantic relationships. Experts have identified that the first seven years of our lives are when we obtain the majority of our belief systems—beliefs that will influence and guide us through the rest of our lives.

It's incredible to think that we obtain so much programming from our families and society that it only takes the first seven years to absorb and learn what is expected of us and our roles in society. Primarily, it sets expectations for gender roles in both personal relationships and professional lives. These expectations—or "beliefs"—keep us trapped in roles that don't serve us and cause pain and suffering as we try to navigate what is expected of us versus what truly serves us.

This early programming can take a lifetime to unravel, and by the time you realize you're not bound by these beliefs, most likely you've already passed them on to your own children—and the cycle continues.

It wasn't that long ago that women weren't allowed to vote, file for divorce, or apply for credit to get a credit card or buy a house. Black women finally got the right to vote in 1965. Landlords could refuse to rent to women until the Fair Housing Act of 1968 was passed. And it wasn't until the passage of the Equal Credit Opportunity Act in 1974 that women could finally apply for credit and buy a home on their own.

There are still millions of women in the U.S. who have one foot in pre-1965 and another in post-1974. Those millions of women had children and raised them according to the belief that women were supposed to be subservient to men and to please them, while men were raised to dominate, control, and manipulate their wives—and not fully participate in raising their children.

My mom was born in 1940, and I was born in 1961. My mother raised us the best she could with the beliefs handed down to her by her mother, and by the societal rules and norms that flooded her world. I inherited many of those beliefs as well and, in turn, passed them down to my children. I was fortunate to have lived through the Women's Liberation Movement of the late '60s and early '70s, and it was then that I started to realize women weren't bound by society's limiting beliefs. I truly believed I could do anything I wanted—and I passed that belief down to my kids.

Unfortunately, that change in gender expectations was limited to professional aspirations.

As far as the marital role, that programming was harder to change. Society still clung to the antiquated belief that women were expected to manage the house and children—even if they earned a degree and entered the professional world alongside their male counterparts. This toxic and unrealistic conditioning is deeply embedded in the subconscious of both males and females by the age of seven, setting the stage for unrealistic expectations in marriage and keeping millions of women trapped in abusive relationships.

No wonder the divorce rate is around 50 percent for first marriages and climbs to almost 75 percent for second marriages. Both men and women are entering the marriage contract with programmed expectations that were set by the time they were seven and reinforced through multiple channels throughout their growth and development. It's the perfect setup for continued domestic abuse.

I was 24 when my first child was born, 31 by the time she turned seven, and I already had two other children who were four or five. I hadn't yet figured out that the beliefs embedded in me at an early age were what kept me trapped in this toxic and abusive marriage. So, I unknowingly passed on to my kids many of those same toxic beliefs.

It's too late for them, and it's too late for my granddaughter, who is almost 14.

So how do we stop the cycle? How do we reach beyond the next generation to end this?

Fortunately, it's much easier to get a message out to the masses through the various social media platforms and the internet than it has ever been in human history. We have to reach out to the generation that still has an opportunity to affect change on the next one coming up. We have to reprogram the youth of today with healthier beliefs and societal expectations that will allow them to enter adulthood and committed relationships with stronger self-worth and self-love. They, in turn, will pass those new beliefs on to their own children—and eventually, the cycle will be broken.

So, what can we do now to empower our children who have already received the subconscious programming? I can only speak from my experience and from the point of view of a female. I was susceptible to the abusive relationship I was in because I was taught to be a people pleaser. I was taught not to honor my own needs and desires but to sacrifice them for the sake of others. We can start there.

It's hard enough to navigate adolescence and the teen years under the best of circumstances. You want to model an environment where the mother's voice is respected by the father so that the kids know they'll also be given a safe space to seek guidance without condemnation. Encourage your children to develop healthy boundaries—and model it for them. Empower your daughters to own their power and not to compromise themselves just to ease someone else's discomfort.

Being of service to each other is a loving act, but it should not be skewed so that service to others comes at a detriment to one's self.

I was raised to be a people pleaser—to put everyone else's needs above my own. I was made to feel selfish, self-centered, or vain if I dared to exert my own needs and desires. Don't do this to your girls. And don't raise your sons to think housework is "women's work."

And remember, you can't just tell your kids with words. They "listen" better by what they observe. If you are not leading by example, you are confusing your children about what their role in society—and in the world—really is.

I'm a survivor of domestic abuse, but I'm not an expert. I can offer some quick advice to those of you already in a relationship—or at the beginning of a new one.

First, trust your instincts. You don't have to know exactly why something feels off in your relationship. If it feels wrong, and your instincts are telling you something isn't right, believe them. That's your higher self—your subconscious—knowing what's off and warning you to step back.

Next, be very cautious of any relationship where they profess their love quickly and shower you with attention and gifts. This is a common tactic called "love bombing," and it's designed to get empathetic spirits to emotionally commit early in the relationship. After the love bombing comes the slow reveal of who they really are. It can be subtle, but it will manifest as a completely different side than the one you first saw. You'll wonder if there's something wrong with them—or worse, question what you might have done to make them act that way.

This is a huge red flag. Again, you need to walk away.

Don't fall for the love bombing. It's a manipulation tactic used against people with big hearts and weak boundaries. The abuser is testing your boundaries to see how far they can push without you pushing back. If your instincts tell you something is off—trust them and back away.

If you're already in a relationship and aren't sure if it's toxic or not, keep it simple and don't overthink it. Ask yourself: How do they make me feel? Do you feel safe bringing up difficult topics, or do you tiptoe around them because they get defensive? Do they bring out the best in you—or do you feel like you have to hide your authentic self?

Whatever you do when starting out in a new relationship—don't shrink yourself in their presence. Don't ever compromise yourself or your self-worth.

Before you get married or fully commit to your partner, make sure that you have your own income stream and your own checking and savings account. One of the biggest reasons victims find it hard to leave an abusive relationship is because they don't have their own money or income. Stay financially independent. You can have a joint account where you each put money in for common expenses like rent, mortgage, utilities, and repairs. Also, make sure you have a credit card in your name. You will need emergency money if you ever have to get away.

If you are married, make sure at least one car is registered in your name. This will give you a vehicle that you can legally take with you if the relationship fails. You need to insist upon this. If your spouse resists, that is a major red flag—and you need to proceed with caution.

You should be the most important person in the world to you. If you haven't figured that out yet, do it now. No one should be more important to you than yourself. No one else will fully know what you are going through or what you need. You need to love yourself enough to know that you deserve all the good things in this life, just like the next person.

You deserve to feel safe and loved.
You deserve to feel worthy and respected.
And you are never too much for the right person.

You can help others who you think may be in a toxic, abusive relationship by looking for these behaviors. Is the woman hyper-independent, doing all the chores inside and out? Do you see the dad helping with the kids—reading them stories at bedtime or giving them baths? Or is it just the mom doing it all?

Does he tease or make fun of her in front of family and friends, then try to cover the intent with, "I was just joking"? And do you laugh along with him instead of stepping in and standing up for her?

Every challenge is an opportunity to grow and to learn to be the best version of yourself. Know this: once you have conquered a problem, you will never be slowed down by that same problem again. It will just be another step up the ladder toward your best self.

As I started my healing journey, I realized that, because of my lack of self-love, I lacked the belief that I deserved to put myself first. Once I learned the lesson that I deserved to love myself and set personal boundaries, I started recovering the power that I had given away to others. I started finding a bigger peace in my soul as I listened to my instincts and followed my joy and passion.

I will end this with how to get the information and support you may need if you are in an abusive relationship:

If you know someone—or suspect that someone you know is in an abusive relationship—stay in communication with them. Give them the number to the National Domestic Violence Hotline: 800-799-7233.

Just as I am not an expert, neither are you. But you can call the hotline yourself and ask what is recommended for family and friends to do in order to support the victim. Don't insert yourself too deeply into their toxic relationship. Instead, encourage the victim to at least talk with someone through the hotline.

Lead with love, compassion, and empathy—but with boundaries.

You are not alone.
You are worthy.
You deserve all the best that life has to give.
So go get it.

My blessings and love to each one of you.

*   *   *   *   *   *   *   *   *   *   *

Empaths walk two phases: naïve innocence and awakened strength. In the first, they love without boundaries, driven by people-pleasing and fear of abandonment, making them prey for narcissists and manipulators. This cycle breaks through devastating abuse, shattering them entirely. But destruction becomes transformation. They rebuild with boundaries, self-respect, and emotional intelligence emerging as dark empaths. They wield their kindness with intention, no longer exploitable but unstoppable.

@myspiritualpath

EPILOGUE

For years, I believed that survival was the end goal. That if I could just make it through the storm—if I could simply outlast the chaos—then peace would naturally follow. But what no one tells you is that survival is only the beginning. Healing... that's the real work. And freedom? That is earned, one brave, trembling truth at a time.

It took thirty-three years to escape a marriage that slowly erased me. And yet, it took nearly ten more to understand that freedom isn't simply leaving the abuser—it's reclaiming yourself from every narrative they ever wrote about you.

I am not the woman he said I was.

I am not small. I am not overreacting. I am not too sensitive, too needy, too much.

I am, in fact, *more*.

More alive. More aware. More whole than I have ever been.

Writing this book was an act of defiance. Against shame. Against silence. Against every single whisper that told me to move on, to forget, to pretend it wasn't that bad.

It was *that* bad. And it deserves to be remembered—not for the pain it caused, but for the strength it demanded.

You've read my story. You've walked beside me through the darkest places I never imagined I'd survive. But I want you to know this: healing is not a straight path. It curves, it dips, it backtracks. Some days, it will feel like you're moving backward. That's okay. Growth isn't linear—it's sacred, spiraling, and often messy.

Now, when I dream, I no longer wake up in terror.

I wake up with breath.

With choice.

With my *own* voice ringing louder than his ever did.

I didn't write this book to expose him—I wrote it to *unearth* me.

And maybe, just maybe, to reach you.

To the woman still doubting her story, still wondering if it "counts," still telling herself, *It wasn't that bad*—yes, it does. And yes, it was.

To the soul quietly bleeding in silence, scared no one will believe her—*I believe you.*

To the one who finally walked away but now faces the bigger battle of *becoming again*—you're not alone.

There's a sacred power in survivors who speak. Our stories are not complaints. They are clarion calls. They are blueprints for the next woman who needs to know: you can walk through hell and still come out *holy*.

I am not who I was. And thank God for that.

I am not the version of me who tolerated crumbs and called it love. I am not the girl who mistook control for protection. I am not the woman who ignored her intuition to preserve peace at any cost.

I am the woman who now owns her silence, her screams, and every sacred moment in between.

And as for the past?

It no longer owns me.

If you're reading this and still finding your way out—I see you. Keep going. One breath, one step, one brave word at a time.

Because the big dark doesn't get the final word.

You do.

And the light? It was always yours.

—Pam

About the Author

Pam Telford, RDH, has served others for over four decades—as a dental hygienist, high school science teacher, and coach. A mother of three and proud grandmother of two, she was born and raised in Yakima Valley, Washington. *The Big Dark* is her raw and courageous account of surviving over thirty years of covert emotional abuse. With unflinching honesty, Pam shares her journey from silence to self-worth, offering a powerful message of healing, resilience, and hope.

THE BIG DARK

A Memoir of Survival, Silence, and Finally, a Voice

For over thirty years, she smiled through the pain. A devoted wife, a mother, a professional—and a prisoner of emotional, psychological, and covert domestic abuse. On the outside, she was the picture of resilience. Behind closed doors, she was slowly disappearing.

In *The Big Dark*, Pam shatters the silence with a breathtakingly raw and unflinchingly honest account of a life entangled with a man who wore the mask of a charming hero—and hid the soul of a manipulative narcissist. From love bombing to gaslighting, from military moves to isolation, from silent screams to loaded threats, this is the anatomy of a trauma bond— and the story of a woman who broke it.

Told with searing clarity, grace, and grit, *The Big Dark* is more than a memoir. It is a lifeline. A reckoning. A reclamation.

If you've ever questioned your reality, minimized your pain, or stayed silent to keep the peace—this book is for you.

You are not alone. You are not crazy. You are not broken. You are waking up.

www.ingramcontent.com/pod-product-compliance
Ingram Content Group UK Ltd.
Pitfield, Milton Keynes, MK11 3LW, UK
UKHW040622211025
8501UKWH00029B/238